Preparing for the Unexpected

Poul Houman Andersen, Hanne Kragh,
Jakob Lauring and Mai Skjøtt Linneberg (eds.)

Preparing for the Unexpected

Design of the future global enterprise

Djøf Publishing Copenhagen
2015

Poul Houman Andersen, Hanne Kragh, Jakob Lauring and Mai Skjøtt Linneberg (eds.)
Preparing for the Unexpected
Design of the future global enterprise

First edition 2015

Coverphoto by Emma Houman Jakobsen
Cover: Bo Helsted
Print: Ecograf, Højbjerg

Printed in Denmark 2015
ISBN 978-87-574-3157-5

Sold and distributed in Scandinavia by:
Djøf Publishing Copenhagen, Denmark
Email: forlag@djoef.dk
www.djoef-forlag.dk

Sold and distributed in North America by:
International Specialized Book Services (ISBS), Portland, USA
Email: orders@isbs.com
www.isbs.com

Sold in all other countries by:
The Oxford Publicity Partnership Ltd, Towcester, UK
Email: djof@oppuk.co.uk
www.oppuk.co.uk

Distributed in all other countries by:
Marston Book Services, Abingdon, Oxon, UK
Email: trade.orders@marston.co.uk
www.marston.co.uk

Content

CHAPTER 1

Preparing for the Unexpected: Design of the Future Global Enterprise

Poul Houman Andersen and Jakob Lauring

> *It was the best of times, it was the worst of times, it was the age of wisdom, it was the age of foolishness, it was the epoch of belief, it was the epoch of incredulity, it was the season of Light, it was the season of Darkness, it was the spring of hope, it was the winter of despair, we had everything before us, we had nothing before us, we were all going direct to Heaven, we were all going direct the other way ...*

This famous first sentence of Charles Dickens' 1859 *A Tale of Two Cities* frames the turbulent events that led up to the French Revolution. Although the story is set in Paris in 1775, it resonates with the uncertainties concerning the impact of globalization. Many in the mature market economies share the feeling that globalization is occurring via a struggle between the traditional world order, in which the Western world dominated economic development, and a new, reorganized world order. A pervasive feature of globalization's impact on industrial activities in mature Western economies such as Denmark is the relocation of business activities from the domestic to the global realm. Early on, in the 1980s and 1990s, the apparel industry in western Jutland relocated its manufacturing to low-cost countries, causing a massive loss of blue-collar jobs. Over the years, however, the new white-collar jobs created in the industry made up for this initial loss and, in the end, left the region better off and better able to confront global competition. This fundamental transformation has become a reference point for many Danish business actors and politicians who have felt the winds of change as globalization has successively impacted additional industries, leading to massive production outsourcing and offshoring. For over three decades, Danish industrial activities have been strongly export driven, and Danish exports have been built on a strong home base, supporting the competitive advantage of Danish firms by means of flexible specialization and localized learning. Cohesion in Danish business has been achieved through institutionalized strengths such as the Danish 'flexicurity' labour market model and system for developing a skilled workforce second to none, a credit-based financial system allowing for long-term investments, and several other characteristic socioeconomic features. Industrial strongholds have been based on these strengths in such diverse areas as shipbuilding, designer furniture, sustainable energy, food, and textiles. However, this recipe for prosperity is no longer as effective as it used to be. An entirely new level of participation in the global division of work is required of Danish industry, and Denmark's position as a natural knowledge hub is no longer taken for granted. Instead, to remain relevant to an increasingly global economy, Danish actors must carefully balance their ability to tap into global opportunities while maintaining local collaboration and focus.

The changes wrought by globalization will likely alter society as we know it. As in several other European countries in recent years, globalization has proven to be a powerful force of transformation in Denmark. Denmark has long been regarded as a relatively open economy, thoroughly enmeshed in international trade. Internationalization started mainly as an export activity in which countries traded goods produced from start to finish in just one country. What has followed with globalization is the break-up of value-chains into smaller and more specialized links, and the global relocation of value-chain activities has become central to the organization and performance of business activities. A broad array of industrial activities has followed this trend in diverse areas such as shipbuilding, footwear, electronics, office equipment, power and machine tools, as well as printing and publishing – to mention but a few. In these industries, production, marketing, administration, and R&D activities are increasingly being relocated or becoming interdependent with activities in other countries. It is estimated that Danish firms now employ more than 1.2 million workers outside Denmark and that over half of the industrial employment in Danish firms is found outside Denmark (DI, 2013).

Denmark shares this pattern of value-chain disruption with a number of mature Western economies. To illustrate the transition of the world's economic activities, London Business School Professor Quah (2011) suggests plotting 'the average location of economic activity across geographies on Earth' (p. 3). According to Quah (2011, p. 1), 'by 2008, from the continuing rise of China and the rest of East Asia, that centre of gravity had drifted to a location east of Helsinki and Bucharest. Extrapolating growth in almost 700 locations across Earth, this article projects the world's economic centre of gravity to locate by 2050 literally between India and China'. Some have suggested that this is a question of upward migration in the global division of work, and that as still more transition economies enter the global scene and offer production capacity and low labour costs, unskilled and semiskilled manufacturing jobs will leave Denmark in favour of more knowledge-intensive work (Danish Ministry of Trade and Commerce, 2005).

Not only are some Danish business enterprises increasingly taking part in global business activities, but Denmark as a society is increasingly touched by global business realities. Denmark is among those European countries with the highest share of the workforce working in foreign-owned subsidiaries. According to Eurostat statistics, over 19% of the private-sector workforce in Denmark is employed by foreign-owned companies (Eurostat, 2014). In some industries, such as information technology, almost half of the jobs are in foreign-owned companies. In view of this development and the increasingly open labour market for knowledge workers, the 'Danish approach' and Danish institutions, such as labour market relationships and relationships between credit providers and business enterprises, are increasingly under pressure. This pressure is already challenging established work and management practices in Danish-based firms and will likely continue to do so in coming years.

Preparing for the Unexpected: What is this Book about?

The debate regarding how globalization will impact the competitiveness of Danish firms and the organization of Danish industry and society is far from new and is unfolding in various forms among various constituents throughout society. This debate is marked by a strong focus on the benchmarks of the relative productivity and innovation capabilities of

Danish business enterprises vis-à-vis the rest of the world. The debate is not limited to business enterprises alone: Some even suggest that the Danish state should be seen as a competitive entity struggling with other states over the rights to the welfare goods of the future.

This book is not simply a tale of Denmark and other mature economies losing ground to countries with lower labour costs, stronger capital bases, and stronger GNP growth. More interesting but missing from the debate is research and discussion about current practices of transformation as Danish business enterprises attempt to cope with the ongoing transformation of their task environments. In 1990, one million workers or one third of the Danish workforce consisted of unskilled workers; by 2011, this number had declined to approximately 600,000. Over the same period, the number of workers with an education equivalent to or exceeding a bachelor's degree more than doubled to approximately 800,000. The consequences of new phenomena such as the surge in robot-enabled production technology and 3D printing for the location and organization of business activities have yet to be seen. We can be sure, however, that these phenomena will profoundly affect the significance and meaning of the flow of people and capital we are now witnessing. These developments have not only led to changes in terms of relocation but also spurred essential changes in the assumptions defining the business enterprise. One way of addressing this challenge is through the late Peter Druckers (1994) 'theory of the business'. According to this theory, an enterprise does not typically lose out because it performs poorly or fails to solve its current problems by being better, more effective, or more cost efficient, as some voices in the global competition debate suggest. Rather, and more fundamentally, it is that the assumptions on which the logic of the business enterprise has been built and is being run no longer fit reality. These assumptions concern both the firm's working beliefs regarding customers, technologies, societal values and norms, its core value proposal, and its mission as well as the firm's key skills and capabilities.

We want to provide an account of the transformation of Danish business enterprises and of how the forces of global transformation are challenging the existing business practices of both domestic corporations and organizations with international experience. These forces trigger a process not only of learning new ways of coping with changing business realities in Denmark and abroad but also of sloughing off old ways and practices, i.e., learning to unlearn and forget theories of the business that have grown obsolete as their basic assumptions no longer fit reality. At the same time, it is an account of how globalization reaches into and changes domestic business practices, sometimes reorienting the theories that drive firm performance.

The rise of new economies, as well as increasing competitive pressure, also entails tremendous growth in the opportunity space for business activities and great latitude to realign the theory of the business. The purchasing power of industry and populations in India and China is already staggering. In these countries, we find societies whose new and growing middle classes have universal needs for which many Danish firms' products and offerings are tailored. Danish providers of branded goods targeting the needs of these segments are only beginning to adjust to these new market realities. Danish companies with global branding footprints, such as LEGO and Bang & Olufsen, have only recently committed themselves to competing for market positions in China and India, although these markets have displayed staggering growth for over a decade. Moreover, with this growth, the increased strain on the earth's resources calls for technologies in several areas in which Danish industry has traditionally specialized. This relates to 'green' areas such as water treatment, sustainable energy production, high-tech conservation agriculture, and heating. Supporting this view, recent OECD research underlines that region-specific advantages – embedded in specialized firms, for example, via skilled labour and innovation capacity – continue to be a significant source of productivity gains for both small and large firms (Pezzini & Byrne, 2007). Although increased business activity is likely to spur exports, thinking in terms of national trade balances and end-to-end domestic production performance may be a testimony to Drucker's point: We have a tendency to measure the future possibilities and growth trajectories of Danish companies based on an assumption from the past, namely, that value-adding activities must mostly be based in Denmark, embodied in products, and then sold to other countries. This perspective does not fit well with a global society in which bringing value to a market is replaced with a notion of co-creating value together with co-constituents in that market. In other words, slogans such as 'made in Denmark' and other country of origin signifiers should perhaps no longer be seen as important trademarks of quality in themselves, as they tend to suggest a rather isolated view of reality in which national borders clearly define activities and in which activities are identified based on their country of origin.

Globalization, on the other hand, is not the same as uniformity and sameness. Rather than seeing the world as increasingly integrated and uniform, businesses are operating in a world of semi-globalization where value increasingly arises from the ability to combine activities effectively across global divides and from discovering opportunities to arbitrage ideas, markets, materials, and people to offer solutions that are novel to specific contexts. Rather than fearing a shift of economic activity from West to East and that the rise of new economic superpowers will lead to the concentration of economic activities there and, in turn, to the demise of Western European economies, we are more likely experiencing a global reshuffling of economic activity as production activities unbundle and increasingly occur in global production networks. The growth in these activities surpasses the growth in international trade as such, suggesting that growing global trade is increasingly governed by global value-chains (Athukorala, 2010).

The Transition Pressure

Although the situation described above is less gloomy than some would predict, this does not mean that the needed repositioning will happen automatically. As the globalization of business activities evolves, there is increased pressure on all actors to display ability to adapt and to proactively seize the opportunities arising from this development. This transition is no simple feat. In a number of respects, Danish firms and related supporting institutions are facing or already undergoing transition towards this end. From the perspective of a Danish manager, the internationalization of business activities is nothing new. However, the existing concepts learned from the gradual internationalization of Danish business activities in recent decades offers only partial insights into the pace and reach of the globalization currently unfolding.

This book is concerned with responses to these ongoing change processes. It addresses the transition challenges facing Danish business actors in a global context, using multiple theoretical perspectives to cultivate an understanding of the international firm and its challenges and organization. We seek to provide various, yet complementary and mutually supporting, insights into the question: How is globalization impacting the management, organization, and development of Danish business enterprises?

The stream of research presented here is based on a basic proposition, namely, that while the development of new business led to organizational change in the era of the manufacturing economy, changes in organizational form will mark the transition to the new businesses of the knowledge-based network economy. We seek to address the complexity and variety of this change through presenting case studies. We also seek to contribute to research into business-to-business marketing in relation to the configuration, evolution, and governance of business networks.

More specifically, we take an interest in how various actors collaborate, coordinate, and share resources at different levels of enterprises that are expanding their activities internationally or that already are multinational enterprises. We will focus on the relationships between institutional forces, organizational actors, group dynamics, and individual agency. We examine how social and organizational structures guide local interaction patterns, recognition, and resource distribution, and how social negotiations between individuals and groups maintain or adjust social and organizational structures. By taking as our departure point the organization of activities that cross sociocultural, organizational, and departmental boundaries, our research efforts combine perspectives from sociology with organization and management perspectives and business-to-business perspectives. Understanding how existing competences can be extended to exploit these business opportunities, how leverage can be found in resources not used to their full potential, how possibilities can be reframed in emerging economies, and how new demands from customers and suppliers in global value-chains can be met and even surpassed are all part of the contingencies faced by managers and their organizations.

In addition, these challenges do not uniformly confront all industrial actors; rather, there is large variation across industries reflecting differences in international specialization. Traditions and differences in institutional settings as well as competitive pressure add to the complexity of the situation, affecting business actors' ability to organize and participate in global production activities. This can be seen in vast differences across industrial sectors in terms of, for example, outsourcing activities.

In the main, the impact of globalization and its consequences for the management, organization, and strategic development of business activities is still unrecognized. Organizational forms, business models, means for generating and appropriating value, and the very nature of what comprises core concepts such as organizations, markets, and employment are up for grabs. With the increasingly global business dynamics, interpretations of such concepts are becoming increasingly transitory in nature. We accordingly refer to *organizing processes* more than to the *organization, economic enterprise,* and *firm* as a more adequate term for identifying the locus of economic organization.

Whereas some changes wrought by globalization are already surfacing and more are about to, there is a large gap between the present state and imagining the opportunities and challenges to come. New managerial mindsets and ways of framing the challenges of organizing, managing, and governing Danish business activities with a global outlook are called for. In many Danish firms, the opportunities created by globalization and how these opportunities will in turn affect globalization are only beginning to emerge. In other industries, changes have been rapid and many actors have yet to recognize them. Take, for example, the Danish wind turbine industry. In the early 2000s, Denmark's position in the wind turbine industry was unrivalled. Most of the world's knowledge of wind turbine design, manufacturing, and operation was concentrated in Denmark. International firms established strong positions in the Danish knowledge hub to tap into specialized knowledge, recruit employees, etc. Over the past ten years, Denmark's position has changed substantially in this regard. Danish firms are still important in the wind turbine industry, but several other geographical areas specializing in and developing wind-energy related technologies have emerged. Although this change has been profound and is recognized by industry actors, several implications of this change seem unrealized at a deeper operational level. One can see this in the case of scientific knowledge. The wind turbine industry has traditionally worked closely with Danish universities and research centres to both conceptualize and test new technologies. Danish universities prided themselves on being among the world leaders in this field. Many Danish-owned suppliers of goods and services still seem think that Danish wind energy knowledge is superior to that of other countries' universities and research environments. At least, their search pattern when it comes to seeking scientific knowledge differs from that of foreign-owned firms as they almost exclusively relate to Danish university research environments. Other Danish industries that have followed similar paths in terms of being unable to effectively meet the changes arising from changing global conditions include, to a greater or lesser degree, the mobile telecommunications industry and the marine industry.

In trying to answer the overall question regarding globalization's impact on the practices of Danish business enterprises, we pose three more detailed questions: 1) What critical managerial and organizational challenges face globally expanding Danish firms? 2) How has globalization impacted 'domestic' business practices in Danish society? 3) How do firms that recognize these challenges actively cope with them?

Overview of the Chapters

In the first part of the book, we address the challenges faced by business enterprises that already have a strong international presence. Danish business enterprises have come a long way in expanding their international activities, evolving from export-based firms into fully-fledged operators across regional divides. In parallel, a certain ethos has developed around the Danish Management Style and Danish approach to organizing international activities, an ethos rooted in Danish norms, traditions, and approaches. Perhaps Danes have grown accustomed to regarding these as virtues, reflecting proud traditions and in some cases even representing a competitive advantage for Danish-based firms. However, fashioning organizational designs and management traditions in accordance with Danish traditions poses challenges as well.

This theme is dealt with in detail in chapter two, 'Open-minded or Self-sufficient? Challenges of Exporting the Danish Management Style to Foreign Business Units'. Here, Klitmøller, Lauring, and Kubovcikova challenge theories suggesting that Danish managers can in all circumstances be expected to be open, inclusive, democratic, and tolerant. They argue that cultural behaviour is not simply an installed mental programme; rather, it is deeply affected by its context and not least by its interaction partner. Internationally oriented Danish managers are accustomed to a specific set of beliefs, based on a strong degree of empowerment, but may change their management style radically when confronted with individuals who are not used to being empowered. Based on case studies of Danish firms, Klitmøller, Lauring, and Kubovcikova suggest a behavioural pattern in which Danish managers at first try to apply a democratic, empowering management style, but if that fails, switch to a fairly autocratic management style. This finding illustrates the weaknesses of relying too heavily on static frameworks based on the theories of authors such as Hofstede (1980).

Not all intercultural interaction takes place face-to-face. Danish multinational organizations increasingly rely on technological media for collaboration and coordination across national boundaries. Virtual work and collaboration have therefore become increasingly important parts of the international business environment. In chapter three, 'Being Close at a Distance: Exploring Technological, Temporal, and Linguistic Challenges to Global Virtual Team Effectiveness', Lindekilde and Klitmøller specifically argue that technological limitations often hamper communication in Danish international organizations and can be viewed as a barrier to creating a shared identity in a work group. Moreover, Lindekilde and Klitmøller argue that virtual team members have difficulties collaborating due to technological limitations and that this challenges communication, identification, and perceived proximity. As such, the perception of proximity becomes more important than actual proximity because perceptions, rather than actual situations, guide actions in organizations.

Perceptions are also dealt with in chapter four, 'Parent Company Arrogance: Perceptions and Consequences', by Lauring, Andersen, Kragh, and Storgaard. They describe how the behaviour and communication of parent company representatives can create a strong impression that parent country nationals are arrogant. These authors outline three actions by parent country nationals that can make subsidiary employees see them as arrogant, namely, ignoring, bypassing, and educating. The three chapters in the first section of the book demonstrate that it is not only important to manage the actual circumstances of globalization, but often equally important to manage subjective notions, perceptions, and expectations derived from interpersonal intercultural interaction that may otherwise derail the globalization process.

The second part of the book focuses on aligning business practices embedded in a Danish institutional context with the changing realities of globalization. Along with the interconnectedness – arising from increasing globalization – of markets for capital, labour, and other resources, Danish work life is facing a transition challenge. Danish work and management traditions have co-developed with and are inseparable from certain societal values, and there is a strong consensus concerning the Danish 'model' of cooperatism. At the same time, Danish firms must align themselves with new contingencies and resources made available by increased globalization as well as with changing conditions for working internationally if they want to remain competitive. This gives rise to many challenges with respect to integrating Danish companies into the rest of the world.

In chapter five, 'Retention of Highly Skilled Expatriates and the Danish Work-life Balance', Normann and Bjerregaard demonstrate that foreign employees arriving at Danish workplaces tend to expect much more social interaction with their Danish colleagues than is the reality in Denmark. The well-developed family-work balance characteristic of Danish work culture seems to contribute to Danes spending fewer hours at work and focusing more strongly on using their time effectively. In this context, Danes seem to find it difficult and inconvenient to incorporate working relationships into the private sphere. This can constitute a barrier for foreigners seeking to adapt to Danish society during their employment in Danish companies.

While the intake of foreign labour is increasingly important for the Danish economy, the relocation of Danish nationals to take up positions or solve problems in foreign subsidiaries or joint ventures is also central to the globalization of the Danish business environment. In chapter six, "Flexpatriation': A View from the Engine Room of Sub-Suppliers in the Maritime Sector', Madsen and Rask start from the increasing expatriation of Danish nationals to foreign countries. More specifically, they set out to study the increasing need for, and consequences of using, 'flexpatriates' as part of a business globalization process. They demonstrate that flexpatriates relocating from Denmark can be seen as centrally placed in the Danish 'engine room of globalization'.

In chapter seven, 'Translating Private Equity in Denmark: The Impact of the TDC Buy-out on the Danish Private Equity Industry', Rocha and Wigan describe how the institutional environment of a local company exerts pressure on international business partners. They demonstrate that private equity firms in Denmark have been subject to diverging pressures emanating from the logics of the private equity field and the national institutional environment. They found that, on one hand, private equity firms in Denmark operate in what is still a predominantly coordinated market economy; on the other hand, these firms control their acquisitions from a managerial perspective originally imported from liberal market economies. This leads to tension between contending business system logics, calling into question the legitimacy of private equity operations in Denmark. The three chapters in the second part of the book all deal with how the structures of Danish society affect the forces of globalization that exert substantial pressure on 'business as usual' in local companies.

The third part of the book treats the strategies and practices applied by firms that have actively transformed their practices to meet globalization's challenges and opportunities in line with the third question posed. In particular, we discuss the organizing of global networks of organizations.

This theme is first taken up by Andersen and Kragh in chapter eight, 'Managing Strategic Transition in an Age of Accelerating Globalization'. They argue that the ability to dynamically fit activities to changing global realities calls for more than merely organizational boundary design and externalization. Corporations need to deal with larger transitional challenges with respect to aligning both organizational designs and managerial mindsets for effectiveness in a globalized business environment. These are important challenges that incumbent firms face when trying to readjust their existing design to overcome the often disruptive changes arising from their task environment. To do this, international business firms must remain flexible.

Another central theme linked to globalization concerns ethics and social responsibilities when responding to local conditions in foreign markets. In chapter nine, 'Collaboration in the Dynamic Organizing of Global Business Networks: CSR in Commons, Protocols, and Infrastructures'. Linneberg and Andersen discuss the notion of collaborative architectures across firm boundaries and provide explorative insights into how shared values and protocols in a community of business actors engaged in corporate social responsibility activities can provide a language for the effective configuration and coordination necessary in globalization efforts. They illustrate the importance of using corporate social responsibility standards to coordinate the value-chain, creating a fit between external stakeholders and internal competences.

This subject is approached from a global sourcing perspective by Ellegaard and Vedel in chapter ten, 'Sourcing Intermediary Profiles in the Global Clothing Industry', While the literature has been relatively silent regarding intermediaries, these authors identify two specific intermediary roles that generate value for buying companies. First, the production specialist specializing in certain products or supply markets can ensure quality, delivery, and services in a way that the buying company cannot with a reasonable resource outlay. Second, the full-service provider can rapidly deliver a portfolio of clothes of various designs to satisfy consumer demand at a highly competitive cost. They conclude that there is no need to avoid intermediaries in global sourcing.

In chapter eleven, 'Models of International Entrepreneurship', Rask and Servais take up the theme of international entrepreneurship. Due to the small size of the Danish economy, international entrepreneurial venturing is essential to Danish business globalization. Rask and Servais outline a model of how and why new international ventures are established and developed. This model can help us understand some of the more recent internationalization processes of Danish firms that have followed in the wake of the increased interconnectivity of global business contexts. This meta-model defines types of international entrepreneurial firms along two dimensions: 1) the degree of geographic diversification measured as the scope of foreign market opportunities and 2) the degree of foreign market commitment measured as the extent of cross-border coordination of resources, actors, and activities.

The final and concluding twelfth chapter, 'Preparing for the Unexpected: Some Tentative Answers', by Kragh, Andersen, and Lauring, summarizes the main findings arising from answering the three research questions on which this book is based. As such, the last chapter bases its discussion of how globalization will impact Denmark in coming years on the findings of the ten previous chapters and provides guidelines for practitioners and policy makers in the Danish business environment.

References

Athukorala, P. (2010). Production Networks and Trade Patterns in East Asia: Regionalization or Globalization?, *Asian Development Bank Working Paper* #56.

Danish Ministry of Trade and Commerce (Erhvervsministeriet) (2005). *Danmark i den globale økonomi*, København.

DI (2013). *Industrien beskæftiger stadig flere i udlandet* (Report). The Confederation of Danish Industry, Copenhagen.

Dickens, C. (1859). *A Tale of Two Cities*, Chapman and Hall, London.

Drucker, P. (1994). The Theory of the Business, *Harvard Business Review*, Sep-Oct, 95-104.

Eurostat (2014): Labour market statistics (accessed online: epp.eurostat.ec.europa.eu/portal/page/portal/labour_market)

Hofstede, G. (1990). *Culture's Consequences*.

Pezzini, M. & Byrne, E. (2007). *Globalisation and Regional Economies: Can OECD Regions Compete in Global Industries?* Publications de l'OCDE.

Quah, D. (2011). The Global Economy's Shifting Centre of Gravity. *Global Policy, 2,* 3-9.

CHAPTER 2

Open-minded or Self-sufficient? Challenges of Exporting the Danish Management Style to Foreign Business Units

Anders Klitmøller, Jakob Lauring and Annamaria Kubovcikova

Over the last decade, the ambivalence existing in the mindset of many Danes has become increasingly apparent. Kuttner (2008) has described how Danish society is, on one hand, characterized by openness to the forces of globalization and, on the other hand, by tight social integration and self-sufficiency. In this chapter, we will investigate whether what has been called the open-minded/self-sufficient paradox also characterizes Danish managers working in international corporations and, if so, how it affects the performance of Danish multinational corporations (MNCs). In doing so, we challenge current research highlighting the ideals of openness and empowerment captured in the notion of the 'Danish Management Style'. While such a style might flourish when Danish managers are working in a national setting, dealing only with employees of the same cultural background, some studies of Scandinavian managers have demonstrated that they radically change their management style in international settings (Bjørn, 1997; Mäkilouko, 2004; Sippola, 2009). In seeking to understand and explore such behaviour, we regard managerial identity as shaped by culturally constituted ideals and actual social interactions (Turner, 2013). The Danish self-perception of being 'open-minded' is an ideal that is continuously reinforced through interaction with other Danes who espouse similar culturally constituted ideals. However, when encountering non-Danes with different perceptions of ideal behaviour, a gap arises between the individual's self-perception of what constitutes effective behaviour in a given situation and how such behaviour is interpreted by others (Stryker, 2002). This mismatch between self-perception and others' perception of the self may lead to an identity crisis likely to elicit detrimental embedded cultural practices such as 'self-sufficiency'. In other words, when Danish managers find that Danish management ideals – an important part of their self-perception – do not yield effective results in an international context, and may even be looked down upon by employees, they may resort to other culturally constituted defensive responses to address the identity crisis that springs from lack of concurrence between perceived effective management behaviour and the values associated with such practices.

To describe the existence of the open-minded/self-sufficient paradox and its relationship with identity formation, we start with a general description of societal responses to specific aspects of globalization, to illustrate the dual nature of Danes' responses and actions. We then link these empirical characteristics to identity theory and the notion of the 'Danish Management Style'. Through interviews with Danish managers and ethnographic field studies in three fully Danish-owned subsidiaries, we will illustrate how the paradox affects the daily management of international organizations, impairing collaboration, communication, and knowledge sharing. We conclude the chapter by discussing the implications of the study for Danish managers working internationally.

Denmark in the Era of Globalization: Societal Context of Danish Managers

According to several observers, the main characteristic of globalization is increased political and economic integration across national borders. However, such forces of global homogeneity often lead to increasing localization and fragmentation on a societal level, as cultural identities and ideals collide (Castells, 1996; Friedman, 1995). This has also been the case in Denmark, most prominently mirrored in the political arena in Denmark's relationship with the European Union (EU) and in immigration scepticism. While the Danish economy is increasingly dependent on international exports, the Danish population remains sceptical regarding the effects of globalization. The tendency towards perceived national self-sufficiency was reinforced after the 11 September 2001 attacks on the World Trade Center and the Muhammad cartoon crisis in which Denmark was heavily criticized, leading to a negative political discourse in Denmark regarding Islam (Andersen & Bjørklund, 2000; Bjørklund & Andersen, 2002).

A cultural paradox arguably exists in Danish society. On one hand, Denmark's economy is open to the world as its companies are export oriented, making observers describe Denmark as an open and tolerant society (Nannestad, 2004). However, a less remarked-on and acknowledged shadow parallels the ideal of 'open-mindedness', namely, the xenophobia and prejudice that run through Danish society (Quraishy & Connor, 1991). There is no denying that as immigration has increased and Danes have been confronted with foreign cultural ideals in social encounters, a tribal culture has emerged that is often closed to Danes not of Danish ethnicity. The question is whether Danish managers, known for their inclusive and democratic management style, display similar tendencies: Do Danish managers display what Andersen (2006, 25) has called 'provincial self-sufficiency' in the international management context and, if so, what consequences does such behaviour have for MNC management?

Danish International Management Practices

In this section, we outline the core elements of what has been called the Danish Management Style. It is an ideal that is well described and measured in the management literature, though we know little of what actually happens to that ideal when managers interact with non-Danes, as occurs in international organizations.

The Danish Management Style

Danish managerial values are arguably based on the national cultural characteristics and societal system of Denmark (cf. Glunk, Heijltjes & Olie, 2001; Schramm-Nielsen, 2001; Suutari, 1996). It is associated with the type of management practiced in other Nordic countries, as this country cluster has a distinct management pattern compared with that of other parts of Europe and, especially, of the rest of the world (cf. Lindell & Arvonen, 1997; Perlitz & Seger, 2004; Ronen, 1986). The ideal of the Danish Management Style is based mainly on Hofstede's (1991) cultural studies of IBM. According to Hofstede's power distance index, Denmark ranks third from the bottom of 40 countries. It has been claimed that nations with a low power distance are characterized by equality, collaboration, and dialogue between superiors and subordinates. In Denmark, management is based on egalitarian values and a democratic political system. Organization charts are flat and hierarchical power distances are small within organizations (Smith, Andersen, Ekelund, Graversen & Ropo, 2003), meaning that employees and employers interact as relative equals in Denmark. Accordingly, the Danish Management Style is considered cooperative and participatory: nobody receives orders from anyone, and executive proposals must be thoroughly explained and justified, rather than being imposed on the basis of authority. In Denmark, managers ask for other people's advice, proposals from executives may be questioned, and counter-proposals can be made. Furthermore, Denmark is described as one of the ten most individualistic countries in the world (Hofstede, 1991), a characteristic manifested in the superiority of individual over group interests and in rather superficial work relationships. Danes are especially proud of their independence, freedom, and autonomy. Consequently, power is weakly centralized and employees participate in business management to a high degree. Hofstede (1991) also ranks Denmark as one of the most *feminine* countries. This cultural dimension stands for modesty and cooperation, and values caring and tender attitudes. This is in line with the ideals of the welfare state, supporting democracy and concern for all members of society. Finally, and perhaps most importantly, Denmark scores low on uncertainty avoidance. Such nations are claimed to be very open to diversity and new ways of thinking (Schramm-Nielsen, 2000).

From Open-Minded Ideals to Self-sufficient Practices

The portrayal of the Danish Management Style as open and inclusive stands in contrast to the recent societal developments in Denmark described in the previous section. In recent years, faced with the forces of globalization, especially increased cultural internationalization, Danes have to some extent displayed a tribal mentality rather than open-mindedness. Hence, the Danish Management Style characterized as participatory, empowering, and inclusive may be exercised mainly in situations in which Danes manage other Danes. Moreover, the discrepancy between recent societal developments in Denmark and the ideal of the Danish Management Style reflects a more fundamental problem with using Hofstede's framework to understand managerial practices. One problem with Hofstede's framework and other similar models is that it addresses *ideals* of cultural values rather than these values as they are practiced, reflecting a static view of culture and international management. Recent studies have illustrated how managerial practices change as they move from a national to an international managerial environment. Bjørn (1997) conducted fieldwork in subsidiaries of Danish companies in Japan and Germany and found that Danish top managers developed a much more autocratic and hierarchical management style than that the Japanese or German managers, who would usually be considered more oriented towards stratification and hierarchy (Bjørn, 1997). This mismatch of expectations made the local workforce hostile to the expatriate managers who, in counter-reaction, changed their style of management to being very domineering and exclusive. Interestingly, Brewster (1995) described almost the same situation when he observed how democratic-minded Swedish managers turned autocratic overnight in England.

To understand such managerial behaviour, and in contrast to the Hofstedian approach, we suggest applying a more dynamic view of identity as shaped through social interaction (Mead, 2001; Turner, 2013). According to socio-psychological theory, identity is based on broader cultural definitions, so the strength of a manager's commitment to a certain identity depends on the expectations and positive evaluations of his or her employees (Stryker, 2002). In a Danish context, the manager's self-perception as an effective leader and the cultural values associated with such behaviour (e.g., open-mindedness) are reinforced through social interaction, since these values are praised by other Danes. This sparks a 'virtuous circle' in which favoured ideals will become embedded in the individual's identity, giving rise to positive emotions such as self-esteem. When the context changes, however, and the Danish manager finds himself in situations in which the ideals and values linked to his or her identity are not positively evaluated, this gives rise to feelings of inadequacy, low self-esteem, and even anger (Turner, 2013). In such identity crises, individuals resort to negative sanctions and bias towards others. The difficulties Danish managers experience when dealing with foreign employees who do not have the same values as themselves are related to the open-minded/self-sufficient paradox, self-sufficiency being a culturally learned response sparked by a state of anxiety and identity crisis when interacting with individuals who hold different cultural values. While Danish managers have the potential to apply an empowering and open approach when dealing with employees (cf. Gertsen, 1988), they may resort to provincial self-sufficiency in international settings if their managerial behaviour is negatively, or merely ambivalently, evaluated by subordinates.

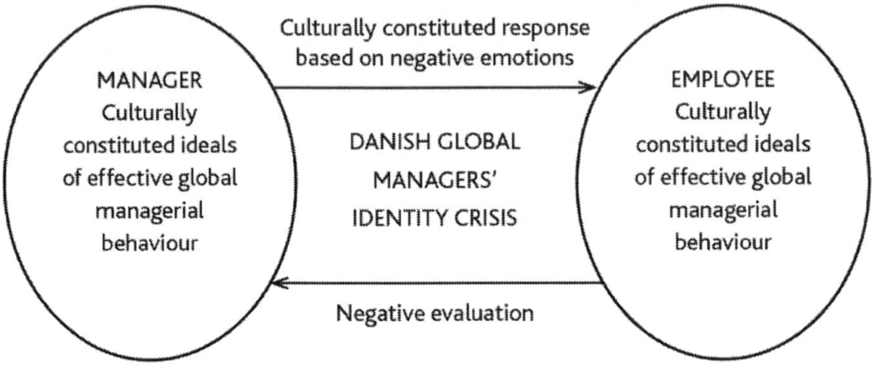

Figure 2.1. Relationship between managers and employees, and their culturally constituted managerial ideals.

In conclusion, there are indications of a gulf between the Danish Management Style as an ideal and in actual practice. To explore the challenge facing Danish managers in international settings, we used semi-structured interviews and ethnographic methodology particularly suitable for capturing the tension between ideal and practice.

Method

Research Design

This chapter draws on interviews with Danish international top managers and on the results of exploratory, ethnographic fieldwork in three Danish subsidiaries in Saudi Arabia, England, and China. Ethnographic fieldwork is a useful research strategy when studying dynamic, fluid, and complex processes related to human behaviour and interaction. It enables the researcher to investigate the implicit ways in which intercultural relations are defined and conceived by groups and individuals. This makes it possible to map how informants talk and think about their own and other groups, and how their implicit understanding of a situation is created, maintained, or contested (Eriksen, 2002). The inherent multi-method nature of ethnographic research helped us increase the internal validity of the study, by giving us the opportunity to triangulate data. Below are the main research techniques employed during three months of fieldwork at each subsidiary.

Participant Observation

By means of participant observation, ethnographic fieldwork offers the unique advantage of generating data on social processes at the level of everyday interactions (Dewalt, Dewalt & Wayland, 1998; Eriksen, 2002; Kunda, 1992). Via an extended process of learning in the studied local setting, researchers gain the ability to recognize and understand the social organization of the observed interactions. This provides an opportunity to register processes that produce and reproduce the social categories applied at the scene (Brubaker, 2002). In the present case, the processes could be observed in the daily dialogues between organizational members in which the negotiation of internal and external categories was debated in a way that would not have been registered in more formal interviews. Furthermore, participant observation also allows the registration of group behaviours such as socialization or boundary creation that are not directly obvious in interviews. Such group processes could be observed by mapping interaction patterns occurring, for example, in offices and the canteen.

The researchers were allowed to move around with few restrictions in all subsidiaries. During frequent walks around the plants, the researchers gradually became familiar with a substantial proportion of the subsidiaries' members at all levels and in all functions. However, as the researchers were not directly connected to any department, there was never any danger of becoming members of any particular group. Altogether, the degree of participation during observation depended on the nature of the activities observed. When observing business meetings, a low level of researcher participation took place; in the canteen and at social gatherings, however, the researchers participated to a greater extent. In addition to the direct observations, numerous conversations with employees were recorded in small notebooks that the researchers kept in their pockets at all times. All such observations were coded in the same way as were the interview transcripts.

Interviews

The interviews took the form of open dialogues between researchers and informants, resembling normal conversations as closely as possible (Bernard, 1995). During the interviews, questions centred on the relations and communication between the Danish managers and host-country nationals, following up on previous statements or observations integrated in the continuously developing interview guide (cf. Alvesson, 2003; Fontana & Frey, 1994). In all, 152 interviews were conducted for the purposes of this study. In China, interviews were conducted with five Danish, one Canadian, and five Chinese managers. In Saudi Arabia, the interviewed group consisted of 16 Danish expatriates and their ten spouses, together with 13 third-country nationals, specifically, six Indian, three Filipino, three Egyptian, and one British employee, for a total of 39 interviews. In England, a total of 90 individuals were subjects of semi-structured interviews, including 28 Danish international workers and 62 English host-country nationals. Fifty-one of the interviewed informants had managerial responsibilities. Finally, we interviewed 12 Danish top managers with extensive international experience from large Danish companies.

Managers were interviewed in their offices while other employees (e.g., workers and secretaries) were interviewed in vacant team-leader offices or meeting rooms. The researchers presented themselves as independent parties, so many local or expatriate employees saw the interviews as opportunities to air disagreements in an anonymous context. The researchers thereby became a means to communicate discontent with the current organization situation to the top management. All interviews were recorded and transcribed.

Analysis

Observations and interview material were analyzed by constructing taxonomies according to Spradley's (1980) guidelines. This implied manually coding the collected data (i.e., printed material, interview transcripts, and observation notes) and sorting them into various categories. The categories were then used to construct a taxonomic tree including a range of subcategories and sub-subcategories. This process was subjective because the sorting of spoken statements and other pieces of information into categories was not always unequivocal. Nevertheless, the process of writing this chapter started from the formed categories, creating narratives as sequences of events (e.g., Clifford & Marcus, 1986; Geertz, 1988).

Results

This section first discusses findings from top manager interviews and then, separately, from interviews at each of the three Danish subsidiaries.

The 'Danish Management Style' as an Ideal

In the early stages of the research, it became apparent that the 'Danish Management Style' was a cultural ideal heavily embedded in the Danish international managers' identities. One notion they used to describe themselves was 'democratic', which they related to Danish society as a whole: 'As we have had democracy in Denmark since 1849, this of course also changes all the preconditions for implementing democratically governed and democratically driven management' (Danish top manager). This self-perception is interesting as it relates managerial aspects to sociocultural features of Danish society. Furthermore, it also illustrates how Danes perceive themselves as better than others at handling some dimensions of management. This belief that the Danes can employ democratic management better than others became even more obvious in the later stages of the research project. Another quotation illustrates the other part of the paradox:

> Well, the biggest problem has actually been dismantling the cultural barriers between the Danes – who acted as if they had better judgment and perceived themselves as superior – and the foreign nationals. To eliminate the arrogance and incompetence that the Danes have been displaying. (Danish top manager)

The contours of the open-minded/self-sufficient paradox are apparent in the above quotations. On one hand, Danish managers are strongly urged to be open-minded and inclusive; on the other hand, these managers display a strong sense of superiority bordering on self-sufficiency. In the remainder of this chapter we seek to explicate the ideal participatory, empowering, and inclusive dimensions of management detectable in the following statements of Danish managers when describing the Danish Management Style:

> The Danish Management Style is very democratic and delegates responsibility. And there is open communication with our employees

> ... trust in other people and expectations of independence, expectations of being able to take responsibility and function independently within a framework. (Danish top manager)

These perceptions support Hofstede's (1991) power distance index, according to which Denmark is a nation with low power distance that emphasizes equality, collaboration, and dialogue between superiors and subordinates. In Denmark, management is based on egalitarian values. Organization charts are flat and hierarchical power distances are small within organizations (Smith, et al., 2003). This ideal is expressed when communicating and obtaining consensus for managerial decisions: 'I try to be very down to earth. I try to communicate a lot – I think it's one of my most important tasks ... the Danish Management Style is very consensual'. These quotations nicely illustrate the abovementioned description of the Danish ideal as cooperative and participatory. However, while Danish top managers expressed a positive view of the Danish Management Style in foreign business units, it became obvious during the study that this style was often not actually applied. We will explore this in the three following cases, examining various aspects of the open-minded/self-sufficient paradox and its organizational ramifications.

Case 1. Danish Management Practices in China

The first case is that of a small Danish subsidiary with four Danish expatriates and approximately 400 local employees. In this Danish subsidiary, both foreign and Chinese managers were aware of the value of collaboration, intercultural communication, and knowledge sharing. When asked directly, they all agreed that sound communication between the two nationalities was a great advantage. The Danish managers claimed that without the knowledge of their Chinese colleagues, their efforts would be similar to those of polar scientists working in the Sahara Desert. One added, 'We would be guessing instead of knowing'. The Chinese managers also valued the idea of intercultural communication, mentioning that although the expatriates knew how to run a business, the Chinese managers were necessary to translate their ideas to fit the local context.

While attitudes towards collaboration and knowledge sharing were generally very positive, actual practice diverged somewhat from that ideal. As one Chinese manager stated, 'Knowledge sharing is like one big conflict here – we don't use each other's ideas'. This could be observed on several occasions when Danish managers contacted former expatriates and other contacts in Denmark to acquire knowledge of the Chinese market, instead of consulting their local colleagues. Moreover, according to the Chinese managers, instead of engaging in dialogue, the expatriates often employed one-way communication. New ideas were proposed to the local managers, but the expatriates did not listen if the answers differed from their own views. One Chinese manager stated:

> I believe that we all have different kinds of knowledge and that this can be used, but frankly, I have not experienced the true benefits of this. Surely, we can get some ideas and learn something we can use in our work, and this is important. But the foreign managers are not familiar with many of the characteristics of the Chinese market, so they should communicate more with us. (Chinese manager)

The above quotation illustrates the Chinese manager's sense that the work relationship was unequal, even though equality was formally espoused. This problem can be illustrated through the following observations of a meeting.

A Danish manager explained the need to improve displays in the franchise shops, saying that it was important that the Chinese shops be as attractive as those in Europe. When asked, the Chinese manager replied that this would be difficult to implement due to the local franchises' reluctance to invest in design, and that patience was therefore needed. The Danish manager responded by firmly stating that to maintain their franchise agreements, they should be required to do better. This ended the discussion. It appeared to the observing researcher that the Chinese manager did not want to openly challenge this resolute statement, though it was obvious to him and the other Chinese managers that the proposal would be more or less impossible to implement in the near future.

Such situations were cited by the expatriate managers as examples of Chinese managers not speaking up due to cultural constraints and because they lacked a sense of responsibility in running the subsidiary. A Danish manager claimed that 'The Chinese are used to strict one-way communication ... The boss is the general and they expect him to be in command'. The perceived hierarchical orientation of the Chinese employees made the expatriates change their management style to fit the perceived local requirements. As a Danish manager put it, 'The Chinese perceive the Danish Management Style as problematic, because I tell them about the target and not so much about how to get there'. This statement expresses the view that the Chinese nationals displayed less independence and initiative than should be expected of employees working in a well-functioning business unit.

Another observed incident illustrated the difficulties associated with intercultural collaboration and dialogue. One Danish manager had the idea of selling Christmas stockings that parents could fill with presents for their children, as is customary in the Anglo-American tradition. The promotion was a fiasco, as most stores responded with statements such as: 'This sock is too big and does not fit' or 'We only received one sock. This must be a mistake. Please send me one more'. Subsequently, a Danish manager claimed that the situation could have been prevented if the Chinese manager had challenged the idea.

Occasions like the above caused the General Manager of the subsidiary to state that establishing dialogue was difficult due to the cultural differences and the resulting relationship between Chinese and foreign managers. As he described it, 'The knowledge sharing is hard. The Chinese people are used to obeying orders and that's the only way they know how to do things in an effective way'. This argument can be interpreted as expressing a perception of the Chinese communication style as not only different but also inferior.

The Chinese managers interpreted the reasons for communication breakdowns differently. As one manager put it, 'My opinion is not important to the foreign managers and often they don't believe me. I give them my opinion two or three times, and the fourth time, I keep quiet'.

One researcher observed incidents that could be interpreted as the expatriates' not treating their local colleagues as equals. For example, the researchers were advised by the expatriates to use simple language and to repeat themselves continuously when communicating with the Chinese managers. In addition, degrading jokes about the locals could often be overheard when the expatriates were speaking together internally. In line with this, the Chinese managers felt that collaboration problems related not only to cultural differences, but also to the convenience of excluding local personnel from some decisions. As one Chinese manager put it, 'The foreign managers always have an idea when solving a problem and it is very hard to change that'. Foreign managers' failure to listen can be related to a statement of the company's Danish General Manager: 'When ideas are proposed, I will consider them, but I normally have an idea as to whether or not they are possible'.

The Chinese managers generally called for more equal relations between the two nationalities. In their view, the organizational culture should, to a greater extent, represent a combination of Western and Chinese values. One Danish expatriate agreed with this; others, however, did not believe that it was possible to forge equal relationships or dialogue due to inherent cultural differences. As stated by the General Manager, 'When you aren't Chinese, you will always have a problem understanding them, and the whole structure of the society and culture will not allow this relationship'. Another Danish manager stated the following:

> There is the Chinese logic and the Danish logic. Neither of them is better than the other, but they are very different. Their language and culture is so different that you sometimes wonder whether we live on the same planet. (Danish manager)

This case illustrates how the cultural differences between the Danish expatriates and the Chinese local managers became clear markers of the group relations that led to communication breakdowns. Danish managers' angry and degrading remarks about their Chinese subordinates seemed to reflect an emotional frustration at the perceived ineffectiveness of the Danish Management Style in a Chinese context. To uphold their image as effective managers, the Danes adopted a more dictatorial style and self-sufficient practices. This was noticeable when the Chinese managers disagreed with the Western managers: The formers' comments would conveniently be ignored by the expatriates, exploiting their superior power position in the corporation. In this case, the inability to listen caused several important and costly mistakes that could have been avoided if the Danish managers had paid more attention to their own reaction patterns when managing in an international context.

Case 2. Danish Management Practices in Saudi Arabia

The second case describes a Danish subsidiary that stationed a group of Danish managers on long-term contracts to oversee the production and distribution of products. The group of Danish international workers had great confidence in the superiority of the Danish worldview and management style. When asked why it was necessary to station Danes in the subsidiary, the expatriates described themselves as more thorough, having a more comprehensive overview and a more developed sense of quality than did the other nationalities they observed in Saudi Arabia. They even believed that, in international settings, the Danes are 'some of the best labourers one can find'. Furthermore, they claimed that the openness of the Danish mentality increased adaptability, making Danes better at cooperating with other nationalities than were Americans or Dutch, for example. One expatriate manager explained:

> There is not one of us Danes who has to be embarrassed by our international skills. We speak English, we speak German, and wherever we go, we can cope. This is because of our understanding, our perspectives on life, and our opinions. (Danish manager)

However, according to them, it was not only their intercultural competences that supposedly suited the Danish managers especially for the job. Supposedly, it was their tolerance and non-discriminatory view of other nationalities and races that gave the Danes an advantage. As one manager put it, 'What characterizes us is that we speak to our middle managers as equal partners. We don't care whether they have light or dark skin. We don't make assumptions about them being idiots'. The self-professed high moral virtues and attitudes of the Danish managers made them unquestioningly in charge of the subsidiary, whereas the Indian, Egyptian, Filipino, or Saudi employees constantly needed directions from management. Due to their particular skills, all the Danish managers agreed that if they left in two weeks, the company would cease to exist. One of the Danes, however, provided a more nuanced view:

> We Danes have a more comprehensive overview than do the other nationalities in the company ... but that may be because we do not involve the other nationalities so much. It may be something self-sustaining in which we build a wall. (Danish manager)

Some of the supposedly missing virtues of the other nationalities may be related to how the company was managed. There also seemed to be another limitation to the Danes' success. According to the Danes, their international and open-minded view met substantial unexpected challenges when confronted with the working practices of the other nationalities in the subsidiary. The empowering management style that the Danish international workers were used to applying at home seemed less useful in their new surroundings. One Dane offered this observation:

> To begin with, you are probably a bit too ambitious or too Danish. You start out by involving the other nationalities too much and then, eventually, you conclude that it doesn't work. Then you learn not to waste your time. You know, the Danish way can take you far, but there is no point dragging it on for the last bit. Then it is like 'You do this and you do that – and that is how it has to be'. (Danish manager)

What the Danes experienced as obstacles to an inclusive management style was interpreted as a lack of independence by the other nationalities. This made the Danes manage in a rather authoritarian manner using only one-way communication:

> In some ways it is easier to work with Indians, Filipinos, and Egyptians, and in some ways it is more difficult. Here you can also make demands – just on a different level ... It is a lot like 'I want it this way!' And then they do it like that until I want something different. So it takes a totally different management style down here. It is more like raising children – not meaning to be offensive. (Danish manager)

The pride of the other nationalities was cited as another impediment to the openness and inclusiveness of the Danish Management Style. According to the Danish managers, the non-Danish employees could not learn because they found it difficult to admit when they were wrong. As one manager put it, 'Pride makes them see problems that do not exist'. Similarly, another Danish manager saw other nationalities' pride as a great barrier to implementing the inclusive management approach. He used a very confrontational strategy to counteract this barrier: 'One of my great pleasures down here is in fact to tell them when they have made a mistake – and get them to admit it'. Due to the difficulties of applying their usual management style, the Danish managers chose to organize the subsidiary like an ethnic hierarchy, very much in accordance with the Saudi tradition. Consequently, to be a manager, one had to be Danish and to be a supervisor, one had to be Egyptian. This practice led one of the non-Danish employees to say that they felt that there was a kind of 'apartheid' in the company. Another informant mentioned that there was a situation in which 'the Danes were divorced from the rest, like feudal landlords'. Naturally, the ethnic hierarchy limited interaction and intercultural learning, the clear division between groups creating a certain suspicion of the other nationalities.

For example, rumours of numerous crimes would spread among the Danes and simple misunderstandings could lead to dramatic stories. As a result of the mistrust, some Danish managers even suggested setting up video surveillance cameras not only in the production area but also in the living quarters of the non-Danish employees.

This scepticism could also be detected in the daily lives of the expatriates. They used harsh language and militaristic vocabulary about the need to beat and kick the workers. They would also often refer to the other nationalities as 'the monkeys' or use other derogatory terms. At the same time, the managers would tell each other that the non-Danish workers were very privileged to work for a Danish company where conditions were better than fair and where they could earn much more than they could in their home countries. However, this quite positive view of the situation was not shared by all the other nationalities. Many non-Danish employees felt demotivated by the exclusive and authoritarian management style that was actually exercised by the Danes. As one Indian employee put it, 'We always just have to say 'yes, yes'. We can never say 'no' to anything. If a manager says it is night when it is day and we object, we will be fined'. An Egyptian middle manager conveyed a similar view regarding the Danish Management Style: 'If you want to work in this company, you have to be like those monkeys that cover their mouth and eyes and ears. We have to be their monkeys'.

While the above describes an extreme case of what can go wrong in the internationalization process of a Danish firm, it still makes important points regarding certain paradoxes of the Danish Management Style in an international context. To begin with, the Danish expatriate workers felt very confident that they were tolerant and open-minded. Yet this feeling was disturbed when they were actually faced with individuals who did not react the way the Danes were used to. When the more empowering and inclusive management styles of the Danish managers seemed to fail, the managers became so frustrated that they radically changed their approach and resorted to being very authoritarian and exclusive. Such emotions and practices could be ascribed to emerging identity crises in the Danish managers when realizing that the values they normally associated with effective managerial behaviour did not render the expected results. This situation is likely to inspire a bias towards Danes as having superior cultural values and against non-Danes as having different and often inferior values. This leads to a 'self-sufficient' feeling, blinding the Danes towards other viewpoints and approaches to work. In conclusion, the case illustrates that it was very difficult for the Danish managers to maintain tolerance and inclusiveness in a working environment differing from the one they were used to in Denmark. Being Danish, the managers simply reserved openness and equality for their national peers; consequently, the collaboration and knowledge sharing was very limited across the nationalities.

Case 3. Danish Management Practices in England

The third case describes the reorganization of an English company after its purchase by a Danish MNC. To oversee the merger, 35 Danes were stationed in this subsidiary of 2,000 employees. The sudden entrance of the Danish employees into the organization prompted some uneasiness among the English employees, causing them to question their own employment status. As one English employee put it, 'Well, they are building a company in England to fill it with Danes and get the English people out as soon as there is an opportunity'. This tension gradually resulted in polarization between the two nationalities. One English manager described the situation as follows: 'For me this company is very much the Danes and the English. The Danes seem to think they come with all the knowledge and if they weren't here, there would be no company'. Gradually, individuals from the two groups came to see each other as members of opposing teams. To communicate efficiently with the English employees, the Danish expatriate workers needed to engage in socialization, meaning, for example, that they should not end a discussion too abruptly, even when patience was running out or they were struggling with the foreign language. The Danes' problem can be described through the words of an English consultant coaching one of the Danish managers. The consultant advised the manager to 'warm' the relationship with his employees, and the Dane responded by asking what tactics would be best for accomplishing the goal. This, among other things, was interpreted as indicating a lack of interpersonal skills. An English manager expressed his opinion as follows: 'The Danes are very capable of understanding their weaknesses. They have a very logical approach to that as well. They address it like mathematics – tell me exactly what I do wrong and how I can do it right' (English manager). A colleague expressed his opinion of the role of emotions:

> The Danish tend to be less emotional. They are very well organized and rational. If it is an English person and you really want to pursue something – if it is a really important issue, you tend to be really emotional about it and really argue and fight for it. Danes are not like that. If they really want something they will not get passionate about it, but they would go for even more rational arguments. In that respect I guess they are a little like the Germans. (English manager)

Although the Danes were more structured in their approach to other people, a number of English employees noticed that the Danes did not use the formal rules and guidelines to the same extent as they did themselves. Instead, the Danish managers would lead by example and expect workers to follow with the same enthusiasm and sense of responsibility. The Danes would train and empower the subordinates and expect the English workers to do the work in the most 'rational' way with as little formal leadership as possible. Disagreements arose when the English workers did not always take the path that seemed rational in the eyes of the Danes. In these situations, the Danish managers felt they needed to work out specific procedures for the workers to do things the right way – i.e., the Danish way.

Accordingly, there was a tendency for the Danes gradually to become more direct whenever they felt their English subordinates did not understand the proper way of working. Sometimes the Danes would even lose their temper in a most inappropriate way in the eyes of the English employees. The Danish managers expected things to be done, if not on the workers' own initiative, then at least according to the guidelines – but that was not always the case in England. The English employees failed to do their jobs without being continuously reminded to the point that the expatriate managers became so frustrated and impatient that they, contrary to their usual democratic management style, started giving some very direct orders.

> Danes that come here they tend to say 'I – think – you – are – wrong – because ...', and there are other ways to say that in English and English people use a lot of humour in the language which Danes don't do. In the beginning, the Danes will be very abrupt, and that pisses people off and makes them do the opposite of what you request. (English manager)

In that way, frustration at the perceived ignorance of the English workers and incomprehension of the more indirect English style of interaction made the Danes come across as very direct or autocratic.

> I have been working in Denmark and I find that the Danes are different from English people in their attitude to work. They expect the employees to do exactly the job they tell them, but with us, that is not the case. That is why people in Denmark don't have procedures as we do. They trust people to do things. (English Manager)

It was rather difficult for the Danes to work in England, because they did not all understand the creation and maintenance of social relationships in the workplace or how to communicate in a less direct fashion – among other ways, through humour. In terms of communication, English humour seems to level social hierarchies while upholding formal relations. Many Danes did not fully understand that. To get through to their English employees, they needed to play along with the game of socializing, meaning, for example, that they should not end a discussion too abruptly, even when patience is running out. Expatriates who did not master the more politically sensitive form of interaction were classified as 'German Danes'.

> What we would be looking for are the more Anglo Danes, not the more Germanic type of people – the more autocratic people that think people will do something just because they tell them to. (English top manager)

The Danish managers, who were expected to be very democratic and inclusive, turned out to be the opposite.

This case describes how Danish managers may react unexpectedly when confronted with other nationalities. More functionalist theories describe Danish national culture as open, inclusive, democratic, and tolerant. However, the results of the research underlying this chapter suggest that Danish expatriate workers may change their management style radically when confronted with individuals who are unused to being empowered. In other words, Danes will at first try to use a democratic, empowering management style but, if that fails, may switch to a rather autocratic style of management. What seemed to happen in the case of the 'German Danes' was that the Danes altered their approach towards their subordinates in reaction to the difficulties of applying their skills in the English context. When the Danes felt that their skills and experience were not producing the usual results, they lost their tempers and started giving very direct orders. Such a reaction can be understood according to a more dynamic view of identity in which the Danes' 'self-sufficient' practices can be interpreted as a culturally based emotional response when faced with unfamiliar interaction patterns and values. In this case, the mutual hostility that gradually developed blocked the collaboration and knowledge sharing between the two groups.

Conclusion

Regarding the challenges of exporting Danish management practices to foreign business units, we found that the future success of Danish companies might be hampered by what we call the open-minded/self-sufficient paradox among Danish managers. Denmark has entered the global era with an ambitious strategy of aiming to compete internationally. Yet Denmark's internal responses to increased globalization have been inconsistent: On one hand, there seems to exist an ideal of inclusiveness and a global outlook; on the other hand, there is some resistance to the EU and to increased immigration throughout the Danish population. We have investigated whether this duality of being both open and closed to the outside world could have influenced the Danish managerial style as practiced in international encounters.

The Danish Management Style is based on participatory, empowering, and inclusive ideals. These ideals are not only conveyed in the relevant literature but are also part of Danish managers' self-perception. The danger of naively seeking these ideals when attempting to understand managerial practices is that they are static concepts that underestimate the iterative, procedural nature of management. From this perspective, a management style becomes a trait-like entity embedded in the individual rather than something negotiated in actual interactions between the manager and his or her employees. To capture a more dynamic view of identity, and to understand how the open-minded/self-sufficient paradox affects Danish managers, we turned to social theories of interaction (Mead, 2001; Turner, 2013). In this light, a manager's commitment to his or her identity as a 'democratic' and 'open' leader is rooted in a positive evaluation of these values by the international staff (Stryker, 2002). This is rarely the case in international settings, as the local personnel may uphold differently culturally constituted values of ideal managerial behaviour. As illustrated in the presented cases, this gives rise to feelings of inadequacy, low self-esteem, and anger when the managers come to realize that their Danish Management Style does not produce effective results. This subsequent managerial identity crisis leads to biased behaviour and 'self-sufficient' treatment of others (Turner, 2013). The present study found that, in international management contexts, the Danish Management Style is extremely difficult for Danes to apply when encountering other nationalities with values different from their own. Consequently, as observed in the studied foreign subsidiaries, the Danish expatriate managers often used approaches that did not correspond to the 'Danish' ideals espoused by themselves and described in the literature.

The challenge for Danish managers is that they are used to leading workforces characterized by informal rules, dedication, motivation, and similar backgrounds to their own. When they encounter employees of different nationalities and with different values, they also evoke reactions that differ from those they are used to. This can cause Danish managers to resort to more authoritarian methods simply to get the job done. This study found that the observed Danes often used one-way communication to simplify work processes and did not listen to their foreign employees or managers. This is consistent with the observation that Swedish expatriate managers who were unprepared for the differences they encountered in England also quickly became autocratic. The confusion and disappointment of expatriate Danes when their management styles do not function could lead to barriers in interaction, knowledge sharing, and dialogue. If this happens, Danish expatriate managers will obtain less key information about the local business environment, such as local ways of organizing work, the local market, and consumer behaviour. In addition, the local workforce will have few incentives to learn from the Danes' expertise. Eventually, these factors could lead to poorer business results.

The chapter demonstrates that there are some challenges in exporting the Danish Management Style, which has often been portrayed as successful in Danish settings. The study uncovered persuasive evidence of the open-minded/self-sufficient paradox, which stems from the core of Danish culture and affects international managerial practices. The Danish ideals of inclusiveness and tolerance are noticeably misaligned with developments within the country in recent decades. Faced with the forces of globalization, Danes, including Danish expatriate managers, must continuously balance being open-minded against being self-sufficient, so as not to jeopardize the future economic success of the country.

References

Alvesson, M. (2003). Beyond Neopositivists, Romantics, and Localists: A Reflexive Approach to Interviews in Organizational Research. *Academy of Management Review, 28*(1), 13-33.

Andersen, J.G. & Bjørklund, T. (2000). Radical Right-Wing Populism in Scandinavia: From Tax Revolt to Neo-Liberalism and Xenophobia. In: P. Hainsworth (Ed.), *The Politics of the Extreme Right. From the Margins to the Mainstream* (pp. 193-224). London: Pinter.

Bernard, R.H. (1995). *Research Methods in Anthropology: Qualitative and Quantitative Approaches.* Thousand Oaks: Sage.

Bjørklund, T. & Andersen, J.G. (2002). Anti-Immigration Parties in Denmark and Norway: The Progress Parties and the Danish People's Party. In: M. Schain, A. Zolberg & P. Hossay (Eds.), *Shadows Over Europe: The Development and Impact of the Extreme Righ in Western Europe* (pp. 105-134). New York: St.Martin's Press.

Bjørn, L.B. (1997). *Managing Uncertainty in Transnational Headquarters-Subsidiary Interfaces.* Aarhus University, Aarhus.

Brewster, C. (1995). The Paradox of Expatriate Adjustment. In: J. Selmer (Ed.), *Expatriate Management: New Ideas for International Business* (pp. 115-135). London: Quorum Books.

Brubaker, R. (2002). Ethnicity Without Groups. *European Journal of Sociology, XLIII*(2), 163-189.

Castells, M. (1996). *The Rise of The Network Society Vol. 1.* Oxford: Blackwell Publishers.

Clifford, J. & Marcus, G.E. (1986). *Writing Culture: The Poetics and Politics of Ethnography.* Berkeley: University of California Press.

Dewalt, K.M., Dewalt, B.R. & Wayland, C.B. (1998). Participant Observation. In: H.R. Bernard (Ed.), *Handbook of Methods in Cultural Anthropology* (pp. 259-300). Walnut Creek: AltaMira.

Eriksen, T.H. (2002). *Ethnicity and Nationalism.* London: Pluto Press.

Fontana, A. & Frey, J.H. (1994). Interviewing: The Art of the Science. In: N. Denzin & Y. Lincoln (Eds.), *Handbook of Qualitative Research* (pp. 361-376). London: Sage.

Friedman, J. (1995). Global System, Globalization and the Parameters of Modernity. In: M. Featherstone, S. Lash & R. Robertson (Eds.), *Global Modernities* (pp. 69-81). London: Sage.

Geertz, C. (1988). *Works and Lives: The Anthropologist as Author.* Stanford: Stanford University Press.

Gertsen, M. (1988). *Expatriate Selection and Inter Cultural Training,* Institute of International Economics and Management. Copenhagen School of Economics and Business Administration.

Glunk, U., Heijltjes, M.G. & Olie, R. (2001). Design Characteristics and Functioning of Top Management Teams in Europe. *European Management Journal, 19*(3), 291-301.

Hofstede, G. (1991). *Cultures and Organizations: Software of the Mind.* London: MCGraw publications.

Kunda, G. (1992). *Engineering Culture.* Philadelphia: The University Press.

Kuttner, R. (2008). The Copenhagen Consensus. *Foreign Affairs, 87*(2), 78-95.

Lindell, M. & Arvonen, A. (1997). The Nordic Management Style in a European Context. *International Studies of Management and Organization, 26*(3), 73-91.

Mead, G.H. (2001). *Essays on Social Psychology.* New Brunswick: Transaction Publishers.

Mäkilouko, M. (2004). Coping with Multicultural Projects: the Leadership Styles of Finnish Project Managers. *International Journal of Project Management, 22,* 387-396.

Nannestad, P. (2004). A Game Real Actors Won't Play? Integration of Ethnic Minorities in Denmark as a Collective Action Dilemma. *International Migration Review, 38*(1), 287-308.

Perlitz, M. & Seger, F. (2004). European Cultures and Management Styles. *International Journal of Asian Management, 3,* 1-26.

Quraishy, B. & Connor, T.O. (1991). Denmark: No Racism by Definition. *Race and Class, 32,* 114-119.

Ronen, S. (1986). *Comparative and Multinational Management.* New York: Wiley.

Schramm-Nielsen, J. (2000). How to Interpret Uncertainty Avoidance Scores: A Comparative Study of Danish and French Firms. *Cross Cultural Management: An International Journal, 7*(4), 3-11.

Schramm-Nielsen, J. (2001). Cultural Dimensions of Decision Making: Denmark and France Compared. *Journal of Managerial Psychology, 16*(5-6), 404-424.

Sippola, M. (2009). The Two Faces of Nordic Management? Nordic Firms and Their Employee Relations in the Baltic States. *International Journal of Human Resource Management, 20*(9), 1929-1944.

Smith, P.B., Andersen, J.A., Ekelund, B., Graversen, G. & Ropo, A. (2003). In: Search of Nordic Management Styles. *Scandinavian Journal of Management, 19*, 491-507.

Spradley, J.P. (1980). *Participant Observation*. New York: Holt Rinehart and Winston.

Stryker, S. (2002). *Symbolic Interactionism*. New Jersey: Blackburn Press.

Suutari, V. (1996). Leadership Ideologies Among European Managers: A Comparative Survey in a Multinational Company. *Scandinavian Journal of Management, 12*(4), 389-409.

Turner, J.K. (2013). *Contemporary Sociological Theory*. London: SAGE Publications.

CHAPTER 3

Being Close at a Distance: Exploring Technological, Temporal, and Linguistic Challenges to Global Virtual Team Effectiveness

Rikke Lindekilde and Anders Klitmøller

Globalization has made the ability of Danish multinational companies (MNCs) to coordinate activities that span vast geographical distances increasingly important. This vast distribution of activities means that MNCs rely greatly on global virtual teams (GVTs) to facilitate collaboration between dispersed organizational units (Jonsen, Maznewski & Davison, 2011; Zander, Mockaitis & Butler, 2012). GVTs consist of individuals who reside in different time zones and countries and who rely primarily on communication technology to complete organizational tasks (Horwitz, Bravington & Silvis, 2006). From the perspective of international organizations, GVTs have many potential advantages: they allow organizations to tap geographically distributed resource pools and, in an era of global economic crisis, technology-mediated communication offers a cost-effective and sustainable alternative to face-to-face collaboration. Yet, as experienced firsthand by Danish international managers, producing effective results often proves more difficult in GVTs than in co-located work groups. Danish managers therefore need to be properly prepared to handle the challenges of such virtual working methods, not least since GVTs are at the heart of the globalization processes currently pressing Danish firms to perform more effectively. This means that competence in using information and communication technologies needs to be improved among Danish virtual leaders, not least in relation to taking on complicated global knowledge-intensive tasks. For while Danish companies have been at the forefront of implementing technological solutions for simple routine work, there is still untapped potential to use digitization for business development and R&D purposes (Ministry of Business & Growth Denmark, 2013).

Making greater use of digitization is by no means easy, however. According to practical experience and existing research, the broad geographical distribution of GVT team members entails a range of challenges that degrade GVT effectiveness. For example, studies have consistently demonstrated that communication deteriorates with increased spatial distance. The lack of physically immediate communication has a negative impact on interpersonal relations, including identification between team members, which negatively affects team members' perception of emotional closeness with each other (Wilson, O'Leary, Metiu & Jett, 2008). This lack of perceived emotional proximity in turn feeds back, affecting communication and identification. A vicious circle is likely to emerge in which team members feel increasingly distanced from each other when they experience communication and identification challenges.

Surprisingly, this relationship between geographical distance, on one hand, and communication, identification, and perceived proximity, on the other, has scarcely been examined in the existing literature (Wilson, Crisp & Mortensen, 2013; Wilson et al., 2008). In particular, the notion of perceived proximity has been paid little attention in studies of the relationship between geographical distance and team effectiveness. The literature has traditionally conceptualized geographical distance and perceived proximity as similar and overlapping notions. Wilson et al. (2008) argue, however, that team members can feel 'far but close', or vice versa, and that perceived proximity, while as important as physical distance, also differs from it when it comes to understanding virtual interpersonal interaction. This means that the potential impact of geographical distance on virtual team outcomes is not fixed but depends on factors that influence whether GVT members feel emotionally distant from or close to each other. Understanding how various conditions inherent in global virtual work influence communication, identification, and perceived proximity could therefore improve our knowledge of GVT dynamics.

Accordingly, this chapter explores how three dimensions of GVT collaboration can challenge team effectiveness due to their impact on the relationships among communication, identification, and perceived proximity. First, information and communication technologies (ICT) could negatively affect communication, identification, and perceived proximity, as the lack of social presence and the lower richness of the media enhance the possibility of miscommunication and misunderstanding (Jonsen et al., 2011; Montoya-Weiss, Massey & Song, 2001). In addition, ICT is asynchronous due to either inherent media limitations or technological challenges (e.g., interrupted Internet service or video feed) that could compound the challenges described above. Second, GVT members are temporally dispersed (Maznevski & Chudoba, 2000), and the coordination challenges arising from time zone differences could add to the communication difficulties, lack of identification, and missing sense of proximity between team members. Third, due to their global geographical dispersion, most team members have to interact in a language other than their own. This factor, often neglected in virtual management studies, severely degrades GVT effectiveness. Language differences have proven to hamper team communication and identification while creating a sense of distance between virtual collaborators (Beyene, Hinds & Cramton, 2009; Klitmøller & Lauring, 2013; Wilson et al., 2013). Whereas extant research has focused on the technological, temporal, and linguistic challenges inherent in ICT communication as individual factors that could damage virtual communication, to our knowledge, no prior empirical study has linked these factors to identification processes and perceived proximity. This could be an important oversight not only for business research but also for Danish international managers. While it is often impossible or inadvisable to reduce the physical distance between members due to the organizational advantages of employees' being geographically dispersed, it might be possible to enhance communication, identification, and perceived proximity between team members, thereby boosting GVT effectiveness. We accordingly ask the following research question: How do technological limitations, temporal dispersion, and linguistic differences affect the relationships among communication, identification, and perceived proximity in GVTs?

The remainder of this chapter is organized as follows. First, we present the conceptual framework used here, which draws on the notions of communication, identification, and perceived proximity and on existing studies of GVTs. This is followed by a methodological presentation in which the two studied Danish MNCs, i.e., SWS and Centro, are profiled and the data-gathering techniques used are outlined. Subsequently, the empirical findings are presented in a thematic narrative format. Finally, we discuss the implications of the results for virtual team management.

Communication, Identification, and Perceived Proximity

GVTs are geographically, culturally, and linguistically distributed diverse teams that rely on technology-mediated communication to undertake organizational tasks (Baba, Gluesing, Ratner & Wagner, 2004; Lipnack & Stamps, 1997). Virtual teamwork allows organizations to position specialists from different functional areas on the same team, regardless of the individuals' geographical locations (Hinds & Keisler, 2002). The far-flung physical distribution of team members is, however, a two-edged sword: while it may offer the organization many potential advantages, including increased flexibility and lower cost, it also represents one of the most challenging aspects of virtual work. Consequently, most literature on virtual collaboration has been concerned with how geographical distance influences team effectiveness (Wilson et al., 2013). The present study found that geographical distance increased conflict, reduced trust, and reduced spontaneous interaction and informal knowledge sharing (Jarvenpaa & Leidner, 1999; Mortensen & Hinds, 2001; Nurmi, 2011). Furthermore, physical distance increases subgroup formation between co-located and distributed team members, with negative consequences for task coordination (O'Leary & Mortensen, 2010; Polzer, Crisp, Jarvenpaa & Kim, 2006). Finally, physical distance has also been found to reduce the affinity between team members, leading to lower responsiveness, less effort, and work delays (Seers, 1989).

The existing literature has paid little attention to the factors that could mediate the relationship between geographical distance and performance. This is because most mainstream studies of GVTs have conceptualized distance in purely objective terms, i.e., as the number of kilometres or miles between team members (Schweitzer & Duxbury, 2010). Recent research suggests, however, that distance or proximity is also a matter of perception (Wilson et al., 2013; Wilson et al., 2008). Studies have demonstrated that people often perceive the same objective distances differently, so what is 'far' to one person may be 'close' to another (De Blij, Murphy &

Fouberg, 2006) depending on a range of factors that potentially influence individuals' perceptions of one another. Communication quantity and quality as well as shared identity between team members have proven to affect the extent to which individuals feel emotional proximity to one another despite being geographically separated (Wilson et al., 2008).

Communication in virtual teams is the exchange of information between two or more individuals, primarily through information and communication technology (Nobel & Birkinshaw, 1998). Studies have consistently demonstrated the importance of communication for virtual team effectiveness (Jarvenpaa & Leidner, 1999; Zander et al., 2012), primarily because communication strengthens interpersonal bonds, in turn increasing information flow between sites (Kraut, Rice, Cool & Fish, 1998). Simultaneously, communication allows team members to develop shared values and categories that strengthen the identification process between individuals (Fiol & O'Conner, 2005). When individuals communicate they start building shared identities related, for example, to their profession or team. Identification is therefore a social process of self-categorization based on interaction with others (Hinds & Mortensen, 2005). As team members start identifying with each other, they establish common ground based on which they can work (Sarker & Sahay, 2002). The more common ground individuals share, the more they communicate, and the closer they feel to one another. This means that both communication and identification are intrinsically linked to perceptions of proximity, i.e., the extent to which one individual feels close to or distant from another (Wilson et al., 2008). It can be argued that even though a relationship exists between geographical distance and performance, this relationship is primarily a mediated one. The relationships among communication, identity, and perceived proximity directly affect the relationship between spatial distance and team outcomes. For example, empirical results from geographically distributed software development projects illustrate how individuals were able to perform well when undertaking very complex tasks (Kogut & Metiu, 2001; Wilson et al., 2008). These virtual team members felt emotionally close to one another due to their intense communication and shared 'hacker identity' (Raymond, 1999). Such cases in which team members feel 'far but close' cannot be explained if we apply a solely objective understanding of distance (Wilson et al., 2008). Instead, we must acknowledge the importance of individual perceptions of proximity and their dynamic relationship with communication and identity (Wilson et al., 2008).

In doing so, however, we must also recognize that work conditions in global virtual environments influence communication, identification, and perceived proximity, thereby affecting team performance. In this chapter we therefore explore how circumstances characteristic of GVTs affect the dynamic relationships outlined above. In particular, we focus on technological limitations, temporal dispersion, and linguistic differences. *Technological limitations* here refer to the limitations experienced by using information and communication technologies relative to face-to-face collaboration. These limitations could stem from a lack of richness in the media themselves, i.e., the fact that, when using the media, one has fewer communicative cues to rely on versus in face-to-face interaction (Daft & Lengel, 1987). They could also take the form of technological breakdowns and discontinuities in video feeds. The notion of *temporal dispersion* captures the fact that GVT members reside in different time zones (Chudoba, Wynn, Lu & Watson-Manheim, 2005), and *linguistic differences* the fact that GVT members usually speak a language different from their native tongue. Technological limitations, temporal dispersion, and linguistic differences have traditionally been associated with *either* communication *or* identification challenges. For example, it has been established that lean media have a negative impact on communication, and that temporal differences reduce identification in virtual teams (Lengel & Daft, 1988; Wilson et al., 2013). No studies, however, have related any of these three factors to the notion of perceived proximity or sought an understanding of how they influence the dynamic interaction among communication, identification, and perceived proximity, potentially mediating the relationship between geographical distance and team performance (see Figure 3.1).

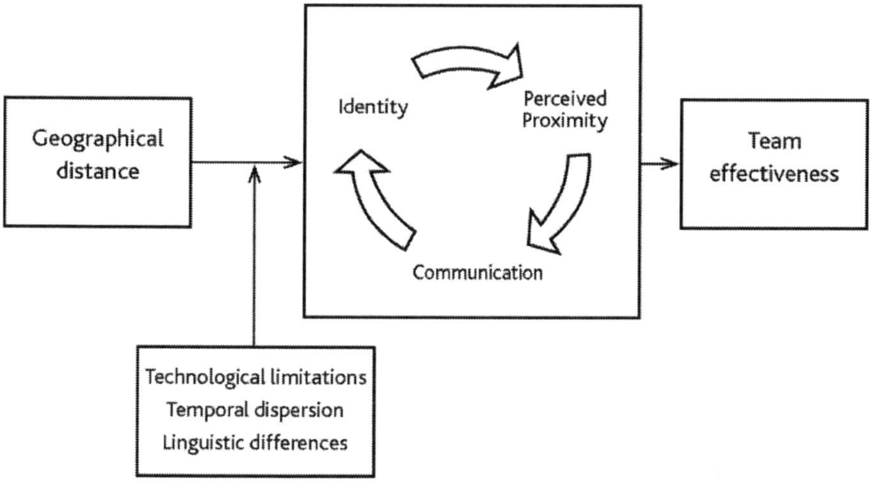

Figure 3.1. The impact of central GVT factors on communication, identification, and perceived proximity (adapted from Wilson et al., 2008).

In the following we describe the qualitative data-gathering technique used in this study. We then move on to an empirical description of the results, describing the challenges related to virtual team performance arising from technological limitations, temporal dispersion, and linguistic differences.

Method

The findings of the study presented here are based on data gathered in two Danish-owned MNCs. The first MNC, here called SWS, produces components for the sustainable energy sector, employs more than 20,000 individuals worldwide, and, at the time of the study, had recently divided its R&D tasks between India and Denmark. This MNC had created several virtual teams to coordinate and oversee various tasks and projects connected with new product development. The second MNC, Centro, is a leading engineering manufacturer that employs 18,000 individuals globally and has about 80 subsidiaries spread over five continents. Over the years, the firm has increasingly used GVTs to manage its decentralized and global activities. These MNCs were chosen because both rely heavily on information and communication technology in their day-to-day coordination of tasks between organizational units. The studied GVTs were all involved in knowledge-intensive tasks such as R&D, marketing, and logistics. Most teams also had Danish managers in key positions, which made the teams particularly suitable for exploring how Danish managers perceive challenges related to virtual teamwork. The GVTs were selected in collaboration with their global HR managers according to the following criteria: 1) the teams were divided between at least two geographically and temporally dispersed sites; 2) the teams did not meet face-to-face more than four times a year; and 3) the tasks undertaken by the teams were knowledge intensive and thus necessitated considerable virtual interaction. Depending on the task, team structure, and project phase, the amount of interdependence varied between team members, who generally exchanged emails, spoke by telephone, and participated in web meetings several times a week.

Initially, our main interest was to gain a broad understanding of global work conditions that could affect the relationship among communication, identification, and perceived proximity as an effect of geographical distance. Rather than seeking an in-depth understanding of the social practices of a particular GVT, we decided to interview various virtual team members and managers. The results presented here are therefore grounded in interviews rather than directly observed behaviour, providing us with information about individual thoughts, feelings, and experiences, i.e., how team members perceived virtual interaction.

Data Collection

84 semi-structured interviews were conducted in the two MNCs. In SWS, 43 employees – members of 14 GVTs – located in India and Denmark were interviewed. In Centro, we interviewed 21 Danish employees and 20 employees of other nationalities, i.e., Indian, German, Swedish, Norwegian, Portuguese, Chinese, American, Hungarian, and Spanish, who were members of 16 virtual teams. The semi-structured interviews took place in vacant meeting rooms or offices, and were facilitated as a guided dialogue between the researcher and the informant. This technique ensured that we obtained answers to the questions outlined in the interview protocol, while simultaneously allowing the informant to raise novel topics related to virtual collaborative processes (Spradley, 1979). Interview questions included 'What challenges do you encounter when communicating with other virtual team members?' and 'What successes have you experi-

enced when communicating with other virtual team members?'. During the interviews, the participants were asked to identify critical incidents illustrating situations in which virtual collaboration and leadership were particularly challenging or particularly well managed (Flanagan, 1954). The interviews, which were audio-recorded and transcribed, lasted approximately one hour each. To increase the accuracy of their responses, interviewees were assured anonymity.

Data Analysis

The data were analyzed using the steps described by Spradley (1980). The researcher involved in studying each MNC first read through the data independently, seeking to identify challenges encountered in the daily management of virtual teams. For each dataset related to an MNC, six to eight main codes, each containing four to six sub-codes, were developed. Subsequently, the themes arising from the coding were compared between the two MNCs, allowing us to identify the most frequently described examples of challenges encountered in virtual collaboration. Based on the participants' own words, we generated an initial list of challenges. During multiple meetings, we discussed our individual interpretations of the themes emerging from our coding scheme and how they challenged communication, identification, and perceived proximity. We alternated between data analysis and literature study to gain a theoretical understanding of our findings and to refine our coding. In this iterative process, the links between global work conditions and communication, identification, and perceived proximity started to emerge. At this stage, we involved a third independent researcher with whom we discussed our findings. This added validity to the coding process and sharpened our interpretations of the empirical data (see Table 3.1). The results of these analytical steps were the three themes, which we have labelled technological limitations, temporal dispersion, and linguistic differences.

Table 3.1. Quotations from the dataset describing the relationships among technological limitations, temporal dispersion, and linguistic difficulties that affect communication, identification, and perceived proximity.

	Communication	**Identification**	**Perceived proximity**
Technological limitations	'There is a technical barrier ... which means that you do not talk confidentially in the same way. It might sound like a bad excuse, but the technology is such a problem, and often you are not able to have a decent discussion when there are more than three or five participants attending a virtual meeting'. 'Our web meetings are usually used for presenting material ... There is less development and discussion going on there ... sometimes we just have to give up or we have to turn off the microphones and cameras to get a better connection ...'	'These web meetings are not made for getting to know people'. 'One or two face-to-face team-building activity days ... to get to know people, would be more effective to get a more 'us' feeling'. 'I can say that I feel that I am not in the same project ... you only have few virtual contacts with these colleagues'.	'I think at virtual meetings some people have this mental block ... They are afraid to speak up'. 'I think, the more we communicate, the closer we will feel, and the closer we feel, the more we communicate'. 'I am supposed to call my colleagues on the virtual project ... but instead I ask the one next to me, since it is easier to ask th one closer to you'.

	Communication	Identification	Perceived proximity
Temporal dispersion	'You easily lose a day or two ... this is really a frustrating barrier, when you just want to get on with your project'. 'When you are at a distance it is not good enough to be able to schedule a meeting in two days. Sometimes you just have to be able to sit down and talk to people, here and now'. 'Then you are struggling just to put up a video or telephone conference with a colleague or your boss ... this is really a frustrating challenge'.	'The time zone challenge is very important. Part of feeling a team is being able to discuss things during the day'. 'When Americans feel excluded from meetings and information in general, we become like teenagers. We want to be heard, but at the same time we want to be independent'. 'You feel neglected! We had a really bad example with a workshop where fifty persons had been invited and here in the US we had to get up at 3.00 a.m.!'	'With a time zone difference of nine hours ... we have difficulties finding each other at the time needed'. 'As a Dane you just don't think of how big this frustration can be ... After being here, I now see that the time zone difference is a practical burden of being a part of this company'.
Language difficulties	'The thing is, the Chinese are not that well educated in English. Some engineers can sit and reply to an email, but on the phone you have to repeat everything over and over again. It just delays everything, so you just want to stop talking with them and send them a mail instead'. 'A couple of times ... there has been total silence at web meetings'. 'Still, Danish managers can't even speak English ... so how can we communicate? A lot of the persons we work with in Denmark just don't know English'.	'When we are discussing important details in a project, you kind of get annoyed with them when you don't understand what they are trying to say – and in the end you just give up'. 'It takes some time to understand each other because we have different pronunciation in English'.	'When you experience things like this [i.e., language barriers], you don't feel that the world is getting smaller. Actually quite the opposite. You feel very far apart'. 'The only doubt was how to get closer to the other colleagues that I don't know, for instance, the ones who are located in Finland'.

Findings

In the following sections we present our findings and demonstrate how technological limitations, temporal dispersion, and language difficulties influence the dynamic relationship between communication, identification and perceived proximity in global virtual work.

Technological Limitations

In the course of our study, it became clear that many of our informants were of the opinion that virtual collaboration was severely hampered by technological limitations. According to the virtual team members, such limitations involved the reliability, convenience, and effective mastery and use of the media available in the organization. Many informants would express frustration with the quality of the available communication technology, as technical problems would cause severe communication challenges in the teams. One informant noted: 'You have to face many technical issues on a daily basis ... this is really a challenge to virtual communication'. This view was supported by several other informants who highlighted the impact of unreliable technology on virtual collaboration:

> When we are facilitating a meeting, the worst thing is when technology messes up, it is frustrating not only for the facilitator, but for everybody ... I think many virtual meetings are postponed for this reason.

The above quotation illustrates how technological limitations could reduce communication frequency. In line with this, another respondent said that the technology used could limit the number of individuals participating in telephone- and web-based synchronous communication:

> It might sound like a bad excuse, but the technology is such a problem, and often you are not able to have a qualified discussion when there are more than three or five participants attending a virtual meeting.

In addition, the technology would, according to the informants, limit the range of tasks that could be undertaken. Functional synchronous media were pinpointed by several respondents as posing a challenge for communication, leading to poor team performance:

> Often our virtual communication is just a cascading of information. Some of the problems at virtual meetings are that you are pulled in different directions. There is so much going on. It is as if they try to squeeze more into the same time ... the natural exchange of information is just not happening at our virtual meetings.

In particular, the informants claimed that communication would be challenged when undertaking more complex tasks: 'Our web meetings are usually used for presenting material to each other. There is less development and discussion going on there'.

In this way, technological limitations could reduce the team member's reciprocal communicative exchanges, in turn hampering identification processes in the GVTs. Informants described how web communication limited the possibility of strengthening social bonds, perhaps because it was more formal and task-oriented than was face-to-face interaction. Consequently, most informants agreed that, even though virtual communication was a necessity in international organizations, face-to-face interaction was preferable for shaping social relationships and fostering a shared team identity. Here, informants highlighted how their adoption of a more impersonal mode of communication reduced the feelings of personal connection and engagement when interacting through technology. As one informant noted, 'I think at virtual meetings some people have this mental block ... They are afraid to speak up. You'll need to meet face-to-face in order to get to know people and what they stand for'. This perception was reiterated by a Danish manager: 'These web meetings are not made for getting to know people'. The communication challenges related to technological limitations also diminished informants' desire to engage with each other virtually:

> These web meetings are so damn boring ... Sometimes there may even be twenty employees participating. This many participants at web meetings also often causes a lot of technical problems and sometimes we just have to give up, or we have to turn off the microphones and cameras to get a better connection ... this makes really bad meetings!

The communication challenges resulting from technological limitations created emotional distance by directly affecting how close team members felt to one another. As stated by one Chinese virtual team member: 'I think, the more we communicate, the closer we will feel, and the closer we feel, the more we communicate'. The lack of perceived proximity also affected communication, worsening team performance: 'I am supposed to call my colleagues on the virtual project ... but instead I ask the one sitting next to me, it is easier to ask the one closer to you'.

In sum, technological limitations could hamper communication and constitute a barrier to creating a shared team identity. This lack of identification would in turn influence the perceived emotional proximity between individuals and degrade team performance.

Temporal Dispersion

The second identified factor that influenced communication, identification, and perceived distance was the temporal dispersion of team members. In particular, employees and managers commented on challenges related to the use of synchronous real-time media such as telephony, web meetings, and videoconferencing when participants were located in different time zones. Specifically, members claimed to encounter difficulties 'finding each other at the time needed', and the greater the temporal dispersion, the greater the communication challenge:

> With a time zone difference of nine hours between California and Denmark, the window of opportunity for contacting each other is very limited, and don't underestimate this! There is practically no overlap in working hours.

It would prove particularly difficult to find the time to communicate when members were located on different continents and divided by big time differences: 'Work time really shrinks as more time zones are crossed, and it [i.e., work time] is almost nonexistent each time we have to include China'. This lack of shared work time delayed communication and caused great frustration, because the team would be unable to proceed with a given task:

> You easily lose a day or two ... this is really a frustrating barrier when you just want to get on with your project. When you are at a

> distance it is not good enough to be able to schedule a meeting in two days. Sometimes you just have to be able to sit down and talk to people here and now.

Even routine tasks, such as scheduling a meeting, could become complex and fraught with interpersonal friction, as noted by one virtual team member: 'Then you are struggling just to put up a video or telephone conference with a colleague or your boss ... this is really a frustrating challenge'. The lack of communication due to time zone differences also posed a barrier to identification, as it could cause team members to feel excluded from informal and ongoing dialogue. For example, a virtual team member stated the following: 'The time zone challenge is very important. Part of feeling like a team is being able to discuss things during the day'. In addition, informants would feel excluded when meetings were scheduled at times when they had difficulties attending. One informant said, 'You feel neglected!', and went on to tell how this happened from time to time: 'We had a really bad example with a workshop where fifty persons had been invited and here in the US we had to get up at. 3.00 a.m.!'

While a GVT manager from the US jokingly listed endurance as one of the most important team member traits, given the conference calls at odd hours, it was not always possible to participate, which severely impacted identification with the team:

> You see, when Americans feel excluded from meetings and information in general, we become like teenagers. We want to be heard, but at the same time we want to be independent. I think we all have our moments of anger and frustration because of this.

The lack of identification and feelings of isolation in turn added to the perceived distance between team members. Members felt that they had drifted apart from one another and from the organization. One informant described this perceived distancing: 'As a Dane you just don't think of how big this frustration can be ... After being here, I now see that the time zone difference is a practical burden of being a part of this company'. Time-zone differences between virtual team members posed a severe challenge to communication, identification, and perceived proximity.

Linguistic Differences

During our study, several respondents pointed out how linguistic differences could challenge the virtual collaborative process. Team members stated that they were often frustrated by differences in the common corporate language, because they slowed the communicative process when using synchronous media. As noted by a Danish manager:

> The thing is, the Chinese are not well educated in English. Some engineers can sit and reply to an email, but on the phone you have to repeat everything over and over again. It just delays everything, so you just want to stop talking with them and send them a mail instead.

As exemplified in the above quotation, individuals were often frustrated with their foreign colleagues when using telephonic and web-based media. In particular, informants highlighted differences in accent as causing communication problems, as described by a Danish manager:

> It is not so much that we do not know the same words. It has more to do with the fact that they speak in this funny tone making it hard to understand. If we discuss something complex, we have to ask again and again, and even then we still misunderstand each other.

According to some informants, this pronunciation problem meant that Danish managers could not lead the GVT effectively: 'Still Danish managers can't even speak English ... so how can we communicate? A lot of the persons we work with in Denmark just don't know English'.

It was not only the accents in verbal conversation that impeded communication in the GVTs, as linguistic differences could give rise to periods of silence in virtual interaction: 'A couple of times when there has been total silence at web meetings, I have tried to translate what I say in English into their native language, for example, Hungarian. For this I have used Google translate' (Danish manager). Accordingly, language difficulties led to miscommunication in the daily virtual work. This would in turn impact identification in the GVTs, as members would start to describe communication in the virtual team in negative terms: 'You look at the ones with language difficulties, they can be really smart, but you just don't know, when you don't understand what they are saying'. Another respondent noted:

> When we are discussing important details in a project, you kind of get annoyed with them when you don't understand what they are trying to say – and in the end you just give up.

Identification processes between team members suffered when language difficulties evoked negative sentiments between team members. The informants felt that this added to the perceived distance between team members, as described by one Danish manager: 'When you experience things like this, you don't feel that the world is getting smaller. Actually quite the opposite. You feel very far apart'.

To conclude, language differences affected the dynamic relationships among communication, identification, and perceived proximity, functioning as a barrier to communication and having a negative impact on the shared identity of virtual team members. Consequently, language differences led team members to perceive each other as distant.

Discussion

Our findings indicate that challenges related to technological limitations, temporal dispersion, and linguistic differences significantly affect communication, identification, and perceived proximity in GVTs. Technological limitations constitute a barrier that reduces team members' communication frequency and quality, which in turn impacts identification and individuals' sense of proximity with one another. Time zone differences tend to reduce communication in general and spontaneous communication in particular, leading to feelings of isolation in the GVT and a lack of perceived proximity. Linguistic differences are also important in the virtual collaborative process, as team members described how language differences slowed communication and prompted negative descriptions, diminishing identification and increasing the sense of emotional distance between members. Our findings suggest that technological challenges, time zone differences, and language difficulties severely impact the dynamic relationships among communication, identification, and perceived proximity, thereby significantly worsening virtual team performance.

With this finding, our study contributes valuable insight into an under-examined area, that is, factors that influence the relationship between geographical distance and team performance. In particular, our findings provide an understanding of the global work conditions that shape perceptions of proximity among team members (Wilson et al., 2008). The results also indicate that, due to technological limitations, temporal dispersion, and linguistic differences, globally distributed teams require an active and persistent managerial focus on building communication, identification, and perceived proximity. Managerial strategies should therefore include planning, clarification of roles, processes, and tasks, as well as training for managers and team members. Furthermore, and as discussed below, managers should seek to encourage communication and create a shared context.

Encourage Communication

In general, managers have to encourage members to practice virtual communication in various forms using various communication tools. Managers should actively support an appreciative and inquisitive approach to communication. Furthermore, they should support language training for team members who want to improve their ability to speak and write the common company language. Regarding language difficulties, another study cited the example of employees holding 'English Fridays' when they spoke only English as a way of gaining comfort with the language (Neeley, Hinds & Cramton, 2012). As both language and communication skills in general improve with practice, enhancing/strengthening these skills would reduce the necessity for frequent face-to-face meetings (Wilson et al., 2008). Managers could also enhance perceived proximity by encouraging conversations in which people discuss daily work issues. Promoting the personal sharing of experiences and emotions would enable all parties to empathize with one another, increasing perceived proximity.

Establish a Shared Context

In general, research demonstrates that one of the greatest problems with global teams is that they do not share the same everyday context. Team members therefore have no idea about the work environment, pace, scale, or scope of their distributed colleagues. This lack of shared context leads to misattributions and less identification, and amplifies the perceived distance among distributed members (Mortensen & Hinds 2001). An important task for GVT managers is therefore to build a 'shared context': in other words, the manager has to work towards compatibility of processes, tools, models, and systems across sites. When team members have access to the same information and share the same tools, work processes, work concepts, and work cultures, the likelihood of misunderstandings and divergent approaches is reduced. A shared context across sites provides the grounding necessary to better make sense of what is said, potentially mitigating harsh assessments of team members and, in turn, reducing interpersonal conflicts. Alignment of context, systems, work concepts, and processes – on the other hand – is often a result of many years of effort, although even movement in this direction may strengthen the platform for collaboration in GVTs. Shared context relates to what Wilson et al. (2008) define as 'common ground' in virtual work. For one person to understand another, there must be common ground between them. When people believe that they share some common characteristic or experience, they project traits or characteristics on others based on real or assumed category membership (Cramton, 2001). Shared context leads to shared identity, and altogether enhances the perceptions of proximity between virtual team members.

Limitations and Future Research

Our findings are limited by choices made in the design of our study. We examined a large number of members and managers of virtual teams to gather a variety of experiences. While our interview strategy allowed for a broad understanding of perception commonalities, it did limit the possibility of observing the interpersonal dynamics within specific teams. Future research could address this limitation by observing how virtual team members overcome challenges related to technological limitations, temporal dispersion, and linguistic differences. Second, our reliance on individual reports limits our ability to confirm team performance outcomes. Future research could address this limitation by obtaining objective measures of the impact of these factors on GVT performance. Furthermore, we might have identified ways of managing the specific challenges if we had studied virtual teams longitudinally. Studying the processes by which the identified factors challenged virtual teams could be an important topic of future research. Finally, the effects of perceived proximity warrant further investigation. In line with our findings, we would expect perceived proximity to predict willingness to work together and beliefs about the effectiveness of collaborating at a distance.

Conclusion

This study has investigated the challenges facing virtual collaboration. Our findings indicate that virtual team members experience difficulties arising from technological limitations, temporal dispersion, and language difficulties, and that these factors challenge communication, identification, and perceived proximity. Our findings also indicate that the more objective notions of distance do not capture the subjective and dynamic relationships that affect perceptions of distance and, in turn, team performance. We believe that the present analysis of challenges facing virtual teams has great potential to make GVTs in Danish MNCs more effective in the future. In particular, our study draws attention to the fact that Danish international employees need to be better equipped to handle the multiple dimensions involved in global virtual work. For example, employees need to be trained not only in the use of information and communication technologies but also how to handle the pressure associated with them and to understand how temporal dispersion and linguistic differences affect team perception. In view of the dynamics of these issues, we maintain that, by addressing these challenges better, Danish companies can enhance their effectiveness when collaborating virtually.

References

Baba, M. L., Gluesing, J., Ratner, H., & Wagner, K. H. (2004). The Contexts of Knowing: Natural History of a Globally Distributed Team. *Journal of Organizational Behaviour, 25*(5): 547-587.

Beyene, T., Hinds, P. J., & Cramton, C. D. (2009). *Walking through jelly: Language proficiency, and disrupted collaboration in global work.* Working paper from Harvard Business School.

Chudoba, K. M., Wynn, E., Lu, M., & Watson-Manheim, M. B. (2005). How virtual are we? Measuring virtuality and understanding its impact in a global organization. *Information Systems Journal, 15*: 279–306.

Cramton, C. D. 2001. The mutual knowledge problem and its consequences for dispersed collaboration. *Organization Science, 12*: 346-371.

Daft, R. L., & Lengel, R. H. (1987). Organizational information requirements, media richness and structural design. *Management Science, 32*(5): 554-571.

De Blij, H., Murphy, A., & Fouberg, E. (2006). *Human geography: people place and culture*. New York: Wiley & Sons.

Fiol, M. C., & O´Conner, E. J. (2005). Identification in Face-to-Face, Hybrid and Pure Virtual Teams: Untangling the Contradictions. *Organization Science, 16*(1): 19-32.

Flanagan, J. C. (1954). The Critical Incident Technique. *Psychological Bulletin, 51*(4): 327-358.

Hinds, P. J., & Keisler, S. (2002). *Distributed Work*. Cambridge: MIT Press.

Hinds, P. J., & Mortensen, M. (2005). Understanding conflict in geographically distributed teams: The moderating effects of shared identity, shared context, and spontaneous communication. *Organization Science, 16*: 290-307

Horwitz, F., Bravington, D., & Silvis, U. (2006). The promise of virtual teams: Identifying key factors for effectiveness and failure. *Journal of European Industrial Training, 13*(6): 472-494.

Jarvenpaa, S. L., & Leidner, D. E. (1999). Communication and Trust in Global Virtual Teams. *Organization Science, 10*(6): 791-815.

Jonsen, K., Maznewski, M. L., & Davison, S. (2011). Global Virtual Team Dynamics and Effectiveness Klitmøller, A., & Lauring, J. (2011). ICT and Knowledge Sharing, in: MNCs: The Role of Media Richness, Uncertainty Avoidance, and Common Language Use, *European Academy of Management*. Tallin.

Klitmøller, A., & Lauring, J. (2013). When global virtual teams share knowledge: Media richness, cultural distance and language commonality. *Journal of World Business, 48*: 398-406.

Kogut, B., & Metiu, A. (2001). Open-source software development and distributed innovation. *Oxford Review of Economic Policy, 17*: 248-264.

Kraut, R. E., Rice, R. E., Cool, C., & Fish, R. S. (1998). Varieties of social influence: The role of utility and norms in the success of a new communication medium. *Organization Science, 9*(4): 437-453.

Lengel, R. H., & Daft, R. L. (1988). The selection of communication media as an executive skill. *Academy of Management Executive, 2*: 225-232.

Lipnack, J., & Stamps, J. (1997). *Virtual teams: reaching across space, time and organization with technology*. London: John Wiley & Sons.

Maznevski, M. L., & Chudoba, K. M. (2000). Bridging space over time: Global virtual team dynamics and effectiveness. *Organization Science, 11*(5):473-492.

Ministry of Business & Growth Denmark (2013). *Report on Denmarks Digital Growth*. http://www.evm.dk/publikationer/2013/29-05-13-denmarks-digital-growth-2013

Montoya-Weiss, M., Massey, A. P., & Song, M. (2001). Getting together: temporal coordination and conflict management in Global Virtual Teams. *Academy of Management Journal, 44*(6): 1251-1262.

Mortensen, M., & Hinds, P. J. (2001). Conflict and shared identity in geographically distributed teams. *International Journal of Conflict Management, 12*(12): 212-238.

Neeley, T. B., Hinds, P. J., & Cramton, C. D. (2012). The (un)hidden turmail of language in global collaboration. *Organizational Dynamics, 41*: 236-244.

Nobel, R., & Birkinshaw, J. (1998). Innovation in multinational corporations: Control and communication patterns in international R&D operations. *Strategic Management Journal, 19*: 479-496.

Nurmi, N. (2011). Coping with coping strategies: How distributed members deal with the stress of distance, time zones and culture. *Stress and Health, 27*: 123-143.

O'Leary, M. B., & Mortensen, M. (2010). Go (Con)figure: Subgroups, Imbalance, and Isolates in Geographically Dispersed Teams. *Organization Science, 21*(1): 115-131.

Polzer, J., Crisp, C. B., Jarvenpaa, S. L., & Kim, J. W. (2006). Extending the fault line model to geographically dispersed teams: How colocated subgroups can impair group functioning. *Academy of Management Journal, 49*: 679-692.

Raymond, E. (1999). *The cathedral and the bazaar: Musings on Linux and open source by an accidental revolutionary*. Sabastopol: O'Rielly and Associates.

Sarker, S., & Sahay, S. (2002). Understanding virtual team development: An interpretive study. *Journal of the Association for Information Systems, 4*(1): 247–285.

Schweitzer, L., & Duxbury, L. (2010). Conceptualizing and measuring the virtuality of teams. *Information Systems Journal, 20*: 267-295.

Seers, A. (1989). Team-members exchange quality: A new construct for role making research. *Organizational Behaviour and Human Decision Processes 43*: 188-135.

Spradley, J. P. (1979). *The Ethnographic Interview*. New York: Holt, Rinehard and Winston.

Spradley, J. P. (1980). *Participant observation*. New York: Holt Rinehart and Winston.

Wilson, J., Crisp, C. B., & Mortensen, M. (2013). Extending Contrual-Level Theory to Distributed Groups: Understanding the Effects of Virtuality. *Organization Science, 24*(2): 629-644.

Wilson, J. M., O'Leary, M. B., Metiu, A., & Jett, Q. R. (2008). Perceived Proximity in Virtual Work: Explaining the Paradox of Far-but-Close. *Organization Studies, 29*(7): 979-1002.

Zander, L., Mockaitis, A. I., & Butler, C. L. (2012). Leading global teams. *Journal of World Business, 47*: 592-603.

CHAPTER 4

Parent Company Arrogance: Perceptions and Consequences

Jakob Lauring, Poul Houman Andersen, Hanne Kragh and Marianne Storgaard

Due to the small size of their home market, Danish companies are often forced to establish themselves abroad and set up foreign subsidiary units. As we learned in the second chapter of this book ('Open-minded or Self-sufficient? Challenges of Exporting the Danish Management Style to Foreign Business Units'), Danish managers do not always have an easy time directing activities in foreign countries, and may find it even more difficult when done from the home country. The misaligned perspectives, mixed motives, and tensions between parent company managers and their subsidiary counterparts constitute an important reality for many Danish companies.

From an international management perspective, dysfunctional relationships between headquarters (HQ) and subsidiaries mean that resources that could have been used to develop the multinational corporation (MNC) are instead spent on addressing resistance and negative emotions. In other words, resources that should be used to create firm value are instead spent in the 'trenches' within the organizational units of the MNC. The standard mixed-motive description of the dilemma is that parent companies prioritize global integration issues to create economies of scale and scope and to share knowledge across the internal network of the MNC, whereas subsidiaries prioritize ensuring local competitiveness and adaptation to the needs of their local market contexts.

This mixed-motive dyad is too simplistic a pattern to advance our understanding of the motives and underlying dynamics operating between MNC units (Ghemawat, 2007). For example, the role of the variation in institutional context in which the organizational units are embedded and the resulting differences in logic have recently been offered as an alternative theoretical perspective for understanding tensions in the MNC organization (Morgan & Kristensen, 2006; Morgan, Kristensen & Whitley, 2001). Parent companies do not always know what is best for their subsidiaries and their involvement in subsidiaries' affairs may subtract rather than add value (Foss, Foss & Nell, 2012). Others have identified geopolitical power relationships as an important context for understanding uneven and unequal parent-subsidiary relationships and the accompanying challenges, as these shape managerial practices and worldviews (Frenkel, 2008). This line of research has focused on the silencing of discordant voices not in line with the core beliefs and ideology of the parent company (Calas & Smircich, 1999; Kristensen & Zeitlin, 2005; Storgaard, 2010).

This chapter examines these alternative perspectives on the HQ-subsidiary relationship. To seek novel insights through interdisciplinary interpolation (Weick, 1989; Morgan, 1989), we apply an alternative theoretical perspective on how the behaviour of Danish parent company managers is perceived by foreign subsidiary managers, analyzing how the attitudes and actions of Danish parent company managers are perceived as arrogant by subsidiary managers. We use social categorization theory and studies of group dynamics to frame what we call parent company arrogance in order to understand silencing and resistance occurring in the relationship. Resistance to adopting uniform practices in multinational corporations has been addressed by another literature stream concerned with the challenging boundedness of practice rather than the emotional and cognitive states of managers (Ferner, Edwards, & Temple, 2012). From this perspective, we can give voice to managerial, individual, and group perceptions not addressed by the dominant literature, but that we believe are critical for understanding the underlying tensions and resulting organizational behaviour. Highlighting the behaviours that drive perceptions of arrogance deepens management researchers' understanding of the dynamics leading to the establishment of lines of defence in parent-subsidiary relationships while providing managers with insight into how to mitigate these effects.

The rest of the chapter is organized as follows. First, we review the literature on arrogance as a phenomenon and the underlying theoretical axioms, discussing how they may be applied in the context of parent-subsidiary relationships. Next, we apply this theoretical framing to case studies, building on extensive field studies of parent-subsidiary relationships in four Danish MNCs. Finally, we discuss our findings, identify how these can inform the existing international management discourse, and outline future implications for management and research.

Theory

Traditionally, four streams of literature addressing parent-subsidiary relationships (Paterson & Brock, 2002) are consulted when analyzing the HQ-subsidiary relationship. These perspectives build on each other to some extent while reflecting the development in research focus that has evolved over the past five decades. We review this literature to address how these four perspectives differ in their underlying assumptions when it comes to understanding and/or explaining variations in and sources of conflict and tension in HQ-subsidiary relationships. We have not reviewed the literature concerned with the impact of institutional distance on these dilemmas, as we are focusing on intrinsic relationship dynamics rather than extrinsic causative or exacerbating factors. Table 4.1 presents a chronological overview of these literature streams and how they frame HQ-subsidiary tensions.

Table 4.1. Overview of research streams treating headquarters-subsidiary relationships.

	Strategy-structure stream	**Headquarters-subsidiary relationship stream**	**Subsidiary role stream**	**Subsidiary development stream**
Dominant theoretical perspectives	Organizational design literature	Contingency and systems theory	Social exchange and resource dependence	Entrepreneurship and agency literatures
Unit of analysis	The organizational structure	HQ	HQ-subsidiary relationship	Primarily the subsidiary
Framing of headquarters-subsidiary tension	Temporary design malfunction or permanent design flaw	Misalignment of environmental challenges faced by subsidiary and HQ formalization and centralization of decision making	Role conflicts between semi-dependent organizational units	Ongoing tensions among organizational units building positions in evolving organizational networks
Example studies of tensions	Bartlett and Ghoshal (1989)	Hedlund (1994)	Andersson, Forsgren, and Holm (2002)	Filatotchev and Wright (2011)

As can be seen from Table 4.1, the dominant perspectives differ in what they regard as important drivers in understanding the conflict aspects of the HQ-subsidiary relationship. More recent research increasingly emphasizes the role of subsidiaries as mandate takers and innovators, placing little emphasis on the parent company role (Egelhoff, 2010; Andersson, Forsgren & Holm, 2007; Cantwell & Mudambi, 2005). For example, Filatotchev and Wright (2011) suggest that managers with local mandates may pursue their own interests rather than those of the parent company. Although these perspectives offer several insights and are backed up by many empirical studies, they have also been criticized for their simplistic assumptions and rather static and macro-oriented understandings of power and of dependence, resistance, and change (Creed, Scully & Austin, 2002; Seo & Creed, 2002). Implicit in all these assumptions is the notion that actors have interests and motives that can be understood within the context of an MNC's organizational structure. They emphasize explanations rooted in a structural-functionalist understanding of the organization as a complete system and underestimate the role played by individual and group factors. Moreover, they tend to cast parent companies as benevolent providers of advice, direction, and master plans promoting the good of the entire MNC (Foss, Foss & Nell, 2012). Several alternative approaches could provide input regarding perceived parent company arrogance that would both complement existing views and challenge the (over)rationalistic premises on which they are based. First, the psychological literature on arrogance as a social phenomenon would be useful in conceptualizing the construct (cf. Weiner, 1994). Second, social categorization theory (SCT) is relevant to understanding some implications of the perception of actions of parent company representatives as arrogant (Tajfel & Turner, 1979; Ashforth & Mael, 1989). Finally, group dynamics theories can help explain some of the outcomes of perceiving others' actions as arrogant (cf. Brubaker, 2002).

Arrogance as a Social Construct

Few regard themselves as arrogant. Arrogance is a socially undesirable trait that can be attributed to individuals or groups based on their combined behaviours and attitudes. Although arrogance is a subjective category on which the perceiver and perceived would rarely agree, this label could have consequences for those to whom it is attached (Haan, Britt & Weinstein, 2007). Although arrogance is a commonly used concept, it is relatively little researched (Hareli & Weiner, 2000; Haan, Britt & Weinstein, 2007), humility – the other end of the spectrum – having received far more attention (e.g., Ben-Ze'ev, 1993; Wosinska, Dabul, Whetstone-Dion & Cialdini, 1996).

Arrogant individuals are generally perceived to be insolent, disrespectful, and self-serving. Interpersonal arrogance is therefore attributed to individuals who supposedly feel that they are better than others. Such individuals are perceived as looking down on their peers, treating them disdainfully and making it clear that they regard their peers as less worthy than their own more important selves (Dillon, 2007). A person may be regarded as arrogant if he or she is perceived to believe that his or her merits and accomplishments are greater than those of others. Accordingly, high achievements combined with high self-esteem could cause individuals to be labelled arrogant (Weiner, 1994). In addition, it is not uncommon to perceive individuals or groups as arrogant if they display little interest in another party's advice. The person offering what he or she believes is valuable advice may feel disrespected and thus find the opposing party arrogant (cf. Weiner, 1985).

Social Categorization Theory

The relevance of social categorization theory (SCT) to understanding organizational behaviour has already been established (Leavitt, 1975; Miller, Greenwood & Prakash, 2009). Building on insights from SCT, Salk and Shenkar (2001) explored social categorization processes in an international joint venture. The SCT perspective, however, also offers important insights into organization theory with respect to understanding social dynamics in complex organizations such as MNCs. Departments, subsidiaries, and other forms of groups in multinational organizations are often seen as political actors competing for scarce resources, such as money, power, or even political initiative (Bouquet & Birkinshaw, 2008; Schotter & Beamish, 2011).

The basic assumption of SCT is that individuals define themselves in terms of group membership, which can be based on similarities in demographic or social characteristics such as nationality, ethnicity, and language (Tajfel & Turner, 1979). In an MNC context, national subsidiaries may well represent categories to which certain values and traits are ascribed internally as well as externally, affecting both interaction and expectations (Vance & Paik, 2005). An important reason for categorization is that individuals are motivated to establish and maintain their self-esteem and therefore categorize themselves into positively labelled units, whereas others are viewed in a more negative light (Kulik & Ambrose, 1992; Vora & Kostova, 2007).

Social categorization could lead to the perception and labelling of members of other business units as being arrogant. Moreover, the fact that parent companies are often successful and powerful business units would add to the probability of parent company representatives' behaviour being perceived as expressing arrogance. For example, in staffing policy, the career opportunities of managers differ depending on whether they work in either the subsidiary periphery or the parent company core (Banai & Sama, 2000; Kostova, 1999). Perlmutter (1969) identified the ethnocentric mindset of managers as another example of perceived arrogance. Pudelko and Harzing (2007) touch on similar issues in discussing the dissemination of HRM policies in MNCs as spurred by either parent company dominance or localization. The consequences of perceived arrogance may include several negative outcomes. Lewicki, McAllister, and Bies (1998) suggest that negative feelings will lead to reinforcing behaviours: suspicion may follow from distrust and lead to cautious and guarded interaction in which the other party's intentions and motives are constantly questioned.

Group Dynamics

International business researchers have used the in-group versus out-group/intergroup behavioural dynamic to account for variations in actions and perception between local groups. For example, this framework has been used to identify the differences between collectivistic and individualistic national cultures (Kirkman, Lowe & Gibson, 2006; Ling, Floyd & Baldridge, 2005). Earley (1993) also links in-group versus out-group categorizations to national culture, proposing that in-group members of collectivistic cultures tend to protect each other more than do members of more individualistic cultures. Finally, in a case study of the organization of knowledge sharing in a Chinese subsidiary of Siemens, Voelpel and Han (2005) use the in-group versus out-group dichotomy to explain the difficulties of transferring global organizational practice between cultural contexts.

While SCT often regards group formation as a unidirectional, linear process, a more dynamic perspective can also be employed. Anthropological studies have demonstrated that the defining of internal norms/values and external boundaries is a process whereby group members actively work to distinguish themselves from competing social units (Barth, 1971). The more challenged the members of a unit feel, the more effort they will put into clarifying in-group boundaries and emphasizing group identity markers (Jenkins, 2000; Yagi & Kleinberg, 2011). Accordingly, certain actions performed by representatives of one group may strengthen the identity and spur the boundary work of members of another (Lauring, 2008). In an international business context, we need to acknowledge that categories such as parent company or subsidiary cannot be understood only as fixed entities and cast as unitary actors, but should also be perceived as categories in which individuals take strategic action based on perceived external and internal relationships and opportunities. Parent company versus subsidiary conflicts should not be understood literally as conflicts between two business units, but as conflicts between individuals and groups that become 'unitized' (cf. Brubaker, 2002). As such, we need to recognize the active work put into shaping perceptions of categories within the MNC. We also need to acknowledge that in-group versus out-group dynamics constitute a reinforcing process that can strengthen negative emotions and perceptions between groups. In other words, when parent company representatives are inconsiderate, dominant, or ignorant of the subsidiary context, being interpreted as arrogant, this could well trigger exclusive boundary work and behavioural patterns (i.e., resistance) among subsidiary employees, who may consequently be portrayed as difficult and obstructive collaboration partners. Moreover, the resistant behaviour of the subsidiary employees may lead parent company representatives to express a less inclusive attitude, which could be interpreted as even more arrogant. Finally, the subsidiary members' attempts to strengthen their internal identity in reaction to external challenges/competition could well make local employees more inclined to classify a range of actions as indicators of parent company arrogance (cf. Janis, 1982).

The theories described above could provide a useful perspective in seeking to understand why subsidiary managers and employees sometimes regard Danish parent company representatives as arrogant and what outcomes this may have. Several negative consequences of perceived parent company arrogance could be predicted from the reviewed literature. First, interpersonal and intergroup conflicts could arise due to emerging negative social categorizations (Tajfel & Turner, 1979). Second, organizational learning potential may decrease due to reduced communication resulting from the perception that parent company managers lack interest in the knowledge and skills of subsidiary units (Gupta & Govindarajan, 1991). Third, subsidiary staff turnover may increase due to a feeling of being looked down on by HQ, leading to the exit of the most talented employees who see better opportunities elsewhere (Ferner, Almond, Clark, Colling, Edwards, Holden & Muller-Camen, 2004; Mellahi & Collings, 2010). Finally, regional initiatives and creativity could be hampered due to a perception that HQ representatives are dictating general policies with little consideration for local circumstances (Cheng & Bolon, 1993).

Methodology

Our unit of analysis is the individual and shared perceptions of Danish parent company behaviour, as we look for incidents of social categorization formation (Ashforth & Mael, 1989). As pointed out by sociological research, individuals are inclined to 'unitize' groups as actors possessing specific intentions and behavioural traits (Bourdieu & Wacquant, 1992). We are interested in incidents in which certain perspectives arise through the categorization and classification of specific events and behaviours in the parent-subsidiary relationship (Brubaker, 2004). We base our study of these formation processes in the context of parent-subsidiary relationships in four MNCs.

Our preliminary understanding of parent company arrogance, of how it is perceived and of its consequences, emerged from an exploratory, single-case study of an English subsidiary of a Danish MNC (hereafter, 'MNC I'). After further exploratory study, it became apparent that perceived parent company arrogance might be a more general feature of the parent-subsidiary relationship. Moreover, it was clear that this concept was complex and called for in-depth qualitative data collection due to its sensitive nature and the strong emotions involved. Consequently, three more studies, i.e., of MNC II, MNC III, and MNC IV, were initiated to verify and elaborate on the initial findings. These were conducted by incorporating the concept of perceived parent company arrogance into ongoing research and by reanalysing and recoding existing interview and observation data. Hence, the multiple case studies that provide data for this chapter draw on four independent research projects conducted at four separate MNCs.

MNC I is a food sector production company headquartered in Denmark with subsidiaries in over 20 countries. The company employs 16,000 staff and has a turnover of approximately EUR 7 billion. MNC II is a furniture industry production company headquartered in Denmark whose products are sold in more than 40 markets worldwide. Its turnover is approximately EUR 100 million and the MNC has offices in seven world regions. MNC III is a global production company in the building material sector headquartered in Denmark. The company's 80 subsidiaries in 45 countries have approximately 16,000 employees and a turnover of approximately EUR 2.3 billion. MNC IV is also a global production company in the building material sector. This company owns manufacturing companies in ten countries and sales companies in just under 40 countries. It is headquartered in Denmark and employs approximately 10,000 people.

Interviews

In all cases, we used qualitative semi-structured interviews loosely following a semi-structured interview guide. The main idea was to apply a 'story-telling' approach, that is, to let the interviewees describe their views on the issue studied as freely as possible, allowing them to interpret questions freely and pursue the themes that they regarded as central. The interview guide was therefore used mainly as a checklist and guide to ensure that comparable data points were collected across the case studies. The themes covered relate to: 1) subsidiary perceptions of parent company behaviour, 2) relationships between parent company and subsidiary employees, 3) the role of expatriates/flexpatriates in inter-unit relationships, and 4) the consequences of perceived parent company attitudes. To each of these themes a number of sub-themes/codes could be attached. For example, in the case of the theme 'relationships between parent company and subsidiary employees', the sub-themes/codes included 1) perceived exclusive language use, 2) perceived lack of consideration, 3) perceived discrimination, and 4) perceived patronization (see examples in Table 4.3).

We specifically asked interviewees to express their overall impressions of the parent company and to provide examples of how their perceptions had developed. At the end of the interviews, interviewees were asked to share any additional information they felt was relevant. At that point, further negative comments on the situation were sometimes expressed. To increase the accuracy of their responses, interviewees were assured anonymity (Siegel, Waldman & Link, 2003).

The interviews, which took place in the interviewees' offices or in available meeting rooms at the workplace, lasted one to two hours. To minimize the effects of the setting and reduce the potential for elite bias, we interviewed individuals from all corporate levels. All interviews were audio-recorded and transcribed, and detailed notes on the interviews and on the researchers' overall impressions were written up the same day as the interview (cf. Eisenhardt, 1989). Table 4.2 indicates the distribution of interviewed personnel from each studied MNC.

Table 4.2. Distribution of interviewees.

Interviews	MNC I	MNC II	MNC III	MNC IV
Local subsidiary employees	62	4	15	2
Expatriates/flexpatriates	28	13	10	1
Headquarters personnel	5	5	11	4
Total number of interviews (n = 160)	95	22	36	7

Following Yin (2009), the qualitative work was undertaken to understand actions and perceptions in their unique contexts. Interviews were supplemented with other sources of data, including corporate documents and field notes from participant observation. These data sources were used to generate questions that were later discussed in interviews and for triangulation purposes. In the final analysis, we used only data that could be verified by more than one source in either one or several case studies.

Analysis

We used an inductive analytical approach relying on an iterative process of comparing theory and empirical data that combined within- and between-case analysis (Eisenhardt, 1989). We coded the data, classified them into emerging themes, and compared our findings with existing theory (see examples in Table 4.3). Afterwards, we discussed the few discrepancies between the sets of coding and decided how to categorize the remaining textual passages. First, we conducted a within-case analysis of the data to understand each case as a coherent whole. Second, we searched for cross-case patterns, comparing the identified topics across the four cases and identifying similarities and differences. Whenever differences in interpretation arose, we returned to the original interview texts and the complementary data sources to decide on the most appropriate interpretation. Working as a group of researchers allowed us to compare the case data in a reflexive way. The data analysis was finalized in a written report sent to each case company.

Table 4.3. Examples of within-case coding using multiple data sources in MNC 1.

Source	Participation	Interview	Observation	Document
Code d.2: Market Knowledge MNC I (UK)	'During a discussion after hours, an English sales manager was very emotional when he tried to explain that the subsidiary could not treat British supermarkets the way supermarkets were treated in Denmark'.	'Up and down is probably the best way to describe the relationship with Denmark. They are able to introduce products into the market with little resistance. In the UK it is different. We get frustrated with them'.	'When a Danish board member turned his back on a speaking English Marketing Manager the English manager was clearly offended'.	'We need to make it clear to our customers that in this company we cherish the long-held values of the hard-working Danish [producers]'.
	– Field notes	– Semi-structured interview with Marketing Manager	– Observation during site visit	– Corporate vision
Sub-code b.1: Language use MNC 1 (UK)	'When I participated in a seminar in Denmark along with employees from England, we found that all speeches were in Danish and that I had to translate'.	'The Danish visitors will talk about us behind our backs and there is nothing we can do about it'.	'English employees are clearly upset when a Danish parent company consultant and a Danish expatriate switch to speaking Danish during a meeting'.	'To all company employees'.
	– Field notes	– Semi-structured interview with English Process Manager	– Observation during meeting	– Translated e-mail header on a Danish language message sent to all MNC employees

Theme: Perceived parent company arrogance
Code d: Perceived consequences of parent company attitudes
Sub-code d.2: Local market knowledge
Code b: Relationships between parent company and subsidiary employees
Sub-code b.1: Language use

Results

The case studies provide numerous examples of how the attitudes and actions of Danish parent company managers toward subsidiary employees and managers are perceived as arrogant by subsidiary representatives. The many instances of parent company managers' arrogance reported by subsidiary representatives can be organized into three distinct categories of arrogant behaviour, which we have labelled *ignoring*, *bypassing*, and *educating*. *Ignoring* describes perceived behaviour in which parent company representatives are perceived as not listening to input from subsidiaries, no matter how relevant and important to the corporate level such inputs might be. *Bypassing* describes perceived behaviour in which the parent company interacts directly with local markets without involving or informing the subsidiaries and thus without acknowledging their relevant knowledge, interests, and competences. *Educating* is perceived behaviour in which parent company managers change subsidiary practices and values to be in line with those of the parent company. All three categories address aspects of social categorization and group dynamics; as such, although each category is described in isolation in the following, the categories are nevertheless interrelated.

Ignoring

This category concerns subsidiary employees' and managers' perceptions that Danish parent company representatives do not listen to their input or viewpoints. Subsidiary managers were frustrated with the fact that parent company managers did not have the requisite insight into the conditions under which the subsidiaries were operating. What is more, subsidiary managers and employees claimed that parent company managers displayed no interest in trying to learn or understand. Subsidiary managers felt ignored when trying to convey to parent company representatives what they perceived as important and relevant information, not just about local conditions but also about matters of more direct corporate relevance.

In one case, relationships between parent company representatives and employees in a UK subsidiary were uneasy because the latter did not feel that their particular challenges were acknowledged by parent company representatives. Expatriates and local personnel complained that they were given ridiculous advice by parent company executives, such as 'just tell the retailers to put our product on the best shelves'. While this may have been possible in Denmark, owing to the dominant home market position of the MNC, it was impossible in the UK. A manager from the UK subsidiary described how parent company managers did not listen to their concerns about what they felt were mistaken expectations concerning the UK market. One interviewee analysed the situation thus:

> Just because it is a big seller in Denmark it is not necessarily the same here. They don't get that. You see them throwing all this money around and you think to yourself – no wonder we are losing money. I don't think they are really listening. (MNC 1)

From the perspective of subsidiary employees, one consequence of the lack of parent company interest in local market conditions was an unresponsiveness to local requests for adaptations to processes and products. For example, one expatriate subsidiary manager explained how parent company managers' unwillingness to change packaging material had serious consequences for the local suitability of the company's products:

> In Europe you can use cardboard for packaging. But in Asia we can't use cardboard because the air is too humid and after four to six months it only has about half of its original stability. Still, they deliver products to China in cardboard packaging! I have tried to ask headquarters 'Why do you do that?' and the answer was 'This is the way we have always done it'. When I argued that it doesn't work, the reply just was 'We don't have time for this'. (MNC III).

This quotation illustrates an important recurring issue in the cases. When subsidiary employees addressed what were important issues for them, parent company managers seemed not to listen. Instead, they indicated and sometimes even explicitly articulated that they did not need external input because they were expecting things to be the same as in the home country. As one Danish expatriate put it, 'I think that it is because it is Danes sitting around talking to Danes. They feel that they are global in their way of thinking, but in fact, they are not'.

Although it may often be unintentional, our study found that subsidiary managers and employees felt that parent company managers were suppressing critical input from outside HQ boundaries and were unreceptive to influences, potential learning, and new perspectives developed in the subsidiaries. As exemplified below, parent company managers seemed to have developed a sense of infallibility:

> There is a great deal of organizational self-esteem in headquarters. I've actually received a great deal of criticism from Denmark [when stationed in Hungary] because my products did not reach headquarters on time. But I just knew that it couldn't be right. So we went to Denmark and we found that the problem arose because headquarters did not move the products from the truck and onto the ramp in time. My products stood waiting outside the headquarters buildings ... And when they realized what the problem was, the Danes got very, very embarrassed. And the problems were solved instantly. But the premise was that it must be the Hungarians who are the idiots ... because Denmark does not make mistakes, so why bother to go check if anything is wrong in Denmark. We saw quite a number of incidents like this. (MNC III)

Summing up, the overall impression is that subsidiary employees often found themselves not taken seriously and not heard by their parent company managers. Important issues were devalued, problems overlooked, and arguments ignored. A repeated shared experience of being ignored added to stereotypical categorizations of parent company managers as arrogant. For example, this is implicit in the irony used by the subsidiary manager in MNC III – 'because Denmark does not make mistakes' – and in the comment of the subsidiary manager in MNC 1, 'I don't think they really listen'.

Bypassing

Another category of parent company arrogance relates to subsidiary staff feeling bypassed. Danish parent company representatives were perceived as arrogant when they, for example, interacted directly with local markets or implemented initiatives that indirectly affected local market operations without asking, involving, or informing subsidiary personnel of their plans and actions. Such initiatives were typically intended to standardize or streamline activities and information at a corporate level, but subsidiary employees often felt offended when parent company representatives interacted directly with local customers, as in the example below:

> So, the marketing department decides that they will send out direct mails about something. And they don't involve us ... They think it is good. I don't think so. They send out a direct mail and they write the names on the label. And they don't know that in Hungary we write the first name second and that's a big problem because we have a lot of names where we have a first name also in the family name. For example, Lazlo Sándor – that can be a Hungarian name, but Sándor is Alexander and Lazlo is Leslie. So these are well-known first names, but who can decide which one is the family name? They think that the local organization is just a barrier to very effective communication with our customers. (MNC III)

In another case, parent company management designed and implemented a new online system intended to standardize information and processes between the MNC and local customers. In doing so, they ignored the fact that implementation would alter communication between subsidiary employees and their customers by shifting much of the daily communication with customers outside the local sales rep-customer relationship. However, an important criterion of success for sales representatives was maintaining close dialogue with customers so as to develop the best possible customer portfolio. In this case, the centrally designed online system, while increasing standardization and efficiency at parent company level, restricted personal dialogue with customers, causing subsidiaries to perceive it to some extent as an obstacle. Furthermore, centralizing a greater amount of information at parent company level left subsidiary staff somewhat vulnerable, as described by a sales consultant:

> I had an appointment where I sat with some customers and I wanted to show them how to order the new nice display for [name of new product], and the day before I had been in the online system and it was okay. [At the meeting] I tried to get in and show this picture and how to order, but it was not in the system. I don't know where it went and why, so after that I called Denmark and they said, no, it is not in the system anymore because of this and this, and we got no information before they actually removed it. (MNC II)

The effect of parent company representatives' bypassing subsidiary staff in attempting to optimize processes globally may also take the form of removing functions or processes from the subsidiary level without either the approval or involvement of subsidiary employees. The subsidiaries may in turn feel that the parent company managers do not understand the implications of such decisions.

> A lot of functions have been removed from the regions and the headquarters haven't really explained why. The communications budget is placed in a central communication office. The IT budget is given to central IT. The only thing that I am now responsible for is employees and travel expenses. And they say that they have strengthened the regions! They just cut it all away, without understanding the consequences. (MNC IV)

For subsidiary staff, the problem with bypassing was that the parent company initiatives intended to increase global efficiency through, for example, centralization and standardization, clashed with the daily requirements of subsidiary managers. In that sense, this category of arrogance is linked to the fact that there were conflicting values between HQ and subsidiaries. Subsidiary representatives perceived the above initiatives as threatening their functioning and, ultimately, their values. What appeared rational from the perspective of the parent company was therefore perceived as irrational from the perspective of subsidiary managers and employees.

Educating

The third category of perceived parent company arrogance encompasses how subsidiary employees regard Danish parent company managers as arrogant when coordinating and aligning activities on a global scale. Parent company representatives of the four case companies seemed to assume that the domestic cultures, values, and practices of the Danish parent companies were superior to those of any of the subsidiaries. Parent company managers appeared to apply an ethnocentric mindset, leading to insensitive conduct generally perceived by local employees as arrogant, 'educating' behaviour.

> For headquarters the objective obviously is to spread the company culture across the world. [They say:] 'We want to be global. We would like to work with different cultures and we also want to understand those different cultures. But everybody must first and foremost understand our common company culture. And everybody has to comply with that regardless of where in the world they are'. (MNC III)

This exemplifies the traditional parent company attitude that the only legitimate organizational knowledge of 'the way we do things' is centrally located in the parent company. Parent company representatives make great efforts to disseminate and teach these values and practices globally. In our study, the parent company managers of one MNC in particular were explicit about their perception of the superiority of Danish Management Style and culture. They were conscious and determined in their efforts to align the subsidiaries' corporate cultures and practices with that style and culture. This led to numerous instances in which parent company managers' efforts to align and coordinate culture within the organization were perceived as arrogance. One expatriate, for example, argued that the Danes seemed to have a certain world map that they brought along when they set out in the world. Based on that map, he claimed, parent company representatives seemed to think that people and practices were, or at least should be, the same all over the world. Another example of such arrogant parent company thinking was provided by a subsidiary employee who reported that parent company managers visiting the subsidiary from Denmark expected that information from the parent company would not be questioned. If subsidiaries had difficulties understanding the information, they, not the parent company, had a problem. The parent company manager felt he had done his job by delivering a message or giving instructions, and he expected everybody to understand and comply immediately.

> Danish managers coming here [i.e., to the subsidiary] tend to think that giving instructions to the production employees is the same in a factory down here as in the factory placed just behind the headquarters in Denmark. [He expects] everyone in the factory to know and understand all the instructions he is trying to convey immedi-

> ately, and if the Chinese do not understand, it must be him or her who is the problem. (MNC III)

In this example, the parent company manager was perceived as arrogant because subsidiary employees sensed that there was only one right way – 'the parent company way' – that it was the objective of the parent company manager to teach to the rest of the world. Subsidiary employees were perceived as less knowledgeable than parent company managers, so they must learn from the higher standards and values of parent company managers. This is also illustrated in the following quotation:

> There has been a tendency that everything coming from Denmark is good and what we have got is less good. We always try to live up to Danish standards. They fail to recognize the good things about this company [i.e., the subsidiary]. (MNC I)

From the subsidiary's perspective, parent company representatives were perceived as arrogant partly because of their ethnocentric assumptions about 'the way things are done' in the organization and partly because they were often overly direct and demanding in attempting to disseminate this 'right way'. One subsidiary manager commented that for each new employee hired in a support function in the parent company, he needed two new employees locally to address their questions. Despite the obvious irony of this remark, it illustrates how subsidiary managers sometimes felt that parent company representatives constantly made demands without considering how they would be perceived from the subsidiary's perspective.

Compared with ignoring and bypassing, educating, as an aspect of perceived parent company arrogance, is more direct and demanding behaviour. It encompasses the way parent company managers correct subsidiary managers' behaviour and the way subsidiary employees are told to change their practices and values in accordance with those of the parent company. This in turn makes subsidiary employees and managers stereotype parent company managers, reinforcing the perception of arrogance.

Discussion and Main Findings

By applying the concept of arrogance along with theoretical perspectives from outside the dominant streams of relevant literature in seeking to understand HQ-subsidiary tensions, we build on existing insights into this phenomenon. When examining perceived parent company arrogance, we find three particular types of action generally deemed markers of arrogance: 1) ignoring, 2) bypassing, and 3) educating. *Ignoring* refers to a situation in which subsidiary employees get the impression that they are not being taken seriously by Danish parent company representatives. *Bypassing* occurs when parent company representatives interact directly with local markets and other local actors without involving or informing subsidiary employees. Finally, *educating* is related to Danish parent company representatives' continuous corrections or adjustments of subsidiary managers' or employees' work practices. Overall, these concepts are well aligned with the constructs concerning how perceptions of arrogance are created. Feelings of being ignored, bypassed, or educated are common among employees in most organizations and may well lead to the labelling of the instigating party as arrogant. In an MNC, however, such feelings could have even more severe and longer-term consequences than in domestic organizations due to the organizational, national, cultural, and linguistic boundaries that may separate parent companies from their subsidiaries. Actions that are interpreted as degrading could induce social categorization, in which parent company representatives are described in a generally negative light. This may initiate the gradual polarization of the two parties, charging managerial discourse across organizational units and leading to both resentment and safeguarding measures. This stifles dialogue and further complicates the management process. The studied cases suggest that a process of escalation exists in which the concepts of ignoring, bypassing, and educating reinforce each other, as shown in Figure 4.1.

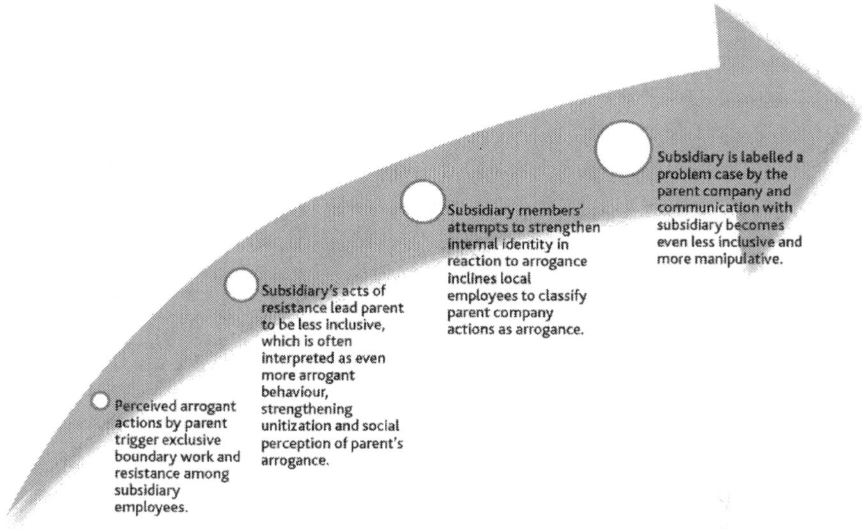

Figure 4.1. The pattern of escalating perceptions of arrogance in MNC subsidiaries.

The process of escalation depicted in Figure 4.1 shows how initially perceived arrogant behaviour and the resulting subsidiary boundary work and resistance may lead to the development of rationales for changing behaviour towards members of the subsidiary among parent company managers. This can be seen as confirming or even escalating parent company arrogance. We think that this dynamic is important for understanding how and why dialogue often fails and tensions rise between organizational units in MNCs; interestingly, this dynamic does not fall into existing and more rationalistic categories used to understand tensions in MNCs.

We also think that the role and importance of arrogance has been overlooked in the organizational literature, so considering it may enrich existing explanations of dysfunctional relationships and tensions between MNC parent companies and subsidiaries. Moreover, by defining three key behaviours that cause subsidiary managers to perceive arrogance, we have taken an important first step in exploring this more deeply. We are not offering an alternative to the existing streams of research in the subsidiary management field discussed in the theory overview, but we believe that the parent company arrogance concept marks an advance from static, macro-oriented perspectives. It offers more processual and micro-oriented theoretical perspectives that may teach us more about the process of managing in an MNC context. In our view, the concept can enrich the meaning and implications of several existing research streams and their research programmes. In particular, we think that we can contribute conceptually to the literature on the HQ-subsidiary relationship, a stream concerned with the quality of this key relationship (Paterson & Brock, 2002). We also believe that our results speak to ongoing research 'puzzles' in the subsidiary role and subsidiary development research streams, conundrums concerning the emergence and resolution of role conflicts (Schotter & Beamish, 2011; Andersson, Forsgren & Holm, 2002). Finally, we believe that research into HQ arrogance is aligned with recent attempts to apply post-colonial perspectives in analysing conflicts and tensions in the HQ-subsidiary relationship arising from, among other issues, ignorance and the 'polyphony of voices and terminologies' used by HQ in communicating with subsidiaries (Kristensen & Zeitlin, 2005, p. 5). We believe that these emerging views also have great potential, as they challenge certain simplistic notions of unitary and universal groupings of interests inherent in most 'mixed motives' research into these HQ-subsidiary relationships.

Implications

Implications for Theory and Suggestions for Future Research

Although this study is a pioneering explorative study of perceived parent company arrogance, it has some straightforward implications for theory and further research in this under-researched area. In theoretical terms, research into parent company arrogance has demonstrated that the theme is a relevant and important subject in international business. Our study therefore addresses an underexplored area in MNC management literature, i.e., how managerial interpretation and attitude formation interact. As our study is preliminary it has several limitations. Nevertheless, we believe that further investigation of the formation of perceptions among managers will take us beyond the sweeping generalizations often made when attributing tensions in parent-subsidiary relationships to cultural differences or simple power games.

Implications for further research are obvious, as both replicating and extending this exploratory investigation may be useful. Replicating the study while trying to avoid as many of its limitations as possible could be worthwhile. Extending its methods to include quantitative ones may also be a useful further research task. Extending the scope of the study to include parent companies from other countries could help us assess the generalizability of our findings. Finally, parent company arrogance could be linked to other central themes of international business research, such as parent-subsidiary power relationships, knowledge sharing, and subsidiary contributions to MNCs' innovation agendas.

Practical Implications

Increasing Danish HQ awareness of the negative consequences possibly resulting from ignoring, bypassing, and educating subsidiary personnel could be a first step towards avoiding them. The possibility of arrogance is often not acknowledged by Danish MNC managers (Storgaard, 2010). The present findings suggest that Danish companies may want to closely monitor and try to counteract the negative outcomes of perceived parent company arrogance. This is crucial, as the damage could otherwise become substantial and difficult to eliminate over time due to group dynamics that could accelerate mutual negative social categorizations. Counter-measures could include cross-cultural awareness training concentrating on the destructive negative reactions that can develop in MNC parent-subsidiary relationships. Interestingly, research from other fields concerned with the role of perceived arrogance in interpersonal relationships finds that attempts to change perceptions of arrogance can increase mutual trustworthiness (Yavas et al., 2004).

Moreover, dialogue and increased interaction should have positive consequences, as the contact hypothesis predicts (e.g., Amir, 1969). According to the contact hypothesis, more frequent communication diminishes the negative effects of social categorizations. In a world of growing market and resource interdependence and where the constitutional order of MNCs is no longer clearly dictated by HQ, understanding and countering processes that may cause organizational tension and increase rigidity are welcomed.

Conclusion

This study has examined parent company arrogance as perceived in international subsidiaries of Danish MNCs. We found three types of action that can cause subsidiary employees to regard Danish parent company representatives as arrogant, i.e., ignoring, bypassing, and educating. Using social categorization theory and studies of group dynamics, we have argued that feelings of being treated with arrogance could have severe long-term consequences in MNCs due to the organizational, national, cultural, and linguistic boundaries that separate parent companies from their subsidiaries. Moreover, perceived arrogance could also result in social categorization in which a general negative image of Danish parent company representatives develops. This could cause the parent company and its subsidiaries to gradually become polarized and group boundaries to tighten. Possible managerial interventions for Danish companies may include disseminating information about this problem as well as dialogue and cultural awareness training specifically tailored to increase understanding and respect between Danish parent companies and their subsidiaries.

References

Amir, Y. (1969). Contact Hypothesis in Ethnic Relations. *Psychological Bulletin, 71,* 319-42.

Andersson, U., Forsgren, M. & Holm, U. (2002). The Strategic Impact of External Networks: Subsidiary Performance and Competence Development in The Multinational Corporation. *Strategic Management Journal, 23*(11), 979-996.

Andersson, U., Forsgren, M. & Holm, U. (2007). Balancing Subsidiary Influence in the Federative MNC: a Business Network View. *Journal of International Business Studies, 38*(5), 802-818.

Ashforth, B.E. & Mael, F. (1989). Social Identity Theory and the Organization. *Academy of Management Review, 14*(1), 20-39.

Banai, M. & Sama, L.M. (2000). Ethical Dilemmas in MNCs' International Staffing Policies A Conceptual Framework. *Journal of Business Ethics, 25*(3), 221-35.

Barth, F. (1971). *Ethnic Groups and Boundaries: The Social Organization of Cultural Difference*. Bergen: Universitetsforlaget.

Bartlett, C.A. & Ghoshal, S. (1989). *Managing Across Borders: the Transnational Solution*. Harvard Business School Press.

Ben-Ze'ev, A. (1993). On the Virtue of Modesty. *American Philosophical Quarterly, 30*, 235-246.

Bourdieu, P. & Wacquant, L.J.D. (1992). *An Invitation to Reflexive Sociology*. Chicago: University of Chicago Press.

Bouquet, C. & J. Birkinshaw. (2008). Managing Power in the Multinational Corporation: How Low-power Actors Gain Influence. *Journal of Management, 34*(3), 477-508.

Brubaker, R. (2002). Ethnicity Without Groups. *European Journal of Sociology*, XLIII(2), 163-189.

Brubaker, R., Loveman, M. & Stamatov, P. (2004). Ethnicity as Cognition. *Theory and Society, 33*(1), 31-64.

Calas, M.B. & Smircich, L.. (1999). Past Postmodernism? Reflections and Tentative Directions. *Academy of Management. The Academy of Management Review, 24*(4), 649-671.

Cantwell, J. & Mudambi, R. (2005). MNE Competence: Creating Subsidiary Mandates. *Strategic Management Journal, 26*(12), 1109-1128.

Cheng, J.L.C. & Bolon, D.S. (1993). The Management of Multinational R&D: a Neglected Topic in International Business Research. *Journal of International Business Studies, 24*(1), 1-18.

Creed, W.E.D., Scully, M.A & Austin, J.R. (2002). Clothes Make the Person? The Tailoring of Legitimating Accounts and the Social Construction of Identity. *Organization Science, 13*(5), 475-96.

Dillon, R.S. (2007). Arrogance, Self-respect and Personhood. *Journal of Consciousness Studies, 14*(5/6), 101-126.

Dubois, A. & Gadde, L.-E. (2002). Systematic Combining: an Abductive Approach to Case Research. *Journal of Business Research*, 55, 553-60.

Earley, P.C. (1993). East Meets West Meets Mideast: Further Explorations of Collectivistic and Individualistic Work Groups. *Academy of Management Journal, 36*(2), 319-348.

Egelhoff, W.G. How the Parent Headquarters Adds Value to an MNC. *Management International Review, 50*(4), 413-431.

Eisenhardt, K. (1989). Building Theories from Case Study Research. *Academy of Management Review*, 14, 532-50.

Ferner, A., P. Almond, I. Clark, T. Colling, T. Edwards, L. Holden & Muller-Camen, M. (2004). Dynamics of Central Control and Subsidiary Autonomy in the Management of Human Resources: Case-study Evidence from US MNCs in the UK. *Organization Studies, 25*(3), 363-391.

Ferner, A., Edwards, T. & Tempel, A. (2012). Power, Institutions and the Cross-National Transfer of Employment Practices in Multinationals. *Human Relations 65*(2), 163-187.

Foss, K., Foss, N.J. & Nell, P.C. (2012). MNC Organizational Form and Subsidiary Motivation Problems: Controlling Intervention Hazards in the Network MNC. *Journal of International Management, 18*(3), 247-259.

Filatotchev, I. & Wright, M. Agency Perspectives on Corporate Governance of Multinational Enterprises. *Journal of Management Studies, 48*(2), 471-486.

Frenkel, M. (2008). The Multinational Corporation as a Third Space: Rethinking International Management Discourse on Knowledge Transfer Through Homi Bhabha. *The Academy of Management Review, 33*(4), 924-942.

Ghemawat, P. (2007). Redefining Global Strategy: Crossing Borders in a World Where Differences Still Matter. Boston: Harvard Business School Publishing.

Gupta, A.K. & Govindarajan, V. (1991). Knowledge Flows and the Structure of Control within Multinational Corporations. *Academy Of Management Review*, 768-772.

Hareli, S. & Weiner, B. (2000). Accounts for Success as Determinants of Perceived Arrogance and Modesty. *Motivation and Emotion, 24*(3), 215-236.

Haan, P., Britt, M. & Weinstein, A. (2007). Business Students' Perception of Arrogance in Academia. *College Student Journal, 41*(1), 82-92.

Hedlund, G. (1994). A Model of Knowledge Management and the N-form Corporation, *Strategic Management Journal, 15*(S2), 73-90.

Janis, I.L. (1982). *Groupthink: Psychological Studies of Policy Decisions and Fiascoes.* Boston: Houghton Mifflin.

Jenkins, R. (2000). Categorization: Identity, Social Process and Epistemology. *Current Sociology, 48*(3), 7-25.

Kim, W.C. & Mauborgne, R.A. (1993). Procedural Justice, Attitudes, and Subsidiary Top Management Compliance with Multinationals' Corporate Strategic Decisions. *Academy of Management Journal, 36*(3), 3502-526.

Kirkman, B.L., Lowe, K. & Gibson, C.B. (2006). A Quarter Century of Culture's Consequences: A Review of Empirical Research Incorporating Hofstede's Cultural Values Framework. *Journal of International Business Studies, 37*(3), 285-320.

Kostova, T. (1999). Transnational Transfer of Strategic Organizational Practices: A Contextual Perspective. *Academy of Management Review, 24*(2), 308-324.

Kristensen, P.H. & Zeitlin, J. (2005). *Local players in Global Games: The Strategic Constitution of a Multinational Corporation*: Oxford University Press, USA.

Kulik, C. & Ambrose, M.L. (1992). Personal and Situational Determinants of Referent Choice. *Academy of Management Review, 17*(2), 212-238.

Lauring, J. (2008). Rethinking Social Identity Theory in International Encounters: Language Use as a Negotiated Object for Identity Making. *International Journal of Cross Cultural Management, 8*(3), 343-361.

Leavitt, H.J. (1975). Beyond the Analytic Manager. *California Management Review, 17*(3), 5-12.

Lewicki, R.J., McAllister, D.J. & Bies, R.J. (1998). Trust and Distrust: New Relationships and Realities. *Academy of Management Review, 23*(3), 438-458.

Ling, Y., Floyd, S.W. & Baldridge, D.C. (2005). Toward a Model of Issue-selling by Subsidiary Managers in Multinational Organizations. *Journal of International Business Studies, 36*(6), 637 654.

Mellahi, K. & Collings, D.G. (2010). The Barriers to Effective Global Talent Management: The Example of corporate élites in MNEs. *Journal of World Business, 45*(2), 143-149.

Miller, D., Greenwood, R. & Prakash, R. (2009). What Happened to Organization Theory? *Journal of Management Inquiry, 18*(4), 273-279.

Morgan, G. & Kristensen, P.H. (2006). The Contested space of Multinationals: Varieties of Institutionalism, Varieties of capitalism. *Human Relations, 59*(11), 1467-1490.

Morgan, G., Kristensen, P.H. & Whitley, R. (2001). *The Multinational firm: Organizing across Institutional and National Divides*: Oxford University Press, USA.

Morgan, G. (1989). *Creative Organization Theory*. Newbury Park, CA: Sage Publications.

Paterson, SL & D.M. Brock. (2002). The Development of Subsidiary-management Research: Review and Theoretical Analysis. *International Business Review, 11*(2), 139-163.

Perlmutter, H.V. (1969). The Tortuos Evolution of the Multinational Enterprise. *Columbia Journal of World Business, 4*(1), 9-18.

Pudelko, M. & Harzing, A.W. (2007). Country of Origin, Localization, or Dominance Effect? An Empirical Investigation of HRM Practices in Foreign Subsidiaries. *Human Resource Management, 46*(4), 535-559.

Riek, B.M., Mania, E.W. & Gaertner, S.L. (2006). Intergroup Threat and Outgroup Attitudes: A Meta-analytic Review. *Personality and Social Psychology Review,* 10(4), 336-353.

Salk, J.E. & Shenkar, O. (2001). Social Identities in an International Joint Venture: An Exploratory Case Study. *Organization Science, 12*(2), 161-178.

Schotter, A. & Beamish, P.W. (2011). Performance Effects of MNC Headquarters-subsidiary Conflict and the Role of Boundary spanners: the Case of Headquarter Initiative Rejection. *Journal of International Management, 17*(3), 243-259.

Seo, M.G. & Creed, W.E.D. (2002). Institutional Contradictions, Praxis, and Institutional Change: A Dialectical Perspective. *Academy of Management Review, 27*(2), 222-247.

Siegel, D.S., Waldman, D. & Link, A. (2003). Assessing the Impact of Organizational Practices on the Relative Productivity of University Technology Transfer Offices: An Exploratory Study. *Research Policy, 32*(1), 27-48.

Sims, R.R. (1994). *Ethics and Organizational Decision Making: A call for Renewal*: Praeger Publishers.

Storgaard, M. (2010). *Lokale syn på globale horisonter: Et kritisk perspektiv på HQ's rolle i den globaliserende MNC*. Aarhus: Aarhus School of Business.

Tajfel, H. & Turner, J.C. (1979). An Integrative Theory of Intergroup Conflict. In Worchel, S. & Austin, W.G. (Eds.) *The Social Psychology of Intergroup Relations*. Monterey: Brooks/Cole Publ.

Vance, C.M. & Paik, Y. (2005). Forms of Host-country National Learning for Enhanced MNC Absorptive Capacity. *Journal of Managerial Psychology, 20*(7), 590-606.

Voelpel, S.C. & Han, Z. (2005). Managing Knowledge Sharing in China: the Case of Siemens ShareNet. *Journal of Knowledge Management, 9*(3), 51-63.

Vora, D. & Kostova, T. (2007). A Model of Dual Organizational Identification in the Context of the Multinational Enterprise. *Journal of Organizational Behavior, 28*(3), 327-350.

Weick, K.E. (1989). Theory Construction as Disciplined Imagination. *Academy of Management Review*, *14*(4), 516-531.

Weiner, B. (1994). Ability Versus Effort Revisited: The Moral Determinants of Achievement Evaluation and Achievement as a Moral System. *Educational Psychologist*, 29, 163-72.

Weiner, B. (1985). An Attributional Theory of Achievement Motivation and Emotion. *Psychological Review*, *95*(4), 548-573).

Wosinska, W., Dabul, A.J., Whetstone-Dion, R. & Cialdini, R.B. (1996). Self-presentational Responses to Success in the Organization: The Cost and Benefits of Modesty. *Basic and Applied Social Psychology*, 18, 229-242.

Yagi, N. & Kleinberg, J. (2011). Boundary Work: An Interpretive Ethnographic Perspective on Negotiating and Leveraging Cross-cultural Identity. *Journal of International Business Studies*, 42, 629-653.

Yavas, U., Benkenstein, M. & Stuhldreier, U. (2004). Relationships between Service Quality and Behavioral Outcomes: a Study of Private Bank Customers in Germany. *International Journal of Bank Marketing*, *22*(2), 144-157.

Yin, R.K. (2009). *Case Study Research – Design and Methods* 4th ed. Thousand Oaks, CA: Sage Publications.

CHAPTER 5

Retention of Highly Skilled Expatriates and the Danish Work-life Balance

Jan Normann and Toke Bjerregaard

Economic globalization has created an international professional space (Wagner, 1998) and facilitated talented individuals' global relocation for work (Froese, 2012). It has led to the diversification of forms of expatriation (Shaffer, Kraimer, Chen & Bolino, 2012), including an increased number of professionals who initiate their own mobility across organizational and national boundaries. Self-initiated expatriates – an emerging resource for international companies – are professionals who on their own initiative (Andresen, Bergdolt & Margenfeld, 2013) take employment in a foreign country, often with no planned time period, the legal employment decision being made by the new work contract partner (Andresen et al., 2013; Inkson & Myers, 2003; Lee, 2005). Mobility across countries has, in this way, become a conventional tendency for many professionals with diverse interests in acquiring new employment experience in the search for global career opportunities (Suutari, Tornikoski & Mäkelä, 2012). This pattern is not captured by traditional notions of global careers, which have primarily been associated with international assignments within companies (Altman & Baruch, 2012).

Many countries, such as Denmark, are engaged in international competition to attract and retain such highly skilled international professionals (DI, 2012). It has been observed that some Danish companies face challenges satisfying their need for specialized, skilled workers from the available Danish labour pool (Oxford Research, 2010). Advancing the understanding and management of challenges relating to retaining highly skilled expatriates is important for companies and governments due to intensified international competition to attract and retain mobile talent (Michaels, Handfield-Jones & Axelrod, 2001). This is especially relevant to global careerists with a boundaryless mindset (Suutari et al., 2012) who often build their careers across countries and organizations, rather than merely within them (Arthur & Rousseau, 1996; Grinstein & Wathieu, 2012). This competition is partly due to demographic change connected with an ageing population combined with a shift in the industrial sector towards a knowledge economy in Denmark and other OECD countries (see the introduction of this book, 'Preparing for the Unexpected: Design of the Future Global Enterprise'). The ability to attract and retain highly skilled international professionals as 'repositories of knowledge' (Bird, 1994) is seen as key to sustaining competitiveness in the face of globalization (Beechler & Woodward, 2009; Schuler, Jackson & Tarique, 2011; Tarique & Schuler, 2010). Yet, in a globalizing business world, there could be specific challenges related to the Danish work-life balance (WLB) in relation to recruiting and retaining foreign highly skilled labour. That is what this chapter is about. It is therefore relevant to examine what expatriates, companies, and other host-country actors should focus on in order to improve WLB for self-initiated expatriates and in that way retain international talent (Mäkelä & Suutari, 2008).

The now rather voluminous research into highly skilled professionals who self-initiate their expatriation revolves around the motives underlying their individual agency in undertaking global career moves (Cerdin, 2013; Doherty, Dickmann & Mills, 2011; Froese, 2012; Inkson & Myers, 2003), i.e., as determinants of mobility decisions and adjustment. An important question concerns how institutional environments influence the global mobility and work experience of such expatriates (Doherty, Richardson & Thorn, 2013; Vaiman & Haslberger, 2013). In the following, we will investigate the challenges facing highly skilled expatriates in Denmark relative to the Danish WLB as partly shaped by broader institutional frameworks.

The remainder of this chapter is organized as follows. First, we present the theoretical background of the research and the methodological considerations. The section 'Retention of Highly Skilled Expatriates and Host-Country Work-life Balance' describes how the Danish WLB influences the work experiences of international talent at the investigated workplaces. Finally, we outline the implications of our findings for international human resource management and suggest directions for future research. Before presenting the Danish case studies in detail, we will briefly discuss a few theoretical issues in relation to WLB.

Work-life Balance and Expatriation to Denmark

This chapter draws inspiration from the literature on the institutional foundations of WLB in various countries and as they pertain to expatriate WLB issues. We first conceptualize WLB, then outline the institutional foundations of WLB in Denmark, before finally examining expatriate issues related to WLB.

Work-life Balance

WLB concerns the positive and negative interaction effects of the multiple roles individuals undertake in their work and social life (Mäkelä, Suutari & Mayerhofer, 2011). Differently stated, WLB can be viewed as the outcome of the interaction between the individual and institutional frameworks, i.e., the individual perception that work and non-work activities are compatible and promote growth in accordance with an individual's current life priorities (Kalliath & Brough, 2008). WLB conflicts arise when individuals cannot reconcile individual aspirations and institutional demands, or when demands from various institutional arrangements are in conflict. WLB conflict in the latter sense exists when: 1) time devoted to the requirements of one role make it difficult to fulfil the requirements of another, 2) strain from participation in one role makes it difficult to fulfil the requirements of another, and 3) specific behaviours required by one role make it difficult to fulfil the requirements of another (Greenhaus & Beutell, 1985). WLB enrichment, on the other hand, occurs when individual aspirations are enhanced by the institutional framework and various institutional arrangements interact in a supporting way. This refers to the extent to which experiences in one role improve the quality of life in the other role when: 1) work and social life experiences have additive effects on wellbeing, 2) participation in both work and social life roles buffers individuals from distress in one of the roles, and 3) experiences in one role produce positive experiences and outcomes in another (Greenhaus & Powell, 2006). While conflict has been and still is the major focus of WLB research, enrichment has recently attracted more attention. Research has traditionally concentrated on the work-family interface, but has recently broadened to treat other types of social life, such as recreational life and friendships (Pedersen & Lewis, 2012; Shaffer, Joplin & Hsu, 2011).

Institutional Foundations of the Work-life Balance in Denmark

A good balance between work and social life is often described as a positive characteristic of Danish society, and Danes are repeatedly rated the happiest people in the world (Helliwell, Layard & Sachs, 2012; OECD, 2011). The Danish welfare model, with its flexible work conditions and social support networks, including maternity leave and childcare facilities (Esping-Andersen, 1990; 2000), not only puts Denmark at the top of the international equality league table but also contributes to a high standard of living in general (OECD, 2012b). Many Danes have a great degree of work flexibility and can often choose to work from home during the week. Employees find it of great value to have a free time allowance and flexible working hours, often preferring more leisure time to higher pay (OECD, 2013).

The institutional framework of WLB is usually a constellation of formal and informal institutional arrangements at various levels. Such institutional arrangements can have regulatory, normative, and cultural-cognitive pillars (Scott, 2008). We can distinguish between welfare models or regimes by how they allocate social responsibilities between the state, market, and family (Esping-Andersen, 2000; Powell & Barrientos, 2004). The liberal, mainly Anglo-Saxon version is based on a minimal state and market mechanisms with a heavy reliance on the individual provision of pensions, healthcare, and services. The continental European version is characterized mainly by employment-linked provision of pensions, healthcare, and social security, but supplemented with an emphasis on family responsibility. Finally, we have the universalistic mainly Scandinavian welfare model in which most services are provided by the public sector (Esping-Andersen, 1990; 2000). The Danish state provides a number of welfare arrangements, ranging from childcare and maternity leave to eldercare, that significantly affect the general WLB for both public and private employees.

The expansion of the Danish welfare state since the 1960s, particularly in terms of social services, has been instrumental in creating high labour market participation for women. Denmark has one of the world's highest enrolments of women in the labour market, approximately 70% of Danish women being active in the labour market (the comparable rate in OECD countries averages approximately 57%). Even so, gender is still a key determinant of inequality in WLB, not only in Denmark, but in all OECD countries. Women in Denmark spend fewer hours on paid work than do men but longer on unpaid activities at home, leaving them less time for leisure and personal care (OECD, 2013). Compared with other OECD countries, Denmark is ranked seventh in terms of fewest number of hours spent at work per year (OECD StatExtracts, 2010). Overall, Denmark ranks the highest in the latest OECD assessment of WLB in all OECD countries (OECD, 2013).

Although corporatism might be on the retreat in Danish society, many arrangements are still made as agreements between state, business, and unions, including arrangements pertaining to WLB. Agreements are often reached at a central national level between these three parties and only later negotiated in detail at the local organizational level between the employer and employees (Pedersen & Lewis, 2012). Unions such as 3F, HK, and DJØF provide in-service training about WLB for their representatives in companies (Pedersen, 2009).

Moreover, in Denmark, management is generally based on egalitarian values and a democratic ethos. Within organizations in Denmark, organizational structures tend to be flat, hierarchical power distances are small (Smith, Andersen, Ekelund, Graversen & Ropo, 2003), and employees tend to communicate as equals. Accordingly, the Danish Management Style is considered cooperative and participatory. In Denmark, managers tend to ask for other people's advice and proposals from executives can be questioned and counter proposals made.

Expatriate Work-life Balance: Expectations and Challenges

Being an expatriate potentially challenges WLB in several ways. Such challenges may pertain to differences between more general elements of expatriate lifestyle or particular cultural backgrounds and the host-country WLB.

First, expatriates are not a homogenous group, instead representing diverse lifestyles and cultural backgrounds. Expatriates come from various cultural-institutional backgrounds differing to various degrees from the host country's dominant WLB. Expatriates may experience differences in both work and social life roles from what they are used to in their home country, and spillover and crossover effects between roles are common (Lazarova, Shaffer & Westman, 2010). WLB expectations vary across nations due to differences in institutional frameworks and individual aspirations. In many countries, work norms requiring long working hours tend to collide with ideals of a strong family life. These variations in the perception and measurement of WLB pose challenges when comparing countries or assessing the match between expatriates from various countries and the institutional framework in a country such as Denmark (Lu et al., 2010; Poelmans, 2003). In addition, variations in individual lifestyle and in organizational procedures and WLB policies will affect the actual WLB for the individual expatriate. Whatever the reason might be, when the relationship between work and social life is not balanced, stress can be significant and result in lack of retention (Deery, 2008; Parkes & Langford, 2008).

Second, differences between host-country WLB and expatriate expectations could relate to certain general characteristics of expatriate lifestyles. Recent studies have demonstrated that expatriates experience specific time-, strain-, and mobility-based conflicts in relation to their WLB (Shortland & Cummins, 2007). Time-based conflicts result from, for example, long working hours, extensive travel, and an expectation of round-the-clock availability. Expatriates are often expected to be constantly available and willing to use weekends and even nights to hold meetings due to overseas colleagues' different time zones (Shortland & Cummins, 2007). Expatriates sometimes experience unsatisfactory family life with too little contact and fewer holidays spent together. This is also related to the strain-based conflicts resulting from lack of energy once the family is together. While both time- and strain-based conflicts can be found in domestic jobs, mobility-based conflicts are more specifically related to the expatriate lifestyle. The transfer of a whole family to a foreign culture far from home both changes and challenges the family's internal dynamics. Both the expatriate worker and spouse assume new roles. Often, a spouse has to give up his or her career and assume a housekeeping role. Children have to establish new social bonds and decipher a new culture (Mäkelä & Suutari, 2008, 2011). Being an expatriate often implies a limited social network in the host country, which can lead to high expectations of opportunities for social networking through work.

Self-initiated expatriates are less embedded in a company than are assigned expatriates and more prone to undertake international relocation for work. Unmet expectations arising from the host-country WLB could result in lower chances of retaining such expatriates in a given country and company. International assignees, on the other hand, work as either expatriates or inpatriates in the host country for a predefined period and with the intention of returning to their home country or moving to another country after completing the term. Even for such expatriates, WLB challenges can still result in expatriate failure. Certain issues concerning the match between WLB in Denmark and expatriate lifestyles will be the same for both types of expatriates. However, there will still be differences in the organizational support given to assigned versus self-initiated expatriates, who are often hired based on local contracts. In the remainder of this chapter, the term 'expatriate' will be used to refer to both types of expatriates, but where there are important differences between the types, they will be highlighted.

Method

The empirical foundation of this chapter is a qualitative study of expatriates in eight companies in Denmark, that is, Novo Nordisk, Vestas, COWI, Grundfos, KMD, Siemens, Danisco, and Estructure. We have sought to convey a broad overview of how the characteristic Danish way of working affects the adjustment and wellbeing of foreign professionals in Denmark. Consequently, we chose to examine a wide range of organizations rather than conduct an in-depth study of one or two companies. This has enabled us to investigate the multiple challenges confronted by highly skilled employees within the selected organizations. The study was conducted by a small group of researchers.

The companies were selected based on their large proportions of professionals with national backgrounds other than Danish. All eight companies were internationally oriented, privately owned, knowledge-intensive organizations. The firms were active, for example, in pharmaceuticals, IT, high-tech, and engineering and were located in Copenhagen as well as in smaller Danish towns. In addition to this regional distribution, the units varied in size, unit status (i.e., HQ or subsidiary), and economic importance. In terms of size, the three largest companies employed more than 32,000 people each.

All eight companies used English as their corporate language. In six companies, English had been used as the official language for over fifteen years, while the others had implemented a language policy more recently. However, all eight companies have experienced a dramatic increase in the use of English over the past five years.

To negotiate access, we contacted organizational gatekeepers by telephone, asking them to identify key people involved in or responsible for coordination and cooperation in multilingual work environments, and our first selection of respondents was made in collaboration with these gatekeepers. Later, we added more respondents to the sample, using a snowball technique relying on insider knowledge obtained from the first interviewees (Bernard, 1995). A total of 56 non-Danish and ten Danish interviewees were included in the sample. About 60% of the respondents had managerial responsibilities. Many were self-initiated expatriates, while a few informants were inpatriates transferred from subsidiaries in other countries to the Danish HQ.

Although the research did involve participant observations, most of the data were collected through qualitative research interviews. The interviews, which each lasted for approximately one hour, took place in the respondent's company, and mostly in private offices or empty meeting rooms.

Depending on respondent preferences, interviews were audio-recorded or documented through extensive note-taking. We concluded our data collection by sending a written report to all interviewees and gatekeepers, asking them to comment on our conclusions. Their responses were subsequently integrated into the data material to ensure that all relevant topics had been addressed and that our results accurately reflected the respondents' intentions.

For the purpose of the analysis, we processed the data in stages, aiming to create an intelligible, coherent whole within the overall context of the study. The process began with a reading of the interview transcripts and reports, which allowed for the extraction and coding of information relevant to the study. In the second stage, we systematized the data under a number of headings adopted from the theoretical framing of the project. Finally, the data, collated in the form of quotations, were assembled and developed into case narratives. The combined data material was coded and categorized into recurrent themes, searching for similarities and differences between attitudes and viewpoints. From these pieces of assembled data, an extensive initial case narrative of more than 300 pages was created. This chapter has been developed from part of this narrative material related to Danish work practices and how they affected the adjustment and wellbeing of foreign employees.

Study Context: The Influx of Highly Skilled Expatriates to Denmark

The exact numbers of expatriates in Denmark as well as worldwide are difficult to determine, but we can get some indications by examining specific schemes aimed at recruiting highly qualified individuals, schemes such as the 'Green Card', Positive List, and Pay-Limit schemes in Denmark. In Denmark, the number of expatriates who get their residence and work permits through the Positive List and Pay-Limit schemes has increased from 33,000 in 2008 to 41,500 in 2010. The influx of highly qualified individuals to Denmark has increased considerably over the past decade (DIS, 2012, 2013). Most highly skilled foreign employees in Denmark recruited under these schemes come from Asian countries. In 2010, 73% of the recipients of Denmark's provisional 'Green Card' for qualified foreigners with university degrees came from just four Asian countries, i.e., Pakistan, India, Bangladesh, and China. These countries accounted for almost three out of five entries to Denmark under the 'Pay-Limit Scheme'[1] (OECD, 2012a). In addition to these schemes, many highly skilled employees are entering the country from other European countries without restrictions and are not registered in connection with their employment.

Retention of Highly Skilled Expatriates and Host-Country Work-life Balance

Many of both the foreign and Danish informants noted that Danish work culture has some special characteristics that differ noticeably from the

1. The Pay-Limit scheme grants access to a work permit to candidates with a written job contract or job offer that specifies the salary and employment conditions, which must meet Danish standards. Annual pay must be no less than DKK 375,000 (see: https://www.nyidanmark.dk/en-us/coming_to_dk/work/pay-limit-scheme.htm).

work cultures of many other countries. These characteristics are described by many Danes and foreigners as the 'Danish way'.

According to many informants observing the 'Danish way', Danes typically work fewer hours than many foreigners are used to, and often start and leave work earlier than foreigners do. Many informants see this as a consequence of giving a high priority to the balance between work and family life in Danish work culture, whereas many foreigners are accustomed to prioritizing work over personal life. An employee with a French background put it as follows:

> If we talk about the lifestyle here, it is also about long-term and sustainable relationships. The workload is often adequate and it is accepted that people leave at 4 p.m. to pick up their children. The style is very much that we must have durable relationships. I do not necessarily think it is like that in our subsidiaries. I do not think it is something special for Novo Nordisk. It is more something special for Denmark. (French expatriate, Novo Nordisk)

Several foreign employees who have their families in Denmark explained that, once they became accustomed to the balance between work and family life in Denmark, they learned to appreciate the extra time it gave them with their families. A female Chinese product manager commented:

> I do appreciate having more time with my son. In China I had a maid to take care of cleaning and cooking. Here I have to do everything myself. Life is very different. In China I had not cooked for many years. I did not have to. Now I have become quite good at cooking and I feel more like a mother for my son. I do appreciate that. (Chinese expatriate, Novo Nordisk)

It is said to be central to the 'Danish way' that Danes' work effort is often determined by the time instead of the task, i.e., Danes typically finish their working day at a certain time regardless of whether or not they have completed the task they are engaged in. In contrast, the task is described as a factor determining when foreigners choose to end their working day. A French product manager, who has worked for a long period in Denmark, explained:

> Where I was working in the US, you generally worked more hours and it was also often accepted to spend more working hours in order to get the tasks done ... You focused more on completing the task than on the time you spent on it. It was not uncommon for us at times to work at weekends or to stay up all night before a deadline. Often you also worked until ten or twelve o'clock at night. But then again you only had a small flat with four other people to come home to. (French expatriate, Novo Nordisk)

When the informants described their experience of Danish work culture, the relationship between working hours and efficiency proved to be a central theme. In particular, many Danes reported observing that Danish employees tended to spend their working hours more efficiently and productively than foreign employees generally did. Many informants justified Danes' spending fewer hours at work than foreigners do by explaining that the Danes often had to go home to pick up children and go shopping, while many foreign workers either did not have family in Denmark or had a spouse to take care of the children.

On the other hand, several Danish informants emphasized that they usually turned on their computers and continued working in the evening when the kids were asleep. The Danes' focus on spending their working hours at the office as effectively as possible was perceived by several informants as accounting for Danes' fewer coffee breaks and less small talk than their foreign colleagues are used to. A Danish Corporate Vice President said that he finds that Danish and foreign work cultures complement each other well:

> It should not be understood in the sense that we want the Danes to be at the office ten hours a day, but it might mean that when they are here they work more efficiently because they have to go shopping before the stores close and pick up the kids. ... I think it is important that it is not just purely Danish or purely foreign departments. Because Danish culture where you have fewer coffee breaks and less small talk also affects the foreigners' working culture. In this way we get the best ... (Danish employee, Novo Nordisk)

While many Danish informants did not find that spending fewer hours at the office affected their efficiency, several foreign employees, in contrast, thought that Danes' tendency to manage their everyday work effort based on time and not tasks could compromise their professional vision and ideals, weakening the company's professionalism and competitiveness in the international market. The Chinese Product Manager who said that she appreciated the extra time the Danish work culture allowed for her family life put it as follows:

> Here private life comes first and sometimes I think that is problematic. The whole business atmosphere is not very aggressive. And I think to do international business sometimes you have to be more aggressive. You have to sacrifice something. (Chinese expatriate, Novo Nordisk)

Danish work culture and WLB therefore differ from what many foreign workers have been used to. Danish employees typically spend fewer hours at work and therefore strive to spend their hours at the office effectively. There seems to be a strong correlation between a strong emphasis on using hours at work effectively (i.e., reducing the time 'wasted' on social interaction with colleagues) and the high level of WLB that characterizes Danish workplaces. This work culture was, on one hand, perceived by several foreign employees with children as greatly benefitting family life but, on the other hand, as compromising to a certain extent the foreigners' professional vision and ideals.

Interaction with Danish Colleagues during Working Hours

Many foreign workers expect and desire greater social interaction with their Danish colleagues, both during and outside working hours, than their Danish colleagues invite.

Many foreign informants describe being surprised to find that their interaction with Danish colleagues during working hours is often of a very professional character. They explain that they are accustomed to having friendly relationships with colleagues, more personal conversations and jokes being a natural part of work life.

That interactions with Danish colleagues were predominantly very professional in nature was explained by several Danish informants as because Danes seek to use their hours at the office effectively. However, several foreign employees also seemed to interpret this as indicating that Danes are not interested in social interaction at work and, in general, are very private, preferring a clear distinction between work and private life. A French employee noted:

> You learn a different way of approaching life. Here you separate family and work, whereas in France you mix them a bit more. In France, you often work until 7-8 p.m., whereas here you finish at 4 p.m. In France, we mix everything and spend more time at the office, but there is more informal conversation. (French expatriate, Vestas)

A Russian employee supported this experience of Danes making a sharper distinction between work and private life than in Russian work culture:

> One difference between Russians and Danes is that Danes are talking about work at work and about women in their spare time. Russians speak about women in working hours and about work in their spare time. In Russia, many decisions are made in the smoking room. There is always a smoking room, and lots of wise decisions are made there. But you also talk a lot about women and vodka. (Russian expatriate, Danisco)

In many cases in which foreigners interpret the lack of social invitations from their Danish colleagues as expressing a general lack of interest in them socially, the Danes' behaviour is likely driven by a desire to get home to their families, rather than by a lack of interest in their foreign colleagues.

Lunch Breaks

Most informants described a general tendency in their companies for Danes and foreigners to have lunch separately. Linguistic diversity seems to be one reason, as the Danes find it more relaxing and less arduous to interact socially in their mother tongue. On the other hand, it is also easier for the foreigners to communicate in English and not to be confronted with Danish. An international employee put it as follows:

> Yes, when we go to lunch they speak a lot of Danish. It is very hard. But yet that is not their problem. They speak their mother tongue. You have to speak that, otherwise it is not easy being let into their circle. (Chinese expatriate, Vestas)

Furthermore, several informants also explained the distinction between Danes and foreigners at lunchtime by stressing that Danes typically begin and end their working day earlier than the foreigners do. As a result of different daily rhythms, Danes tend to be hungry for lunch earlier than the foreigners are. A Danish employee explained:

> Actually, it is often the case that the Danes have lunch together in the canteen, and a little later the foreigners go together for lunch. I think it is because foreigners generally begin their work day a little later, and they also have lunch later. The Danes often begin their work day earlier and therefore they also have lunch earlier. Many foreigners do not have family and friends here, whereas we have families to come home to – I think it has got something to do with that. (Danish employee, COWI)

According to this view, the Danish family-work balance indirectly helps limit the foreigners' perceived opportunities for social interaction with Danes at lunchtime. While many Danish employees have families, several foreign workers explained either that they did not have family in Denmark or that they had a spouse who took care of the children. The fact that both Danish parents typically work outside the home may partly account for the different daily rhythms of Danes and foreigners. This ultimately seems to indirectly affect the opportunities for social interaction between Danes and foreigners at lunchtime.

Social Interaction outside Working Hours

As with social interaction during working hours, many foreign informants also expected and desired social interaction with their Danish colleagues in the private sphere outside working hours. Many foreign informants regarded it as a natural part of receiving new employees to be invited by management and colleagues to social gatherings after working hours. Many foreign informants were therefore surprised to find that they were not welcomed as expected at the Danish workplace. A British employee shared his experience of what it was like to start working in a Danish firm:

> Something that I was surprised about, actually, is that within the three or four months I was living here on my own, I just wondered when one of the senior people in our department would say, 'Come

> out and see us for the weekend and have brunch on a Sunday'. But nobody did. I think that is what the Danish character is like. It is not unfriendliness; it just does not cross their minds. (British expatriate, COWI)

Many foreign informants regarded it as a general feature of Danish culture that Danes are typically very private and 'homebound', often preferring to see family and old friends to forming new friendships. As noted, Danes are perceived to distinguish sharply between work and private life and between colleagues and friends. Foreign professionals often find it much more difficult and time consuming to create a new local social network with Danes than they have experienced in former destinations. A foreign professional said that 'It takes time to build relationships and trust between people. Danes are more private and closed than people in southern cultures' (Romanian expatriate, Grundfos). An Italian employee elaborated further:

> Danes are on one side and the expats on the other. It has always been like that. In the canteen or anywhere ... it is a cultural issue. ... I do not have any Danish friends; I do not think that any of the expats have Danish friends. It is difficult to make friends with the Danes since they have their own friends. They do not open up. They explained it to me: They are friendlier in the beginning than anybody else, but in the long term, they would not make friends – it would take a long, long time. And usually we would not have the patience to wait for that. If you want to be a friend, be a friend – we do not want to mess around for years to be able to trust each other. (Italian expatriate, COWI)

Several Danish informants were aware of foreigners' expectations to socialize after working hours, but they said that this was not integral to Danish culture and that such socialization could be difficult to combine with family life:

> Socially, we are probably not good in Denmark at receiving people. In the US, people were incredibly good at saying, 'We are going there in the weekend, would you like to join us?' Here it can be hard to get access to their social life. It is probably because of our

> background. We see each other very much at home and we meet with family and old friends most of the time. We are not as outgoing and it probably requires something more to take people home than just going out. We do not go out to restaurants a whole lot in Denmark. (Danish employee, Novo Nordisk)

Another Danish employee said that he found it difficult and inconvenient to combine family life and work life the way that many of the foreign employees expected:

> It is a big challenge for us when we get a Chinese or an American employee, because they come with high expectations of having a social network here at work. But it can be a little hard to take the obligation on oneself and take colleagues home when we work as many hours as we do. Or if you are going to the zoo and then just have to explain to the family that a couple of colleagues are joining us as well. (Danish employee, Novo Nordisk)

There seems to be a common expectation in the families of several Danish informants that both parents are responsible for allocating joint time to the family on weekends. If one parent suddenly allowed labour relations to impinge on this family time, it would disturb the joint agreement, as expressed above by the Danish employee. This is an approach that, according to Hofstede's (1991) masculinity/femininity dimension, seems to characterize societies like that of Denmark where there is a large overlap between gender roles. In these communities, there is typically a strong emphasis on equality between the sexes and sharing family responsebilities between men and women. An imbalance could be created between the partners if one party nurtured work relations during family hours.

Even though the lack of social interaction with Danes is seen as a cultural issue by many foreigners, it can be difficult for some foreign informants not to interpret this lack of interaction, in part, as an indication of personal failure. Several foreign informants reported thinking: 'What have I done? I am here all alone, and no one has invited me home?' (Lithuanian expatriate, Grundfos). Another employee put it as follows: 'Danes are friendly to foreigners during the time they are forced to socialize with them' (Hungarian expatriate, Grundfos). She said that there was no more socializing after work when the Danes returned to their families, and added: 'It is very lonely'. Many foreign informants said that it took time to learn to regard the lack of social invitations as due to different (work) cultures rather than personal failure.

In this regard, language is also highlighted as an important factor affecting the degree of social interaction between Danes and foreigners. There seems to be a close correlation between the foreigners' Danish skills and the number of Danes in their social network, both during and outside working hours. Most foreign informants find that Danes, while generally possessing high written and oral English proficiency, are very reluctant to speak English. Despite Danes' high English proficiency, both foreign and Danish informants noted a tendency for linguistic uncertainty among Danes when they had to speak English. A Lithuanian employee cited an example of this:

> We went to a lecture at Grundfos, and since it is an international organization the lecture was held in English. After the lecture, the lecturer asked if there were questions, but there were no questions. Then he asked if there were any questions in Danish. And then it turned out that people had questions and it ended up becoming a discussion among the Danish participants. Unfortunately I cannot tell you what was discussed, because I did not understand. (Lithuanian expatriate, Grundfos)

Danes' sense of linguistic uncertainty or inadequacy when, they have to speak English, is highlighted as helping limit the interaction between foreigners and Danes. This seems to occur more often in social than in purely professional interaction. A Danish senior engineer explained the problem:

> You lose a lot if everything has to be in English. The majority is able to manage and know many words on a technical level, but when it comes to the small talk about everyday stuff and emotional things, it often gets really difficult. (Danish employee, COWI)

In this regard, several foreign informants explained that, early in their time in Denmark, they realized that, if they wished to strengthen social interactions with Danes outside working hours, they needed to learn Danish. One foreign informant affirmed this:

> If you want to be a part of Danish culture, and live in the country as you did at home, talk to your neighbours, talk to people when you are out shopping, know what is happening in the world around you, it is important to speak Danish. Because despite the Danes' good English skills, they do not speak English in private. (Dutch expatriate, Grundfos)

While the foreigners generally said that few Danes were part of their social networks, networks created among the foreigners seemed to be important for the foreigners' experience of wellbeing in Denmark. Most foreign informants said that they had a strong social network of foreign colleagues, and that they often socialized after working hours. Some of these networks are fairly formal in nature, involving joint excursions, cultural events, and the like, while others are more informal networks in which foreigners meet for dinner or a drink. The vast majority of foreign informants said that these networks were the lynchpins of their social life in Denmark and crucial to enriching their spare time. A Bulgarian employee described such a network:

> Something that is really good in this company is that they have this globetrotter club. It is quite good, also because the person in charge has some really good ideas. They know how to organize good meetings with colleagues and we go visiting museums and castles. Places where, if I was not invited, I would probably never have gone. And I would have missed that from Danish culture. We have also gone to a typical Danish Christmas dinner. If you wait for your Danish colleagues to invite you, you will wait for a long time. (Bulgarian expatriate, Novo Nordisk)

Besides enriching their spare time, these social networks – several informants claimed – provided access to understanding, experiences, and knowledge that improved how the expatriates felt at work. As one expatriate employee said, 'It is all connected – if you do not feel good in your private life it affects your performance on the job and vice versa' (Romanian expatriate, Grundfos).

Many foreign employees entered the Danish workplace expecting to be included in their Danish colleagues' social life outside working hours, assuming that this would be a natural part of welcoming new colleagues. Most expatriate informants did not find that Danes invited such interaction and found it difficult to form friendships with them. Instead, formal and informal networks between foreign colleagues played a central role in foreigners' social lives outside work and were of great significance to most foreign informants' experience of wellbeing in Denmark.

Social Networking and Professional Performance

Besides the Danish WLB, other factors affected the recruitment and retention of highly skilled foreign labour. Several foreign informants described a close correlation between the degree of uncertainty about practical and cultural issues and the quality of their professional performance. Several informants found that when their companies made extra efforts to help them integrate, both during and outside working hours, it helped them adjust more easily to the Danish workplace and society. While some described successful company initiatives, most informants emphasized that it would facilitate their adaptation to Danish life if companies in general more actively supported and cared for the wellbeing of foreign employees – even outside working hours. A Chinese employee said:

> I was lucky because I knew a lot of people in Denmark from working at the factory in China. So they could help me out with some of the things and I easily found a flat. But no one at Vestas was assigned to help me, and I did not think HR had time to help me. So I asked a lot of questions to friends and people at the office. But it is different from how it is done in China, since there you will have a person assigned to help you out in the beginning. (Chinese expatriate, Vestas)

Discussion and Concluding Remarks

Many studies have been devoted to understanding how self-initiated professional expatriates undertake global career mobility through individual agency. Even so, the literature on self-directed expatriation tends to lack contextualization and seldom reflects the multilevel nature of such processes (Al Ariss & Crowley-Henry, 2013). Management theory regarding self-initiated expatriates tends, in various ways, to cast relatively little light on how global mobility and work experience are institutionally moderated. This study speaks to recent calls for more context-specific, self-initiated research into the expatriate experience (Al Ariss & Crowley-Henry, 2013; Vaiman & Haslberger, 2013).

When foreign professionals arrive at Danish workplaces, they tend to expect much more social interaction with their Danish colleagues – both during and outside working hours – than their Danish colleagues generally invite. As expatriates, they often confront the challenges of developing a new local social network in their host country. However, the high level of family-work balance characteristic of Danish work culture, as shaped by broader institutions, seems to contribute to Danes' spending fewer hours at work and focusing more strongly on using their hours there more effectively than many foreigners are used to. This work culture and, in particular, family-work balance partly reflect broader institutional frameworks. This seems to influence the fact that social interactions tend to be significantly downplayed among Danish employees. In this context, Danes seem to find it difficult and inconvenient to integrate working relations into the private sphere, as Danes generally distinguish more sharply than foreigners do between work and family life. Instead, the formal and informal networks among foreigners uncovered here play a crucial role in the foreigners' social life and experience of wellbeing in Denmark.

When social interaction with Danish colleagues fails to meet foreigners' expectations, this can impede their efforts to adapt to Danish society during their employment in the Danish company. The fact that expatriates often have very few Danes in their social networks outside working hours seems to have a negative impact on their professional performance and opportunities to gain professionally from social networking. Previous research documents that low host-country embeddedness may drive expatriates to relocate (Mahajan & De Silva, 2012; Reiche, Kraimer & Harzing, 2011; Tharenou & Caulfield, 2010). When expatriates integrate into social networks of highly transient professionals, rather than host-country nationals, their host-country embeddedness and retention will weaken. In this vein, the WLB of Danish work culture, as shaped partly by broader institutions, can constitute a challenge for companies in the international competition to attract and retain global talent (Tung, Worm & Petersen,

2008). As in other countries where a similar type of WLB prevails, Danish WLB could at some point be challenged by the forces of globalization. According to the present study, some factors indicate that this is likely.

Companies and public organizations in host countries with a WLB that runs counter to the expectations of many foreign professionals could develop various initiatives to compensate for this. One simple initiative would be to communicate relevant information to prepare both host-country employees and newly recruited international professionals for potential challenges. Another possible initiative would be to make holding social or outside-workplace events involving expatriates part of the job description of host-country employees, or to reward employees for taking such initiatives. Furthermore, public organizations could, for example, in collaboration with companies, hold various social networking events for expatriates and facilitate their use of local leisure offers, such as various cultural or sports facilities. Such initiatives should also facilitate social networking with host-country nationals, to ensure that international professionals do not merely integrate into their own separate, international communities disembedded from the local context.

References

Al Ariss, A. & Crowley-Henry, M. (2013). Self-initiated Expatriation and Migration in the Management Literature: Present Theoretizations and Future Research Directions. *Career Development International, 18*(1), 78-96.

Altman, Y. & Baruch, Y. (2012). Global Self-Initiated Corporate Expatriate Careers: a New Era in International Assignments? *Personnel Review, 41*(2), 233-255.

Andresen, M., Bergdolt, F. & Margenfeld, J. (2013). What Distinguishes Self-Initiated Expatriates from Assigned Expatriates and Migrants? A Literature-based Definition and Differentiation of Terms. In M. Andresen, A.A. Ariss, M. Walther & K. Wolff (Eds.), *Self-Initiated Expatriation: Individual, Organizational and National Perspectives*: Routledge.

Arthur, M. & Rousseau, D. (1996). *The Boundaryless Career: A New Employment Principle for a New Organizational Era* Boston, MA.: Cambrigde University Press.

Beechler, S. & Woodward, I.C. (2009). The Global 'War for Talent'. *Journal of International Management, 15*(3), 273-285.

Bernard, R.H. (1995). *Research Methods in Anthropology: Qualitative and Quantitative Approaches*. Thousand Oaks: Sage.

Bird, A. (1994). Careers as Repositories of Knowledge: A New Perspective on Boundaryless Careers. *Journal of Organizational Behavior, 15*(4), 325-344.

Cerdin, J.-L. (2013). Motivation of Self-Initiated Expatriates. In M. Andresen, A.A. Ariss & M. Walther (Eds.), *Self-initiated Expatriation: Individual, Organizational and National Perspectives*: Routledge.

Deery, M. (2008). Talent Management, Work-Life Balance and Retention Strategies. *International Journal of Contemporary Hospitality Management, 20*(7), 792-806.

DI. (2012). Sådan Ligger Landet – Globaliseringsredegørelse 2012: Dansk Industri (The Confederation of Danish Industry).

DIS. (2012). Tal og Fakta på Udlændingeområdet 2011: The Danish Immigration Service.

DIS. (2013). Tal på Udlændingeområdet pr. 31.01.2013: The Danish Immigration Service.

Doherty, N., Dickmann, M. & Mills, T. (2011). Exploring the Motives of Company-backed and Self-initiated Expatriates. *International Journal of Human Resource Management, 22*(3), 595-611.

Doherty, N., Richardson, J. & Thorn, K. (2013). Self-Initiated Expatriation and Self-Initiated Expatriates: Clarification of the Research Stream. *Career Development International, 18*(1), 97-112.

Esping-Andersen, G. (1990). *The Three Worlds of Welfare Capitalism*. Oxford: Polity Press.

Esping-Andersen, G. (2000). *Social Foundations of Postindustrial Economies*. Oxford: Oxford University Press.

Esping-Andersen, G. (2000). The Sustainability of Welfare States into the Twenty-First Century. *International Journal of Health Services, 30*(1), 1-12.

Froese, F.J. (2012). Motivation and Adjustment of Self-initiated Expatriates: the Case of Expatriate Academics in South Korea *The International Journal of Human Resource Management, 23*(6), 1095-1112.

Greenhaus, J.H. & Beutell, N.J. (1985). Sources of Conflict between Work and Family Roles. *The Academy of Management Review, 10*(1), 76-88.

Greenhaus, J.H. & Powell, G.N. (2006). When Work and Family Are Allies: A Theory of Work-Family Enrichment. *The Academy of Management Review, 31*(1), 72-92.

Grinstein, A. & Wathieu, L. (2012). Happily (Mal)Adjusted: Cosmopolitan Identity and Expatriate Adjustment. *International Journal of Research in Marketing, 29*(4), 337-345.

Helliwell, J., Layard, R. & Sachs, J. (2012). World Happiness Report: The Earth Institute, Columbia University.

Hofstede, G.H. (1991). *Cultures and Organizations: Software of the Mind*. London ; New York: McGraw-Hill.

Inkson, K. & Myers, B. (2003). 'The Big OE': Self-directed Travel and Career Development. *Career Development International, 8*(3), 170-181.

Kalliath, T. & Brough, P. (2008). Work-life Balance: A Review of the Meaning of the Balance Construct. *Journal of Management and Organization, 14*(3), 323-327.

Lazarova, M.B., Shaffer, M.A. & Westman, M. (2010). Elucidating the Positive Side of the Work-family Interface on International Assignments: A Model of Expatriate Work and Family Performance. *Academy of Management. The Academy of Management Review, 35*(1).

Lee, C. (2005). A Study of Underemployment among Self-Initiated Expatriates. *Journal of World Business*, 40, 172-187.

Lu, L., Cooper, C.L., Kao, S.F., Chang, T.T., Allen, T.D., Lapierre, L.M., Spector, P.E. (2010). Cross-cultural Differences on Work-to-family Conflict and Role Satisfaction: A Taiwanese-British Comparison. *Human Resource Management, 49*(1), 67-85.

Mahajan, A. & De Silva, S.R. (2012). Unmet Role Expectations of Expatriates, Host-country National Support, and Expatriate Adjustment. *International Journal of Cross Cultural Management, 12*(3), 349-360.

Michaels, E., Handfield-Jones, H. & Axelrod, B. (2001). *War for Talent*. Boston: Harvard Business Press.

Mäkelä, L. & Suutari, V. (2008). *'The Work-Life Conflicts and Related Coping Strategies among Managers with Global Careers'*. Paper presented at the Proceedings of the 34rd Annual European International Business Academy (EIBA) Conference, Tallinn, Estonia.
http://eiba2008.ttu.ee/public/Papers/57.pdf

Mäkelä, L. & Suutari, V. (2011). Coping with Work-Family Conflicts in the Global Career Context. *Thunderbird International Business Review, 53*(3), 365-375.

Mäkelä, L., Suutari, V. & Mayerhofer, H. (2011). Lives of Female Expatriates: Work-life Balance Concerns. *Gender in Management, 26*(4), 256-274.

OECD. (2011). *How's Life?* : OECD Publishing.

OECD. (2012a). *International Migration Outlook 2012*: OECD Publishing.

OECD. (2012b). *OECD Economic Surveys: Denmark 2012* (Vol. 2012): OECD Publishing.

OECD. (2013). *How's Life?* 2013: OECD Publishing.

Oxford Research. (2010). The Expat Study 2010. Denmark: Oxford Research A/S and the Copenhagen Post.

Parkes, L.P. & Langford, P.H. (2008). Work-Life Balance or Work-Life Alignment? A Test of the Importance of Work-Life Balance for Employee Engagement and Intention to Stay in Organisations. *Journal of Management & Organization, 14*(3), 267-284.

Pedersen, V.B. (2009). Work Life Balance – Hvad Betyder det Egentlig? *Psykologisk Set, 26*(74), 23-30.

Pedersen, V.B. & Lewis, S. (2012). Flexible Friends? Flexible Working Time Arrangements, Blurred Work-life Boundaries and Friendship. *Work, Employment and Society, 26*(3), 464-480.

Poelmans, S. (2003). Editorial: The Multi-level 'Fit' Model of Work and Family. *International Journal of Cross Cultural Management, 3*(3), 267-274.

Powell, M. & Barrientos, A. (2004). Welfare Regimes and the Welfare Mix. *European Journal of Political Research, 43*(1), 83-105.

Reiche, B.S., Kraimer, M.L. & Harzing, A.-W. (2011). Why Do International Assignees Stay? An Organizational Embeddedness Perspective. *Journal of International Business Studies, 42*(4), 521-544.

Schuler, R.S., Jackson, S.E. & Tarique, I. (2011). Global Talent Management and Global Talent Challenges: Strategic Opportunities for IHRM. *Journal of World Business, 46*(4), 506-516.

Scott, W.R. (2008). *Institutions and Organizations: Ideas and Interests* (3rd ed.). Thousand Oaks, CA: Sage Publications.

Shaffer, M.A., Joplin, J.R.W. & Hsu, Y.S. (2011). Expanding the Boundaries of Work-family Research: A Review and Agenda for Future Research. *International Journal of Cross Cultural Management, 11*(2), 221-268.

Shaffer, M.A., Kraimer, M.L., Chen, Y.P. & Bolino, M.C. (2012). Choices, Challenges, and Career Consequences of Global Work Experiences: A Review and Future Agenda. *Journal of Management, 38*(4), 1282-1327.

Shortland, S. & Cummins, S. (2007). Work-life Balance: Expatriates Reflect the International Dimension. *Global Business and Organizational Excellence, 26*(6), 28-42.

Smith, P.B., Andersen, J.A., Ekelund, B., Graversen, G. & Ropo, A. (2003). In Search of Nordic Management Styles. *Scandinavian Journal of Management, 19*, 491-507.

Suutari, V., Tornikoski, C. & Mäkelä, L. (2012). Career Decision Making of Global Careerists. *The International Journal of Human Resource Management, 23*(16), 3455-3478.

Tarique, I. & Schuler, R.S. (2010). Global Talent Management: Literature Review, Integrative Framework, and Suggestions for Further Research. *Journal of World Business, 45*(2), 122-133.

Tharenou, P. & Caulfield, N. (2010). Will I stay or Will I go? Explaining Repatriation by Self-initiated Expatriates. *Academy of Management Journal, 53*(5), 1009-1028.

Tung, R.L., Worm, V. & Petersen, S.A. (2008). How Small Nations Fare in the Global War on Talent: The Case of Denmark'. *Journal of Small Business Strategy, 19*(1).

Vaiman, V. & Haslberger, A. (2013). Self-Initiated Expatriates: A Neglected Source of the Global Talent Flow. In V. Vaiman & A. Haslberger (Eds.), *Talent Management of Self-Initiated Expatriates: A Neglected Source of Global Talent* (pp. 1-15). London: Palgrave Macmillan.

Wagner, A.-C. (1998). *Les Nouvelles Elites de la Mondialisation: Une Immigration Dorée en France*. Paris: Presses Universitaires de France.

CHAPTER 6

'Flexpatriation': A View from the Engine Room of Sub-Suppliers in the Maritime Sector

Mona Toft Madsen and Morten Rask

New managerial mindsets and ways of framing the challenges of organizing and managing Danish business activities must now be governed according to a global outlook. A key element of Danish companies' globalization efforts in past decades has been the use of expatriate assignments. In many companies, expatriate assignments are used systematically as part of management development, which, if the timing is right, may help the expatriate climb the management career ladder (e.g., Feldman et al., 1992). In companies with less formalized career trajectories, expatriate assignments have been used on an ad hoc basis to manage and coordinate the company's activities at a given foreign location and to build bridges between the company's foreign and local business units (e.g., Feldman et al., 1992; Collings et al., 2007). In parallel, an increased number of business flights has been observed, starting in the early 2000s (Ruskov, 2011), indicating that expatriation is increasingly complemented with business travel. Research into cross-cultural management and international human resource management (IHRM) has touched on such alternative assignments and travel arrangements (e.g., Black et al., 1999; Bonache, 2006). 'Frequent flyers', 'business commuters', and 'international business travellers' are terms used to describe different forms of international business travel. Mayerhofer et al. (2004a, b) used the term 'flexpatriation', which alludes to expatriation, to define a certain form of business travel not characterized by relocation. Flexpatriates are understood as 'those who travel for brief assignments, away from their home base and across cultural or national borders, leaving their family and personal life behind' (Mayerhofer et al., 2004b p. 1371). Mayerhofer et al. (2004a) further defined flexpatriates as those business travellers who frequently change their location across national borders. An assumption based on this definition might be that flexpatriates have broader access to various cultures while expatriates become specialized in one specific national culture.

Research into alternative international arrangements remains limited (Welch & Worm, 2006), not least in a Danish context. This is unfortunate because international relocation is an important element of Danish firms' globalization efforts. From a career perspective, it can be claimed that, while most firms have policies for traditional expatriation, substantially fewer firms have formulated policies governing extended business travel (Brookfield, 2011). For example, the IHRM literature does not explicitly suggest any procedures for handling compensation for flexpatriates. In other words, based on the literature and our empirical study, one rarely finds written procedures and/or contracts for flexpatriate work. Instead, the pattern seems to be that travel is deemed an inherent part of the job of, for example, a Business Area Manager, Marketing and Customer Relationship Manager, or Sales Manager. This has the practical implication that these managers are responsible for specific decision making and coordination tasks at their job's home base in HQ even while abroad. Although international business travel is not a new empirical phenomenon, we lack knowledge of who these travellers are, the purposes of their travels, and the specific tasks they undertake when abroad.

This chapter investigates the phenomenon of flexpatriate assignments in Danish firms, making suggestions regarding how flexpatriate assignments may naturally grow out of the maritime sector's structure and organization. More specifically, our research concerns flexpatriates' own perceptions of what they do when abroad and their experience of bringing their jobs' home base responsibilities with them on their travels.

Globalization through Expatriation

Traditional expatriate assignments have been studied in the field of cross-cultural management and international human resource management (IHRM) (Bonache, 2006; Collings & Scullion, 2006). The term 'expatriate' refers to an employee on a long-term posting outside his or her home country during which the employee's family and personal life are relocated (Mayerhofer et al., 2004a, b). After having spent a period of time abroad, repatriation is initiated and the expatriate returns home. For the traditional expatriate, international experience, financial gain, and enhanced career opportunities within the organization are the main motivators for embarking on international assignments (Dowling & Welch, 2004). However, research into expatriate assignments has revealed that companies and potential expatriates often experience challenges (Collings et al., 2007). For example, it can be difficult to find the right candidate and, apart from the high costs of traditional expatriation, relocating families and the process of repatriation can also often be problematic (Collings et al., 2007; Harvey & Novicevic, 2006).

Globalization through Flexpatriation

In the words of Collings and Scullion (2006, p. 154), 'there is a need to go beyond studying the traditional expatriate assignment in order to also examine the emergence of newer, short-term, international assignments'. Expatriation is costly, and there is a shortage of leaders willing to accept long-term international positions (Dowling & Welch, 2004). A growing literature has identified the potential of flexpatriate arrangements (Mayerhofer et al., 2004a; 2004b). It is claimed that such international travel arrangements have been used frequently for years, but that they have not been formalized and hence not investigated in depth. What job characteristics invite flexpatriate rather than expatriate arrangements? It has been suggested that, due to changes in infrastructure and IT opportunities, flexpatriate arrangements might have increasing potential (Mayerhofer et al., 2004a).

Other parts of the literature on international business and business travel have suggested that expatriate leaders have recently largely been replaced with local leaders (Rostgaard & Christensen, 2010a, b). In other words, firm internationalization has evolved into firm globalization, meaning that local leaders are preferred (Rostgaard & Christensen, 2010a). This has potentially increased the demand for another kind of boundary spanner. More specifically, as surveys have demonstrated, international business travellers are increasingly used (Pricewaterhouse-Coopers, 2010), while expatriates are less often used in some countries

(Rostgaard & Christensen, 2010a, b). It has been claimed that 'flexpatriate assignments facilitate a global understanding of company operations and the development of global competence more effectively than a long-term placement in one location' (Moore in (Mayerhofer et al., 2004a, p. 651).

Context of the Study: The 'Danish' Maritime Sector

Denmark is a global maritime sector leader despite the country's small size (Invest in Denmark, 2014). For example, Maersk, which is the world's largest operator of container ships and supply vessels, was founded and is still headquartered in Denmark. Historically, Denmark has hosted huge shipyards such as B&W, Danyard, and Aarhus Flydedok; increased global competition, however, has meant that most shipyards are now located in South East Asia (Normander, 2006). Though this shift has obviously had a major impact on Danish shipyard sub-suppliers, according to the Danish Export Association, only ten of 110 members among these sub-suppliers have chosen to move their own production to China (Normander, 2006). For example, around 100 shipyard sub-suppliers export goods worth approximately DKK 15 billion annually to China (Boutrup, 2012), constituting a substantial trade generating a natural demand for extensive business travel in the sector. While the sub-suppliers' production is mostly in Denmark, their customers, the shipyards, have concentrated their activities in Japan, South Korea, China, and Taiwan. Moreover, the shipping companies themselves are distributed all over the world.

The sub-suppliers to the shipbuilding industry therefore represent an interesting context for the study of flexpatriation. The findings reported in this chapter derive from a qualitative study in which we used semi-structured interviews (Flick, 2009) to address the research aim presented above. The interviewees were selected via the Danish Export Association (Danish Export Association, 2011), where a contact person was asked to identify eight relevant companies in which people who fit our definition of flexpatriates could be contacted. In dialogue with our contact, we concluded that the maritime sector represented what could be called an extreme case (Patton, 2002), since most collaboration between suppliers, shipyards, and shipping companies occurs across countries and is characterized by frequent travelling. All eight interviewees were males from

Danish sub-suppliers in the maritime sector with an extensive travel schedule and/or responsibility for staff with travel obligations, as well as for their own travel arrangements.

Findings: Trends Affecting Travelling and Work Conditions for Flexpatriates

Improved infrastructure and better access to information and communication technology (ICT) are factors often cited in our study. They have changed the whole way the business world functions, and for flexpatriates their impact is especially profound. For example, smartphones have made it possible to receive and answer e-mails even when one is on the way to dinner with a customer in China. If not before, it is at least possible to answer e-mails in the hotel room after a long day with customers or other network members. As well, business travellers can complete various kinds of paperwork outside normal working hours and maintain continuous contact with spouses and children by means of ICT. There is also a downside to this constant accessibility, as it can be very difficult to define when work starts and finishes. Even when they are not travelling, flexpatriates in particular will experience the impact of different time zones in their network:

> And when it's after lunchtime, they wake up in the United States, and they start responding to what you sent them yesterday. So when you get home, you can start all over, because you did not deal with the European part of the business. I went to bed at 3 a.m. yesterday because there was work to do in the United States, and I get in this morning – totally nuts. You have to do this, when you are online 24/7 and you try to be engaged. The problem is that we have different time zones, and as Europeans we can match all three zones in the middle of the day.

Being accessible 24/7 is crucial to one's job as a flexpatriate. According to our informants, members of the older generation used to have a 'lone wolf' attitude to the jobs and their careers, accessibility primarily being established by physical presence, measured as the number of travel days needed. Younger flexpatriates apparently emphasize the downside of extensive travel, and accordingly use social media and ICT much more to support and/or as an alternative to travel. In the 1980s and 1990s, business trips lasted longer and were less structured and efficient:

> We have had salespeople who told about the beginning of their work life: they travelled to Singapore, and then they sent home a fax saying that they had arrived safely. They stayed in Asia for two weeks, visited customers, and arrived home with a pile of papers. Later they faxed the customers a proposition. To communicate in that way – oh my God, from [when] a customer makes an inquiry, until he gets a proposition ... it could take months.

Another aspect of travelling a few decades ago was the lack of access to communication channels. The older generation of travellers got used to having little contact with HQ and their families when abroad:

> I think it becomes sort of a lifestyle for many people. I know colleagues in other companies who are close to retirement – they are scared to death because they'll have to stop travelling. And I know people who, if they have to sit at their desk for more than three weeks, they just have to get out. So of course a lot of the travellers like it, but they only complain because they believe they have to do that. [laughs] But in fact, I think most people who travel like it. It has become a lifestyle in some ways.

One interviewee explicitly distinguished between flexpatriates and wannabes:

> We have a guy here ... he has so many travel days, and he is the kind of guy, it would not be a problem if I called him one evening and said that we were going to Tokyo the next morning. He would just throw everything away and leave – the suitcase is packed, the passport is ready, and he would know exactly which flight to take! I mean most of the others ... and now we talk generations, right? If I asked one of our young salespeople here, he would have to find out whether this could fit with the programme, he would have to call home, find out whether it could fit with the family situation – I

> think you see a difference between the real dedicated flexpatriates and the wannabes.

Several informants recognize this difference between the older and younger generations of flexpatriates and, among other factors, explain this in terms of changed gender roles in the family. In addition, changed travelling habits are used as an explanation:

> But that was in another time and context: ordinary people did not go abroad to exotic places. Most people today would fly twelve hours to go on holiday, or maybe not everyone, but it has become more common ... So getting to see the world through your job has more or less lost its meaning, and that is why I say I could imagine that younger people have their reservations about it, since they have already been abroad. They did that after high school or during holidays. The 'exotic' thing has gone and I think that takes the top off your motivation.

This change in travel habits might have influenced how most people, not least flexpatriates, think about crossing national borders. As noted in the above quotation, the world has become 'smaller', and using trips to unusual locations as an incentive for flexpatriate work has lost its lustre. On the other hand, the more relaxed approach to other cultures has advantages as well. The global – or geocentric mindset, as Perlmutter (1969) would call it – concerns how to 'develop the best men from everywhere in the world for key positions everywhere in the world' (Perlmutter, 1969, p. 12). In other words, although specific cultural traits and habits are embedded in specific countries and regions, there are broader patterns regarding global work. According to our study, very detailed background information on specific national cultures provides only intuitive guidelines, while a broader global understanding seems to help the informants even more:

> Of course, you know there are things you have to be aware of when you go abroad, things you have to familiarize yourself with before you rush to Brazil and make a fool of yourself. But if you behave politely and are interested, you will not get into trouble. And if you happen to take a business card with one hand, it will also not be the

> end of the world. [laughs] I always take it with two hands, though, and people will know that I travel a lot in Asia. [laughs] Just smile, be open and interested. I notice when I meet people that they have two kids, for example. Then I can always ask about them, which it is something that works in all cultures.

Compared with expatriates located in a specific country, for example, for three years, flexpatriates are more flexible. Representatives of Danish maritime sector sub-suppliers naturally often travel to Asia to visit shipyards, but they also travel to other parts of the world to visit shipping companies, agents, sales offices, etc. In that sense, they might develop a relatively broad cultural perspective over time. As indicated in the above statement, informants in our study seem to develop rules of thumb that they think can help them everywhere. Another informant raised the matter of displaying humility:

> When you meet with other cultures you have to meet them with humility and openness in order to build up relations. That is important. I do not know, but I would think it has more to do with personality than formal education.

This informant implicitly emphasizes that cultural understanding is a matter of behaving well in a dynamic and globally oriented way more than having been trained in specific national cultural traits, a point made by proponents of building global mindsets rather than specializing in particular cultures (Osland et al., 2006).

Changes in the general travel and IT conditions for business travellers have made it easier to travel while keeping in touch with HQ, family, and friends. At the same time, improved access to IT and transport make it possible to extend the working day, which can be a double-edged sword. Apart from this, the working relationships and conditions in the maritime sector are rather complex, as will be discussed in the section below.

Danish Maritime Sub-Supplier Context: Relationship Building and Expert Support

As mentioned above, the context of this study is the maritime sector, which can be seen as an extreme case of globalization as all shipyards have moved to Asia in recent decades, while the customers (i.e., the shipping companies) and many sub-suppliers have remained in Europe and the United States. This has affected the entire sector, including the sub-suppliers whose representatives were interviewed in this study. An informant from a sub-supplier that delivers to the shipyards elaborates on how the sector works:

> In the global maritime sector, we operate using a so-called maker's list. The shipping company buys a ship and develops a maker's list concerning where they intend to buy, for example, pumps. And the shipyard develops a list in which they offer the pumps for a certain price. Then you reach an agreement as to who should be on the final maker's list, as there might be four companies, and then you know that someday you will have to talk to those four shipyards.

Integral to getting on a shipyard's maker's list is to build relationships. Furthermore, some interviewees' responsibilities largely entail visiting customers and negotiating prices and/or technical specifications of the products involved. This is often time-consuming, as individualized, customer-adapted solutions have become more common. Project management and/or more direct transfers of technical expertise exemplify other flexpatriate tasks. The debate over HQ standardization versus local adaptation was also treated in the interviews, as the choice of strategy greatly influenced flexpatriates' jobs.

The Danish sub-suppliers in the maritime sector were formerly characterized as having customers and suppliers located a few miles away. Today, they are distributed around the globe, making travel essential to the job. Apart from technical and sales expertise, travelling to build good relationships with customers, and in some cases with customers' customers, is integral to the flexpatriate job.

Our interviewees also mentioned that internal relationship management is especially important when one's company has sales offices (or other subsidiaries) in Asia. China is a central country in the maritime sector, and the country and its workforce are undergoing rapid changes. Chinese workers now have relatively strong incentives to leave their current employers for more challenging or better paid jobs in other companies. One informant said that an important reason for travelling to China was to deal with this challenge:

> When I am in China, it is also a way of building up relations with the people out there, all of them. I spend a lot of time talking to all of them, listening to their worries and pleasures, and I follow what happens in their families. We have a high employee turnover rate, and that is what we are trying to stop. We have not lost anyone for a while, but within the last two years we have lost two salespersons. Not because they were unhappy, but they realized that they could go to German and Swedish companies that had just started and get paid double. Apparently those companies did not know the [local] wage level.

The context of the company and the entire sector heavily affect the kinds of competences needed to realize a firm's international strategy, for example, by integrating and coordinating activities through relationship management.

Flexpatriate Responsibilities Regarding Global People Management

In line with Bartlett and Ghoshal (1989), we believe that the great challenge of any organization as it becomes larger and more diverse is to keep its core values alive. This is important for being able to coordinate and integrate the global activities of a firm. One informant, the vice president of a company delivering pumps to shipping yards, emphasized conflict resolution as one of his important responsibilities:

> When you work in our matrix organization, the person responsible for maritime has a sales responsibility of, for example, 300 million Danish krone. The Chinese guy has a sales responsibility of, for example, 100 million Danish krone in China, across sectors. Here we have a potential area of conflict. The guy responsible for China

> might say, 'My friend, I don't have enough resources right now to work in maritime'. The maritime guy would then try to put pressure on him, and argue that a new product has to be introduced now, that he must find resources. So ... [one] sometimes ... [has] to pour oil on troubled waters, to get the matrix to function right.

Another vice president from a very large company explained that, although a formalized set of company values existed, he needed to practice global management more informally:

> You know, we have our employee engagement [i.e., talks about internal company value material], which demands that I should be visible in order to set the agenda. A lot of these issues could easily be managed using modern technology, but without face-to-face dialogue, you can transfer as much information as you want, but if you do not have direct dialogue, you are not really certain that things will actually happen. If we do not have a common understanding of our values, we will not develop a common culture and we will never be able to make things happen. So that is why I travel a lot.

Another informant, an executive, indicated the importance of executive visibility in the subsidiaries:

> In an organization like ours, where you have one guy sitting in Singapore referring to the sales manager in China, who again refers to the sales director in Denmark, it is a long way home. Therefore, I go down there, we spend the whole day together, we can talk, and I can meet his family. You see, we develop a different relationship there, because if he calls me, we talk for an hour in which he makes his report, and then I turn to something else. So it has a lot to do with relationships. All of these tasks could have been done through the phone – you know specific functional tasks. But to arrive in Singapore, show up at the office and say, 'Wow, nice new offices', and say hello to new employees – this is not the same as having phone conversations.

People management is needed in all companies and is an even bigger task when the company is global, especially when the company's relationships are widely distributed globally, as is the case in the maritime sector.

Discussion and Implications

The subject of our empirical study was flexpatriates from Danish sub-suppliers in the maritime sector. Our intention was to identify flexpatriates' typical job titles, determine their main responsibilities, and to discover how the sectoral context as well as more general tendencies in travellers' work conditions affected these responsibilities. Furthermore, we wanted to identify potential future challenges and opportunities afforded by flexpatriation. We were especially puzzled by how flexpatriates dealt with playing what we saw as a double role, namely, being responsible for various strategic and operational tasks at HQ while being abroad much of the time.

Broadly, our findings emphasize that Danish sub-supplier companies in the maritime sector are characterized by strong international collaboration, using flexpatriates as mediators between HQ and local sales offices, between sub-suppliers and shipyards, and sometimes between shipyards and shipping companies. The following discussion of our findings will be structured around three main topics: 1) general changes in travelling conditions for business travellers, 2) the impact of the context of Danish maritime sub-suppliers, and 3) the typical responsibilities of flexpatriates from Danish sub-supplier companies in the maritime sector. Based on a discussion of these findings, we will identify a few challenges and opportunities that might accompany flexpatriation in the future. An overview of factors affecting flexpatriation can be seen in Figure 6.1. Some of these factors are general in nature, affecting all companies that collaborate globally, while others are more sector specific. Global people management is another relevant factor in the maritime sector that may occasionally become particularly urgent for sub-supplier companies in this sector, as flexpatriates function as boundary spanners between shipping yards, shipping companies, and internal subsidiaries. Although we are aware that most flexpatriate tasks overlap, for example, that internal relationship management and external relationship management are intertwined, we have nevertheless categorized the findings as illustrated in Figure 6.1.

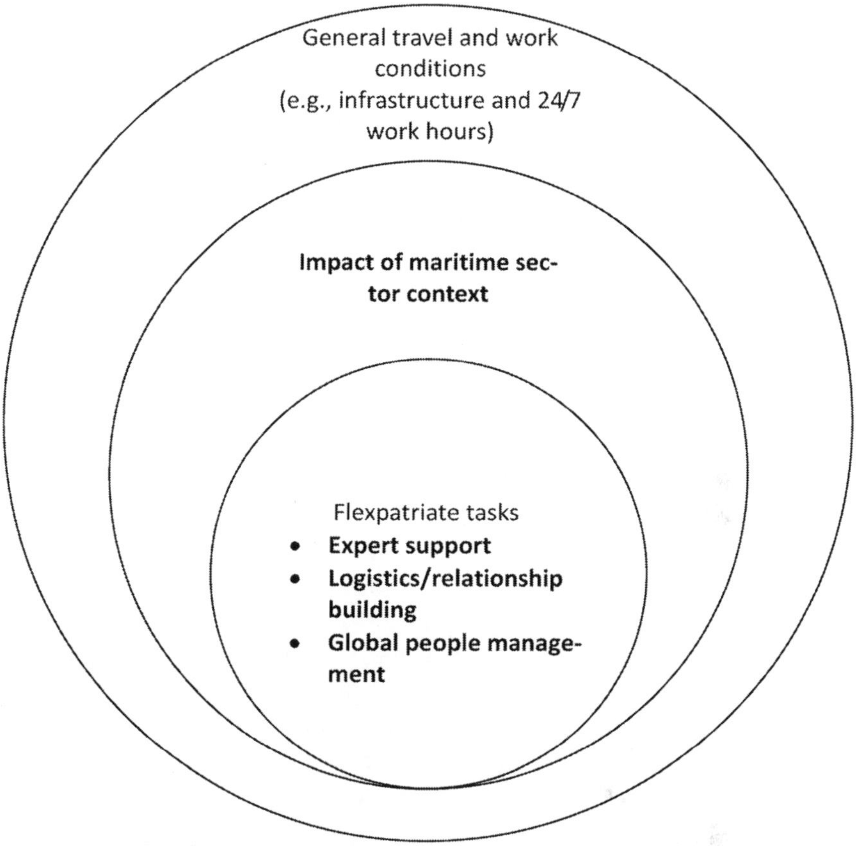

Figure 6.1. Elements of flexpatriation in Danish sub-supplier companies in the maritime sector.

The Influence of Broader Changes in Business Travel Conditions

Earlier research (e.g., Mayerhofer et al., 2004a, b) has identified the importance of improved infrastructure, which our empirical study confirms. More specifically, changes in the airline industry mean that a business traveller can now fly to new destinations, at lower prices, and more frequently. At the same time, improvements in IT and communication channels in general have made it realistic to travel while remaining in touch with family, friends, HQ, and other collaborators on a daily basis. Moreover, virtual communication has made it possible to work across time zones – in other words, around the clock – which has potential downsides. Altogether, these changes in work conditions for business travellers make it possible to go abroad without neglecting responsibilities at HQ. Compared with expatriate work, it might be easier for the flexpatriate to work in the evening, in the airport, and on the flight. In other words, flexpatriation often extends the working day by several hours, simply because it is possible. This might not always be possible for an expatriate who has relocated his or her family and has a spouse and children waiting at home.

According to informants in our study, one effect of access to cheap flights is that many people have been abroad even before starting their careers. Most people can afford holidays to destinations such as Thailand, China, and Brazil, so the opportunity to travel to such destinations through work might no longer be seen as pleasant and/or prestigious. Moreover, as a flexpatriate with HQ responsibilities, there will probably be little time for exploring. Instead, a long trip to, for example, China is approached as a necessary part of the job, offering time to get something done during the flight or at the hotel room in the evening. Again, the situation is different for an expatriate: although he or she has a busy work schedule, there will still be chances to go on private excursions with the family. Business travel is not a new phenomenon, but certain changes in infrastructure and communication channels have made it easier to travel and undertake operational work at the same time.

When asked explicitly about cultural differences, our informants indicate that they do not see national cultural training as useful, but that they instead rely on more globally accepted values such as openness, friendliness, and curiosity. This brings to mind contemporary theoretical debate on the importance of global mindsets rather than understanding specific national cultures (e.g., Osland et al., 2006).

The Impact on Flexpatriation in the Context of Danish Sub-Suppliers in the Maritime Sector

The main changes in the sector are that customers' ship building activities are now concentrated in South East Asia while the ship owners are globally distributed, a pattern justifying constant travel by sub-supplier employees. As the activities in South East Asia are often very specialized, leading to small individual purchase volumes, it is uneconomic to establish subsidiaries. The flexpatriates from sub-suppliers therefore become the needed boundary spanners in the sector.

Danish Maritime Sub-supplier Flexpatriates' Typical Tasks

Examples of identified flexpatriate job titles are CEO, business area manager, sales manager, and marketing manager. Their job titles naturally describe our informants' tasks as flexpatriates, but it might be fair to categorize the typical tasks into three broad groups, namely, expert support, logistics/relationship building, and global people management. *Expert support* concerns various kinds of sometimes very specific technical advice, for example, on how to adapt a standard product to fit the customer's context (e.g., adapting an air conditioning system to a specific climate), or negotiations (e.g., regarding prices, quality, and/or delivery).

The *logistics/relationship building* category of flexpatriate tasks often concerns relationships between HQ and customers and/or customers' customers, often involving, for example, a sales agent speaking the local language. This part of the job is largely concerned with building trust and, according to our study, is crucial. At the same time, it is uneconomic to have local units in all countries, so an expatriate assignment would seldom be an option. In addition, a sub-supplier cannot send an inexperienced person for such a task, and more experienced employees who are settled with family are often unwilling to become expatriates. Another aspect of flexpatriate relationship building concerns retention. In our study, the matter of key employee retention was raised by a sales manager as something that was crucial in the maritime sector in China, where there are many offers for competent employees.

Global people management has to do with internal *people management*, a rather broad category with various sub-categories; for example, raising the company profile and strengthening company culture across countries were duties our informants found demanding, though important. They emphasized in various ways that, while many tasks can in practice be undertaken virtually (e.g., spreading company values via intranet or inquiring about a business case via e-mail), to ensure that tasks are completed properly and that people are 'on the same page', relationships must be cultivated and subsidiary/sales office employees must believe that they are making a difference and that HQ cares about them (and to some extent about their families as well). Furthermore, people management sometimes entails resolving specific conflicts between employees with different responsibilities (e.g., disagreements concerning resource use, language, or culture that engender misunderstanding), for example, in a matrix organization.

Implications for Practice and Research

As Denmark is a small country, the use and management of international relocations is important for companies domiciled there. While earlier work in the IHRM area identified challenges with international business travel, it usually emphasized business travellers' lifestyle, Work-life balance, and private life in general, for example, by highlighting the risk of divorce and alcoholism (e.g., Mayerhofer, 2011; Tahvanainen et al., 2005). However, even from the employer's perspective, the widespread use of flexpatriates can have long-term practical implications: for example, playing a double role, as flexpatriates arguably do, can reduce work effectiveness, work quality, and potential knowledge exchange if it is the combination of easy travelling access, long working days, and 24/7 work availability that has led to increased use of flexpatriation.

However, flexpatriation does offer advantages over expatriation. First, it obviously saves money when a flexpatriate goes abroad to undertake specific tasks while continuing to be in charge of his or her obligations at HQ. Second, this form of assignment offers considerable flexibility, which expatriate assignments do not. Moreover, our study indicates that flexpatriates could become more globally minded through their dynamic interaction with various nations, rather than becoming specialized in specific national cultures, which sometimes leads to expatriates choosing to stay in specific nations.

However, a limitation of our study is that we have talked only to the older generation of flexpatriates. When they started their careers, they were more or less isolated from HQ when abroad, and therefore did not generally have to fill two jobs or play a double role. In addition, they began their careers at a time when foreign travel was regarded as 'exotic', so, in many ways, they approached flexpatriation as an exciting 'lone wolf' lifestyle. They now accept, with some regrets, that things have changed. They have opinions on how things have changed and start from the assumption that the new generation has a different approach to the job. Future research could shed light on the new generation of flexpatriates and the potential conflict arising from double-job issues.

References

Bartlett, C.A. & Ghoshal, S. (1989). *Managing across Borders: The Transnational Solution*. Cambridge, MA: Harvard Business School Press.

Black, J.S., Morrison, A. & Gregersen, H.B. (1999). *Global Explorers: The Next Generation of Leaders*. New York: Routledge.

Bonache, J. (2006). The Compensation of Expatriates: a Review and a Future Research Agenda. In G.K. Stahl & I. Bjørkman (Eds.), *Handbook of Research in International HRM* (pp. 158-175). Cheltenham, UK: Edward Elgar.

Boutrup, C. (2012). Dansk Maritimeindustri på Offensiv i Kina. *Business.dk* 6. december 2005. Opdateret 26. maj 2012.

Brookfield. (2011). *Global Reloation Trends – 2011 Survey Report*: Brookfield Global Relocation Services.

Collings, D. & Scullion, H. (2006). Global Staffing. In G.K. Stahl & I. Bjørkman (Eds.), *Handbook of Research in International HRM* (pp. 141-157). Cheltenham, UK: Edward Elgar.

Collings, D.G., Scullion, H. & Morley, M.J. (2007). Changing Patterns of Global Staffing in the Multinational Enterprise: Challenges to the Conventional Expatriate Assignment and Emerging Alternatives. *Journal of World Business*, (42), 198-213.

Danish Export Association. (2011). *THE DANISH MARITIME GROUP – a Member of the Danish Export Association*.
http://www.dk-export.dk/page1502.aspx [2011, May 17].

Dowling & Welch. (2004). *International Human Resource Management: Managing People in a Global Context* (4th ed.). London: Thomson Learning.

Feldman, D.C. & Thomas, D.C. (1992). Career Management Issues Facing Expatriates. *Journal of International Business Studies* 23(2), 271-293.

Flick, U. (2009). *An Introduction to Qualitative Research* (4th ed.): Sage Publications.

Harvey, M. & Novicevic, M.M. (2006). The Evolution from Repatriation of Managers in MNEs to Patriation in Global Organizations. In G.K. Stahl & I. Bjørkman (Eds.), *Handbook of Research in International HRM* (pp. 323-343). Cheltenham, UK: Edward Elgar.

Invest in Denmark. 'The Danish Maritime Industry'. 2014. Ministry of Foreign Affairs of Denmark. January 13, 2014.
http://www.investindk.com/Clusters/Maritime-industry.

Mayerhofer, H., Hartmann, L.C. & Herbert, A. (2004a). Career Management Issues for Flexpatriate International Staff. *Thunderbird International Business Review, 45*(6), 647-666.

Mayerhofer, H., Hartmann, L.C., Michelitsch-Riedl, G. & Kollinger, I. (2004b). Flexpatriate Assignments: a Neglected Issue in Global Staffing. *The International Journal of Human Resource Management, 15*(8), 1371-1389.

Mayerhofer (2011). Recognising Diversity in Managing Work-Life Issues of Flexpatriates. *Equality, Diversity and Inclusion- An International Journal* 30 (7), 589-609.

Normander, B. (2006). Den miljøtunge industri på vej væk. *Global Økologi*. Maj, pp. 9-11.

Osland, J.S. (2008). Overview of the Global Leadership Literature. In M.E. Mendenhall, et al. (Eds.), *Global Leadership: Research, Practice, and Development*. London: Routledge.

Osland, J.S., Bird, A., Mendenhall, M. & Osland, A. (2006). Developing Global Leadership Capabilities and Global Mindset. In G.K. Stahl & I. Bjørkman (Eds.), *Handbook of Research in International HRM* (pp. 197-222). Cheltenham, UK: Edward Elgar.

Patton, M.Q. (2002). *Qualitative Research and Evaluation Methods* (3rd ed.). Thousand Oaks, CA: Sage Publications.

Perlmutter, H.V. (1969). The Tortuous Evolution of the Multinational Corporation. *Columbia Journalmellemrum? of World Business*, *4*(1), 9-18. http://search.ebscohost.com/login.aspx?direct=true&db=buh&AN=5543148&site=ehost-live

PricewaterhouseCoopers. (2010). *Managing Tomorrow's People – Talent Mobility 2020: Themellemrum? Next Generation of International Assignments*. http://www.pwcias.com/webmedia/doc/634064113481631618_hra_mgt_tmr_ppl_apr2010.pdf

Rostgaard, A. & Christensen, J.R. (2010a, September 10). Ud med de Danske og ind med de Globale Værdisæt. *Berlingske Nyhedsmagasin*.

Rostgaard, A. & Christensen, J.R. (2010b, September 10). Udlændinge i spidsen for danske virksomheder. *Berlingske Nyhedsmagasin*.

Ruskov, J. (2011, May 4). Comeback til Business Travel. *Berlingske Nyhedsmagasin*.

Tahvanainen, M., Welch, D. & Worm, V. (2005). Implications of Short-Term International Assignments. *European Management Journal 23*(6), 663-673.

Welch, D.E. & Worm, V. (2006). International Business Travellers: a Challenge for IHRM. In G.K. Stahl & I. Bjørkman (Eds.), *Handbook of Research in International HRM* (pp. 283-301). Cheltenham, UK: Edward Elgar.

CHAPTER 7

Translating Private Equity in Denmark: The Impact of the TDC Buy-out on the Danish Private Equity Industry

Robson Rocha and Duncan Wigan

Private equity firms play a substantial role in advanced economies and an increasing role in developing economies. One of the world's largest private equity firms (PEFs), Kohlberg Kravis and Roberts, indirectly employed 560,000 people in the United States in 2007, making it the second largest employer in the country, just behind Walmart. McKinsey and Company includes Kohlberg Kravis and Roberts among four new power brokers in global capital markets. Private equity (PE) controlled 5% of the value of companies listed on US stock markets, 3% of those in Europe, and approximately 0.5% of the USD 167 trillion global capital market as of 2006 (McKinsey 2007, pp. 3-15). The PE business in Denmark has increased in importance. Between 1991 and 2008, PEFs acquired 205 Danish companies; between 2005 and 2008, 114 companies were acquired by PE, indicating its growing significance over time. Data from the Danish Economy and Business Ministry indicate that PEFs employed 6% of the Danish workforce in 2009. 63% of companies acquired by PE belonged to the manufacturing sector, while the service sector accounted for the greater number of jobs among the acquired companies. According to a Danish Venture Capital Association annual report, Danish companies owned by PEFs employed 584,000 workers globally in 2011. Of these, 49,000 employees, a decreasing proportion, work in Denmark. Not only TDC, but other important flagships of the Danish economy, such as ISS, Falck, and

Copenhagen Airport, are owned by PEFs. Over the last two years, the PE business has been consistently identified in the national media as a key source of wealth and competitiveness for the Danish economy. The national industry association, the Danish Venture Capital Association (DVCA), has enjoyed considerable success in presenting a positive image of and gaining acceptance for PE in Denmark. This is despite the fact that the leveraged buy-out (LBO) of TDC[2] by a consortium of foreign PEFs had previously challenged the legitimacy of the PE field in Denmark. Specific characteristics of this LBO transgressed what is commonly considered legitimate behaviour in Denmark, which has a coordinated market economy. We will elaborate upon the specifics of this case below.

It is perhaps unsurprising that many local actors resisted and questioned the legitimacy of PE in Denmark when the contrast between its logic and that of the Danish system was cast into sharp relief by the TDC LBO. What was perceived as a short-term profit-making strategy, an alien managerial model, and overly aggressive financial engineering contrasted sharply with a system known for longer-term strategies, cooperation across institutional spheres (including components of the firm, such as labour and management), and more conservative approaches to profit extraction and financial strategy. The managerial tools and modi operandi deployed by PEFs are often in clear tension with what has been understood to constitute the Danish business system. To understand how foreign PEFs disrupted field legitimacy, local actors resisted specific PE business strategies, and PEFs responded to this, we explore how a PE managerial logic was first absorbed and then reconstructed locally by various social groups. To investigate the processes by which this alien logic was translated and adapted, it is necessary to evaluate the role played by actors located at various levels of the Danish business system. When an alien logic enters an institutional environment, it will likely meet resistance, leading to its translation and adaptation to local norms, rather than exclusion. Accordingly, it is essential to investigate how various actors have interacted to enact strategies for shaping the PE industry in Denmark. Taking a broadly constructivist perspective, we avoid considering firms to be unified and independent actors, instead raising larger questions about how to conceive relationships between business and so-

2. Tele Danmark A/S was renamed TDC in 2000.

ciety, between forms of ownership and national institutional environments, and the interaction of these with the globalization of economic activities.

The chapter does not focus on evaluating PEF performance. Instead, we examine how institutional heritage, or various nationally bounded administrative heritages (Bartlett & Ghoshal, 1989), affect the processes by which imported business strategies disrupt, attain, or maintain legitimacy. This chapter therefore investigates the legitimacy dynamics catalyzed by a relatively new way of financing and controlling firms in a business system considered a coordinated market economy. We demonstrate that PEFs are under pressure to satisfy diverse expectations simultaneously, so as to achieve external legitimacy, or 'licenses to operate', in various countries and business systems. We investigate how PE resolves countervailing institutional pressures emanating from the friction between a universal model and its local translation. We then examine how local actors are affected by the actions of foreign PEFs, and how these local actors in turn respond. To do so, we explore the acquisition of TDC by a transnational consortium of PEFs.

The introduction to this volume raises several urgent questions concerning the overarching problem of how globalization affects the management, organization, and evolution of business enterprises. Insofar as globalization involves transverse forces disrupting extant patterns of business relationships, our case exemplifies the tensions and dynamics unleashed by globalization and how a clash across borders (both geographic and normative) is regulated and resolved to both domesticate and shape the specificities of contemporary change. We concur with the editors of this volume that global dynamics are destabilizing widely accepted concepts such as 'markets, organizations, and employment'. In turn, we confirm that 'organizational structures guide local interaction patterns' to illustrate how translation as 'social negotiation between individuals and groups' modifies societal and organizational structures. In doing so, they produce an outcome representing a temporally stable and incrementally evolving partial resolution of the contradictions emerging from the interaction of global dynamics where nationally bounded institutional configurations may emerge.

Private Equity: Optimal Global Benchmarking or Financialized Capitalism

PEFs employ heterogeneous strategies in managing their acquisitions. Depending on the skill set within the PEF, the economic characteristics of the markets or sectors in which the PEF operates, and broader macroeconomic conditions, particularly liquidity conditions in global financial markets, a PE fund can easily switch focus, temporal horizon, and management strategy. This chapter focuses on the strategy of the LBO, though we note that it is inadequate to equate one such strategy with PE in general. PEFs engaging in LBOs, or debt-fuelled acquisitions, solicit investor funds and deploy debt to buy mature firms and take them out of public ownership. This is distinct from venture capital funds, which provide seed money for immature and usually high-tech firms with highly uncertain prospects. By reengineering the acquired firm's finances and restructuring its operations, PE aims either to return the firm to public ownership through an initial public offering or sell on the acquired firm privately at a higher price. The PEF manages acquired companies for a limited period of two to seven years. After this period, any profit is distributed between the firm, the general partners, and the investors – the limited partners – who constitute the PE fund. Both PEFs and PE funds are usually limited-liability partnerships, which protects their managers and investors from responsibility for the full cost of any losses incurred within their acquisitions. Each PE fund is time limited and investors commit a sum at the beginning of the fund's existence, which they must divulge to the fund firm as and when requested. Solicited capital is usually deployed in the first two or three years of the fund's life. PEF revenue arises from two sources. First, the firms charge investors approximately two percent of invested funds annually for management services. Second, the PEF is entitled to 20% of profits after reaching a 'hurdle rate' usually set at approximately 8% of invested funds. While the financial crisis has led to the renegotiation of these contract terms in some cases, this remains the dominant model.

Their detractors claim that PEFs are secretive asset strippers that amass short-term and outsized windfall profits by loading acquisitions with debt, systematically reducing tax liabilities, and restructuring employment relationships along neoliberal lines (Erturk et al., 2008; Froud & Williams, 2007; Morgan, 2009). In this view, PE generates a dangerously leveraged exposure to firm performance by concentrating equity and increasing the role of debt in the acquired firm's financial structure. The consequence, in this view, is that the acquired firm may well generate excess returns to investors and the PEF, but at a heavy cost, as PE renders its acquisitions acutely vulnerable to swings in the cost of financing. Furthermore, there is concern that the extraction of value in the present might rely upon its reduction in the future as acquired firms become less flexible in the face of change and retain a lower capacity for adaptation. In other words, the short term is traded against the long term. Treating the firm as a disaggregated body of assets has generated acute concerns regarding the social embeddedness and function of the firm, raising anxieties regarding the subordination of all stakeholder interests to the immediate interests of legal ownership. As such, the issue plays into a renewed concern with the socio-political content of the legal constitution of the firm (Ireland, 2010). From this perspective, by using various mechanisms of value extraction, PE exploits legal and liquidity conditions to concentrate future wealth generation – which it renders increasingly uncertain – in the present. The PEF is understood as inserting itself between various stakeholders and manipulating a complex of relationships (among investors, politicians, financiers, employees, and customers) so as to maximize, or massage into existence, what critics call a mirage of profitability.

On the other hand, proponents of PE hold that PEFs force economic upgrading, increase competitive capacity, promote innovation, create employment, and ameliorate the weaknesses associated with the public corporation. Following Jensen (Jensen & Meckling, 1976; Jensen, 1989), supporters argue that PE offers an optimal resolution to the problem of limited company owners being separate from the point of control, while managers are inadequately incentivized to maximize returns to ownership; in so doing, PE can maximize the efficiency and thereby social utility of the firm. PE corrects market prices by identifying and rectifying the undervaluation of assets and resolves the problems associated with the separation of ownership and control. In improving the acquisition's performance, PE generates tax returns to the state, increases employment, and adds to the general stock of wealth via returns to investors (Morgan, 2009). The 'market triumphant' view holds that LBOs sharpen incentives arising from ownership to improve performance and discipline the firm on the basis of increased debt vulnerability. A need to meet a regular debt repayment and the absence of spare cash will ensure management focus. Furthermore, the specialized and sophisticated skills a PEF will bring to bear in managing an acquisition enable PEFs to impose global best practice within acquisitions. PE is, in these terms, necessarily a force for the greater good.

This dichotomous reading of the economic role and social value of PE has led to a series of vociferous debates across the UK, Germany, the European Union, and Denmark (UK Treasury, 2009; EU Commission, 2010). However, these polarized debates may be blinded to the real complexity of the PE business. Detractors tend to focus on LBOs and associated processes of 'asset stripping' and 'gearing'. Supporters, in contrast, rely almost exclusively on the claim that PEFs are uniquely capable of resolving the agency problem and optimizing resource allocation. We argue that this dichotomous reading of the business is misplaced. PE encompasses a wide range of business models, ranging from the ideal-typical LBO to rebranding and medium-term growth strategies. Our interest here is not so much to evaluate the claims of or adjudicate this debate; our aim is rather to understand the implications of the construction and maintenance of reputation and legitimacy for institutional dynamics and change in a national business system. The dichotomous nature of the debate surrounding PE provides a suitable context in which to take on this challenge. We argue that it is how legitimacy is negotiated that defines institutional enactment and change in this case.

Private Equity in Denmark

Denmark has been widely understood as a clear exemplar of a coordinated market economy (Hall & Soskice, 2001) where broad participation in decision making has been an important component of national industrial regimes. While Denmark has liberal labour market characteristics, such as low levels of employment security (the famous 'flexisecurity system'), the Danish business system is typified by a strong trade union movement and a tradition of cooperation between labour market actors (Madsen, 2006). An agreement establishing cooperation committees was established in Denmark as early as 1947 by the labour movement and private employers' associations. Firms are embedded within networks of trade and industry associations and engage these associations to solve a variety of incomplete contracting dilemmas and create important non-market collective goods. Organizational power is dispersed across various stakeholders represented on the supervisory board and most decisions are consensual (Kristensen & Rocha, 2012; Rocha, 2009). Several legal provisions encourage owners to develop long-term, relational contracts with investors in a stakeholder system in which various groups, in addition to owners, are given a strong voice in firm management. On the face of it, these features are at odds with the PE model, in which, for example, PE management is assumed to be able to make frequent and significant changes to acquisition strategies, structures, and practices without reference to consensual decision-making procedures, as would be expected in the typical governance regime of a coordinated market economy. Crucially, in this market environment, ownership conduct is assumed to be circumscribed by a host of national institutional complementarities in the interest of long-term, socially embedded competitive optimality. In contrast, PE evaluates assets according to a global standard and ostensibly raises the spectre of Veblen's pecuniary definition of modern business civilization wherein the differential advantage of capitalist managers (mere 'money capitalists') '[takes] precedence over the economic advantage for the community; or rather the differential advantage of ownership is alone regarded in the conduct of industry under this system' (Veblen, 1908, p. 107). This chapter aims to understand how these two very distinct logics are enacted and negotiated locally.

Methodology and Data

This research focuses on the acquisition of Danish companies by PEFs. The present study involves an in-depth case study covering the period from the initial privatization of TDC through its acquisition by the PE consortium, Nordic Telephone Company (NTC), to its partial resale in the 2010 equity sale. Case studies permit deep exploration of how the institutional contexts in which PEFs are embedded affect the way they are controlled and coordinated and, in turn, how PEFs control and coordinate the impacts of the PE field on the specificities of the institutional context and its social foundations.

Data were collected using three techniques: (1) semi-structured, one-to-one interviews, (2) semi-structured group discussions, and (3) the study of written and electronic documentation. Informants were chosen according to guidelines for 'purposeful sampling' (Lincoln & Guba, 1985) using a 'snowball or chain sampling' strategy. The authors chose informants who would be able to cast light on the main research question concerning changes in legitimacy over time based on auto-description within a discursive field.

The collected data were coded and categorized to facilitate abstraction and theory construction. Coding proceeded primarily on two levels: 1) using a list of concrete terms grounded in the data (e.g., PE, shareholder value, maximization, restructure, outsource, performance, strip, and returns); 2) using a list of more abstract terms (e.g., legitimacy, reputation, ideology, globalization, capitalism, and state) based on terms found in the literature (see Eisenhardt, 1989). During axial coding, the authors developed further conceptual domains by comparing themes within and between transcripts (Corbin & Strauss, 1990). The translations are the authors'.

Destabilizing and Reconstructing Field Legitimacy in Denmark

The narrative of the TDC case starts with the agglomeration of regional telecoms by the Danish parliament in 1990, creating a single telecoms giant. Like many state-owned entities in the 1990s, Tele Danmark A/S was fully privatized by 1998. Given the then prime minister's later central role in opposing PE, first in Denmark, and then across Europe, it is ironic that Poul Nyrup Rasmussen was the prime minister during this process and during the wave of privatization in the 1990s. This initial privatization opened up the possibility of PE influencing the Danish system. Large corporate assets previously regarded and protected as national champions now became exposed to the global marketplace. The point of analytical interest here is that, as noted above, at the core of institutional theory lies the notion that institutional constellations impose an endogenous logic of path dependence on actors who drive and interact with institutional transformations (Whitley, 1999). Relationships between institutions within an institutional environment, such as Denmark, will often constrain change and, where there is change, partially define that change. In this case, however, the actions of rule makers generated outcomes quite different from those intended. Privatization in Denmark was intended to create an ownership democracy, not to permit what some would subsequently understand to be the disembedding or dismembering of a national champion via an alien business model. This sentiment has been reflected not only in the political discourse surrounding the buyout, but also in academic literature claiming that firms constituting the infrastructural architecture of a nation should not be exposed to the full force of the global market. On this basis, we claim that the literature on institutional change needs to be sensitive to the fact that, while institutions evolve along path-dependent lines, this evolution is marked by a substantive element of contingency. Rule followers may enact institutions in such ways that the results differ markedly from those originally intended. The present case demonstrates that, while extant institutional constellations do constrain change, the path of transformation is not predefined and actors seeking to control the path of change will often not be entirely successful.

Following the full privatization of Tele Danmark A/S, SBC, an American firm specializing in the telecoms sector, bought 42% of the company's shares. In 2004, SBC sold its holdings on the Danish and New York stock exchanges. At this juncture, and directly reflecting the importance of TDC as an infrastructurally significant and central component of the Danish coordinated model, TDC's 'charter' was amended so that no single shareholder could own more than 12% of its equity. As PE had at this stage only just appeared on the public radar, this change likely reflected a proactive defensive move. In 2004, an offer to buy the firm made by the US PEF, Blackstone, was rebutted. Subsequently, TDC's board removed the restriction on ownership concentration, opening up the possibility of a PE-led acquisition. As a director of one of the most powerful Danish pension funds explained:

> So part of the deal between government and these American buyers [i.e., SBC] was that there should be a change so that no one but the Americans could have this over 12% [equity stake]. It was a poison pill. When they left the company, some of us supported that it should be taken out. All these limitations on ownership, it was said, were supposed to protect the shareholder. No, it was to protect the management. That is my basic point. So if there is no takeover risk for management, the company will be hijacked by daily manage-

> ment and the board, and it is the shareholders who are hijacked. (PF director)

In 2005 TDC received a buy-out offer of USD 76 billion, or USD 382 per share. The offer included a 'control premium' to existing shareholders of 44.7% over the prior three-month average share price. The bid was led by NTC, a consortium with a regional focus set up by five giant foreign PE funds: Apax, Permira, Blackstone, Providence, and Kohlberg Kravis Roberts & Co. The Danish pension fund ATP, one of the larger shareholders, rejected the offer, blocking the 90% threshold necessary to compel remaining shareholders to sell. 'For a very long time, we had been very critical of the way the board managed the company. In our opinion, there was a lot of low-hanging fruit in the company. In that respect, we did not think the offer ... reflected the possible value of the company. In that way, it was strictly an investment decision. It caused a lot of fuss internally' (PF Director). Consequently, TDC was not taken into private ownership and was subject to the usual reporting requirements for listed companies. Ultimately, Nordic Telephone Company secured an 88.2% stake in the fourth largest European buy-out to that time.

In 2005, TDC had more than 13 million European customers and was a typical diversified firm theoretically undervalued in the equity market and, given previous state ownership, financial market conditions, and dominant trends in corporate governance, ripe for restructuring. TDC was widely considered a national champion, operating as a quasi-monopoly in the Danish telecoms market and characterized by a corporate governance regime associated with the coordinated market economy. For example, according to interviewed union representatives, the initial takeover of Tele Danmark by SBC in 1998 was accompanied by the inability of the new American owners to understand the specificity of Danish labour relations with their emphasis on co-determination.

NTC's strategy in acquiring and restructuring TDC incorporates many elements commonly associated with the negative perception of LBOs: leverage, gearing, equity concentration, tax optimization, asset sales, large managerial fees and remuneration, initial reductions in employee numbers, and redefined employment contracts. Consequently, a vociferous debate emerged at all levels of Danish society concerning the legitimacy and consequences of the new ownership model. This debate, reflecting European concerns, maintained its intensity over time as the restructuring and exit strategy unfolded amidst an initial liquidity glut, a surfeit of cheap money, and then the global financial meltdown. Interestingly, the most notable protagonist in this debate has been the former prime minister, Poul Nyrup Rasmussen, who, as noted above, was in office during the TDC privatization process but has vehemently and consistently campaigned against the consortium and the PE business model, while pushing at the national and regional level for greater regulation of the PE industry.

The important point in this context is that TDC, which may not be representative of the activities of PE in Denmark more broadly, was the catalyst for vociferous public debate over PE in Denmark. Significantly, this debate has very much been delimited and defined by the studied case. Indeed, the PE business model existed in Denmark well before NTC's takeover of TDC, but the question of the legitimacy of the business model only arose in the wake of the TDC buy-out. TDC put the PE business on the map. One leader of the PE business in Denmark made it quite clear that the TDC case catalysed a strong focus on the issue of legitimacy:

> Around the time of TDC, we realized that case was so bad for private equity because it involved a cocktail of big non-Danish, non-European, US private equity [funds] buying a business with which we all had some sort of connection. It is on the borderline between public and private. It very much involved who should own Danish industry. It involved big payments to our CEO in a public-dash-private business. It was people who came in, probably without doing a lot of research about culture, and they simply did not introduce themselves. You can say that TDC was such a big acquisition, and involved so many issues, that for us it was very important to say that now we basically need to establish a platform. We need a license to operate, because if we do not have it, it will be so easy for everybody, for Poul Nyrup and other politicians, to attack. So we said, OK, we need to establish a framework for private equity to operate in this country. You cannot be this big and important, and then just close the door.

Significantly, public concern over the fact that TDC had quickly moved from being a major source of corporate tax revenue to paying nearly nothing in taxes to the Danish state prompted, at least symbolically, a significant change in the taxation of PE in Denmark. As a result of the DKK 2 billion reduction in tax revenue from seven large companies, the liberal government reduced the deductibility of PE fund interest payments. The main source of the difficulty was that PEF acquisitions were afforded tax deductions on interest payments arising from debt incurred in the buy-out, while interest payments from the acquired firm, which theoretically compensated for deductions, went abroad, where the Danish tax authorities had no jurisdiction. This phenomenon was exacerbated in relation to foreign PEFs. According to the Danish tax authority, the legal change was enacted specifically in reaction to the TDC case, which from one year to the next moved from being one of the most important contributors to Danish tax revenues to making virtually no contribution at all.

On the face of it, this amounted to a critical challenge to the success of the PE model in Denmark, as the tax change struck not only NTC and TDC, but Danish PE more broadly. At this juncture, the industry, led by Denmark's largest and longest-standing PEF, Axcel, bolstered the role of the industry association, the DVCA, whose main focus was to legitimize PE across Danish society. A DVCA employee stated that:

> We are a kind of a communicator for all this, for the buy-out guys, as they were pretty closed at that time. Since then, the DVCA has become more organized ... Christian Friigaast ... he made the whole community organize and we are the spearheads of that organization. And since then we have had ... a very, very good network among politicians. I come from the public service, just across the street. I was a public servant so I have a very good network among our civil servants. What we do is lobby a lot and what has happened since then is that, since we started organizing, we have actually been modelled ... and we publicly can see how often we are quoted in the press.

Interviewees employed in the PE business or related financial institutions consistently contrast the strategies of PEFs with features of a coordinated economy, drawing parallels between PE and capitalism, opposition to PE and socialism (interpreted as regressive political control). This discourse is firmly situated in a particular deinstitutionalized conception of economics, the economy, and economic assets. Each is understood as necessarily apolitical, the proper subject of 'scientific' evaluation, and naturally unfolding outside of historical time. As such, institutional transformation in any society follows a universal logic emanating from the exigencies of the global market. When confronted with common criticisms of the industry, the DVCA responds, 'Yes exactly, because there is some argument against capitalism. It is also an argument against those who make a lot of money. ... It is not an argument against private equity; it is an argument against capitalism'.

Notably, arguments against PE did not rest purely on a negative evaluation of the ethics of certain practices and strategies; competition featured as well. Players in other industrial sectors argued that they were placed at a tremendous disadvantage vis-à-vis PE regarding their chances of attracting risk capital. Insofar as PE could gain a differential advantage in terms of financing techniques and related fiscal exposures, traditional industrial players in the Danish institutional environment were placed at a structural disadvantage. Our interviews confirm that industrial players felt at such a disadvantage.

The PE sector, which had existed for almost two decades in Denmark, was suddenly subject to intense debate over its legitimacy as a direct consequence of the NTC acquisition of TDC. In this context, the perception that PEFs threatened the 'Danish model' rapidly spread through Danish society. A critical mass favouring intervention and greater regulation emerged across various segments of society, so that even the liberal government became inclined to impose more exacting regulation on PE. Figure 7.1 shows the extent to which the number of articles in Danish media treating the issue of PE mirrors the chronology of the TDC buy-out. This demonstrates the catalytic role of the TDC buy-out and how this case circumscribed the patterns of institutionalization in, and institutional dynamics surrounding, the PE field in Denmark.

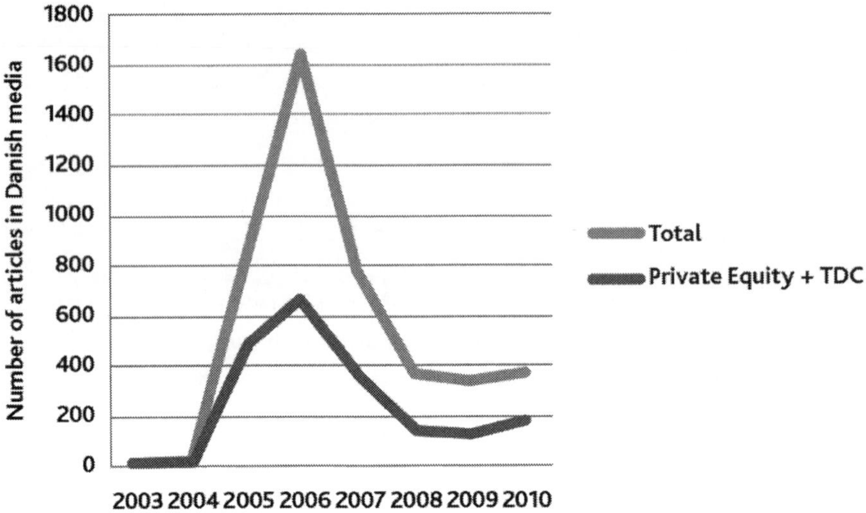

Figure 7.1. Media coverage of private equity over time (source: Infomedia).

The possibility of deducting interest from tax payments had commonly been exploited by Danish PEFs. However, the sheer size of the deduction in the case of TDC generated outrage among the public. As a result of the reduced tax revenues and growing public pressure, the liberal government reduced the deductibility of PE interest payments (Thomsen et al., 2008). Table 7.1 presents the legislative changes enacted in Denmark as a direct consequence of the TDC LBO; the law from 2007 is known as the 'TDC law'.

Table 7.1. Legislative changes targeting private equity (source: Retsinformation).

Year	Effects of legislative changes
2007	Reducing the tax deductibility of interest payments
2008	Broadening the classification of taxable companies
2009	Eliminating the differential treatment of capital gains and income tax for private equity employees

One Swedish PE manager highlighted the significance of the 2007 law:

> Prior to this law you could deduct all the interest, but now there is a limit to interest deductibility, so you can only deduct 21.3 million Danish Kroner of interest. Even though you have 100 million in interest, you can only deduct 21.3 million.

As a direct consequence of the debate surrounding the buy-out of TDC, legislation was enacted designed precisely to corral the activities of PE in Denmark and reduce the ability of PEFs to enjoy competitive advantages not readily available to other firms operating in the same environment. A collision between an alien institutional logic and the normative and cognitive framework undergirding a national institutional complex led to the renegotiation of a 'social license to operate'. This change was important in ameliorating both the public furore over the case and the political conflict between interested actors. Furthermore, legislative innovation succeeded in hitting the target, i.e., big multinational PEFs. Local PEFs, that had been acting in greater accord with local expectations, have been less affected by the changes. Several interviewees cited the TDC case as the singular trigger of the tax changes that generated persistent fears of future legislative intervention. The impression was that the rules of the game may well change again, depending on government and public sentiment towards PEFs. The managing partner of a Danish PEF highlighted this:

> We do not merit the 'higher earner' label here because we are a small fund. But I know people who have left the country, who are living in London now, so in real terms they [i.e., the government] have lost money because of that tax [regulation]. But it looks nice. These guys were actually paying for part of the tax reform, because they deserved it. This was kind of the spirit even in a right-wing government, and therefore you can say that the fear is obviously what might happen now, if they somehow want a scapegoat, for something – you never know.

Table 7.2. Clashing models, normative criteria, translation, and domestication of private equity.

	Universal institutional logic	**Unacceptable PEF strategies**	**Acceptable PEF strategies**	**Translated institutional logic**
Success criteria	Maximizing investor returns	Downsizing and outsourcing aiming exclusively at management enrichment	Contributing to local development and upgrading laggards	Related to rate of return, but firms must be locally responsive
Tax	Tax optimization	Tax evasion	Tax paying	Reduced opportunities to avoid taxes Partners pay income not capital gains tax
Financial structure	Use of high levels of debt in buy-outs	Short termism, increased financial fragility, and windfall profits	Efficient capital structure and incentivized management	Reduced opportunities to deploy high leverage Reduced deductibility of debt
Corporate governance	Solving the principal-agent problem through active ownership	Top-down control and secrecy	Cooperation with other economic actors	Solving the principal-agent problem via active ownership, but with deference to the 'Danish model', i.e., sensitivity to a broad range of stakeholders
Managerial strategy	Focusing on core competences	Asset stripping and harvesting low-hanging fruit	Producing profits through efficiency gains, development, and growth	Less 'aggressive' asset management, greater industrial focus, and growth through focus on core competences
Public relations	Private	Closed	Open communication with stakeholders	Following industry guidelines Explicit communication strategies

Significantly, other actors have since altered their perception of PE. Trade unionists accept that while PE raises a series of difficult challenges, in some cases the changes wrought are both competitively optimal and inevitable, given the conditions of globalization. This constituency, commonly considered the most negatively affected by PE activity, accepts this activity as long as the 'Danish model' is respected and the competitiveness of laggard Danish firms is improved. In 2010, Harald Børsting, Chair of the Danish Trade Union Confederation and one of the most powerful actors in the Danish economy, distinguished between good and bad finance firms in the DVCA annual report:

> Both good and bad financial firms exist today. The good financial firms contribute to economic development and increase employment through the development of firms and workplaces; the bad ones achieve their results through lower tax payments. This sector of the economy has developed, and has started acting in a different way.

Table 7.2 summarizes how the universal PE logic is defined by actors in the sector, how local actors characterize PE according to their normative and cognitive expectations, and the parameters that now define the translated PE logic in Denmark.

This brief examination of the PE buy-out of TDC and the debate that simultaneously arose from, and partially determined, the process highlights how institutional enactment relies on a contest between agents over legitimation. Debates about legitimacy arise at the intersection of the national and universal level and both constrain and enable contingent and path-dependent change. Actors are continually renegotiating the enactment of the regulatory regime, establishing new perceptions of what is and is not considered acceptable and sometimes provoking unintended changes by transgressing institutional boundaries.

Discussion and Conclusion

We have analyzed how PEFs gained legitimacy in Denmark and how this process was mediated by national actors and institutions. We suggest that PE has been progressively legitimized via a particular discourse of universal 'freedom' (Rose, 1990). However, we have also illustrated how contests over legitimacy mobilized actors to shape institutional change. Institutions have been seen as crucial for reducing uncertainty (DiMaggio & Powell, 1983). Coping with institutional expectations through seeking legitimacy has been fundamental to this uncertainty reduction. Yet, firms are subject to multiple institutional environments and logics whose demands do not necessarily coincide. Foreign investors and powerful Danish stakeholders had quite different expectations about how PE should function when taking over a large Danish company. PE management may adopt organizational practices that, while deviant in the host economy, are legitimate in the home country or field in which the PEF is situated, if they are able to play at the intersection of different institutional environments, such as international financial markets and national institutions. This imposes new exogenous transformative forces on national institutions, and PE actors may thus be able to leverage their strengths to reshape the national institutional environment. The present case indicates that neo-institutionalism and business systems approaches both seem to underestimate and underspecify the agency of organizational actors in avoiding conformity and shaping institutions.

In seeking external legitimacy, well-positioned and well-resourced actors may be able to influence the basis on which legitimacy is attained and change patterns of acceptable behaviour. The contest over what is considered acceptable, instead of leading to continuity, generates change in established institutional patterns. Actors have the agency to respond, resist, shape, and negotiate institutional change through institutional enactment. Institutional reproduction is based on the assumption that actors have unexamined assumptions, worldviews, and cognitive patterns that are difficult to change. However, this is not confirmed by our observations and analysis. In the same organizational field, actors may have quite divergent expectations about how PE should function. This chapter demonstrates that agents of change are not uniquely institutional entrepreneurs or rule makers. In the present case, foreign PEFs played a fundamental role in enacting institutions, disregarding the question of national legitimacy when they could gain support and acquiring resources in other business environments. The capability of PEFs to proactively resist and avoid, rather than passively react to, local business system environments should not be underestimated.

We describe and analyze institutional change as a process partially determined by contestation over legitimacy. We argue that any economic system comprises heterogeneous actors who, to improve their positions, are likely to reinterpret institutionalized rules when enacting them. We demonstrate that economic actors are always participating in struggles to maintain, as well as to change or even subvert, institutionalized rules and legitimized practices, creating disputes that in turn generate a slow but incessant dynamic of cumulative change. As a result, although extant institutional environments materially affect transformative contests, institutional reproduction is only temporarily possible. From time to time, disputes over interests and norms among and within social groups may wreak havoc on institutionalized rules and force embedded groups to restructure internally, reordering their positions and interests. Simply stated, institutions reproduce, but via a contingent evolutionary process.

To address the overarching theme of this collection, namely, the relationship between globalization and the Danish political economy, our analysis suggests that increasing interactions between the Danish system and global economic forces are likely to generate conflicts over the terms of those interactions and the standards of legitimacy that govern them. Furthermore, such conflicts will be resolved by compromises between actors and by incremental institutional adjustment co-determined by Danish and global actors, norms, and models. As this collection goes to press, heated debate is unfolding over the acquisition of a large minority stake in the state-owned energy monopoly, DONG, by the somewhat notorious US investment bank, Goldman Sachs. Notably, much of this debate is a function of the experience of the TDC buy-out. Most importantly for the present discussion, iterative episodes of globalization will continue to be governed by concerns over legitimacy, and the precise nature of changes driven by contemporary globalization will be the function of the balance of forces between actors attempting to define the basis on which legitimacy is established. As such, globalization itself is not only characterized by widely recognized historical and material forces, such as the increasing financialization of an expanding world economy, imperatives facing firms to internationalize, or the proliferation and development of information communication technologies, but also by ideas, norms, and contests regarding what is considered appropriate and legitimate.

References

Corbin J. & Strauss A. (1990). *Basics of Qualitative Research.* Thousand Oaks: Sage.

DiMaggio P.J. & Powell W.W. (1983). The Iron Cage Revisited—Institutional Isomorphism and Collective Rationality in Organizational Fields, *American Sociological Review*, 48(2), 147-160.

DVCA (2010; 2011; 2012). Private Equity Funds: A Report from DVCA on Good Governance in Private Equity Funds, DVCA: Copenhagen. (Originals in Danish).

Eisenhardt, K.M. (1989). Building Theories from Case Study Research, *Academy of Management Review*, 14(4), 532-550.

Erturk.I., Froud, J., Johal, S., Leaver, A. & Williams, K. (eds) (2008). *Financialization at Work: Key Texts and Commentary*. London: Routledge.

Froud, J. & William, K. (2007). Private Equity and the Culture of Value Extraction. *New Political Economy* 12(3), 405-420.

Hall, P. & Soskice, D. (eds.) (2001). *Varieties of Capitalism: the Institutional Foundations of Comparative Advantage*, Oxford: Oxford University Press.

Ireland, P. (2010). Limited Liability, Shareholder Rights and the Problem of Corporate Irresponsibility. *Cambridge Journal of Economics* 34(5), 837-856.

Jensen, M.C. & Meckling, W.H. (1976). Theory of the Firm: Managerial Behaviour, Agency Costs and Ownership Structure, *Journal of Financial Economics* 3(4), 305-360.

Jensen M.C. (1989). Eclipse of the Public Corporation, *Harvard Business Review*, September-October.

Kristensen P.H. & Rocha R.S. (2012). New Roles for the Trade Unions: Five Lines of Action for Carving out a New Governance Regime, *Politics & Society*, 40(3), 453– 479.

Landsorganisationen (1999). Report on Private Equity. Trade union confederation, LO: Denmark.

Lincoln, Y.S. & Guba, E.G. (1985). *Naturalistic Inquiry*. Beverly Hills: Sage.

Madsen P.K. (2006). 'How Can It Possibly Fly? The Paradox of a Dynamic Labour Market in a Scandinavian Welfare State', in Campbell J., Hall A. & Petersen O.K. (eds.) *National Identity and the Varieties of Capitalism: The Danish Experience.* Montreal: McGill University Press.

McKinsey (2007). The New Power Brokers: How Oil, Asia, Hedge Funds and Private Equity are Shaping Global Capital Markets, McKinsey Global Institute: McKinsey & Company.

Morgan J. (2009). *Private Equity Finance: Rise and Repercussions*, Palgrave Macmillan: Basingstoke

Rocha R.S. (2009). The Impact of Cross-Border Mergers on the Co-decision Making Process: the Case of a Danish Company, *Economic and Industrial Democracy* 30(4), 1-26.

Whitley R. (1999). *Divergent Capitalisms: the Social Structuring and Change of Business Systems*, Oxford: Oxford University Press.

CHAPTER 8

Managing Strategic Transition in an Age of Accelerating Globalization

Poul Houman Andersen and Hanne Kragh

Understanding the drivers of globalization and how they affect the organization and management of business enterprises is an increasingly salient topic for managers. Several underlying drivers of change spur the dynamics of globalization. Global trade and investment flows have surged in recent years. In 2010 – a year of financial crisis – world merchandise exports were up 14%, growing four times faster than world GDP (WTO, 2012). All economic sectors are directly or indirectly affected by the challenges and opportunities brought on by the increasing distribution of value-chain activities, new factor and product markets, and the steady decline of established and mature economies. The importance of local advantages, such as proximity to customers and supply bases, seems to be decreasing as customers relocate a still wider range of activities (Leamer & Storper, 2001). Moreover, information digitalization continues to afford new possibilities for organizing business activities and appropriating value on a global scale. The ability to deploy and gain from knowledge assets is increasingly recognized. At the same time, transportation costs are decreasing rapidly, reducing the overall importance of physical distance. Finally, the economic growth of the so-called BRIC countries has changed the world's economic centre of gravity with respect to the locus of investment and trade (Quah, 2011). Although this development has been emerging for some time, it is only recently that managers have come to realize that the magnitude and rate of these changes call for a qualitatively different organizational response in the business enterprise (Mathews, 2006a).

For firms to become, or stay, sufficiently agile and flexible in this new world order, new organizational forms are called for. For new ventures, this 'gale of creative destruction' is part and parcel of the contemporary business realities that managers and employees must accommodate, and even thrive in. However, for firms that are already established internationally, the shift in business conditions and underlying dynamics requires that they engage in a fundamental process of strategic reinvention and transition. Decreasing transportation costs, together with global trade liberalization and information digitalization, have changed the conditions for doing business in almost all industries, forcing managers to reconsider how their firms relate to the marketplace. This is a process not only of organizational change through learning but also of shredding existing notions concerning established business practices. On one hand, managers in established firms already have experience of doing business internationally. Established routines, organizational forms, and managerial mindsets are tuned to a specific understanding of international opportunities and how these can be exploited. On the other hand, such competences were often honed to be effective in a world where international operations were organized very differently and not exposed to today's competitive demands and business opportunities. In these cases, yesteryear's core competences may well be today's core rigidities (Leonard-Barton, 1992), adding to the complexity of the transition process.

This chapter investigates the strategic transition faced by established international firms in light of the above changes and challenges. We seek to answer the following question: How do established firms rebalance their existing activities to deal with the emerging global business realities? In particular, we look at changes to organizational forms, managerial mindsets, and firm boundaries. The chapter is explorative and attempts to conceptualize the challenges of the strategic transition by examining the examples of three Danish international firms. Each firm has undergone fundamental strategic changes in attempting to respond to or anticipate substantial changes in their operating environment. Although all these changes have to do with organizational form, managerial mindsets, or firm boundaries, the paths chosen by the three firms differ, as do the outcomes of their endeavours.

The chapter proceeds as follows. First, a brief discussion of strategic transition in internationally experienced firms establishes the relevance of focusing on three fundamental and interrelated elements of organizational restructuring: organizational form, managerial mindsets, and firm boundaries. Next, we outline the nature of the expected changes and conceptualize managerial response as a process of rebalancing the three elements. We then present three case firms, describing and analyzing their transitions. We conclude by discussing managerial implications and opportunities for further research.

Strategic Transition in International Organizations

Especially in established international organizations, strategic transition is neither swift nor trivial, but calls for careful balancing of operational and strategic demands. As pointed out in the literature on organizational transition (Miller & Friesen, 1980; Cule & Robey, 2004), organizational transition: 1) unfolds over time and 2) reflects complex and multiple relationships between environmental, strategic, and organizational variables. Organizational transition has been likened to the process of changing tires on a vehicle in motion (Eisenhardt & Brown, 1998). Such transition is difficult because of the need to maintain existing business while implementing radical changes in an organization. Naturally, this gives rise to widespread frustration over priorities, chains of command, coordination, and resource allocation decisions.

When it comes to describing and understanding the processes of strategic transition as an enterprise evolves and changes its international commitment, the international business literature is largely silent (Kristensen & Zeitlin, 2005; Andersen, 2008). As Kristensen and Zeitlin (2005) note, it is remarkable how little the international business literature emphasizes the difficulties involved in taking steps to change business enterprises' international presence or commitment. Other streams of literature are highly aware of these challenges, which include overcoming organizational inertia and resistance, unlearning, and inculcating new ways of thinking. In an early seminal contribution, Greiner (1998) described organizational transition as a series of evolutions and revolutions, the revolutionary phases being characterized by significant upheaval of existing management practices, organizational structures, and processes. More specifically, the upheaval process is typically described as one of: 1) 'unfreezing' existing routines, processes, and ways of thinking by justifying change processes, making them accepted as relevant and necessary; 2) 'moving' these to a new organizational trajectory; and 3) 'refreezing' these new trajectories, ensuring that the newly grafted organizational practices become part of the organization (Kotter & Cohen, 2002).

Opposed to this view of change as an episodic and intentional event that disrupts an otherwise stable order of things, others see change as continuous and constantly emerging (Weick & Quinn, 1999). From this perspective, organizational change consists of endless modifications in structure and managerial processes, while the role of management is to redirect ongoing change, rather than occasionally initiating change projects limited in time and scope. The processes underlying such change have been described as freezing, rebalancing, and unfreezing (Weick & Quinn, 1999). As we are concerned with the ongoing rebalancing efforts of firms as they try to adapt to changed business conditions while holding on to workable parts of existing business models, our view of change corresponds more closely to this conceptualization of change. Despite some case companies having initiated large, carefully planned change projects to adapt to changes in their environments, we view these as part of longer-term ongoing change processes. Furthermore, we view the ability of managers to continue to make sense of ongoing changes in their surroundings as a key determinant of future competitive advantage, a view in accordance with the 'freeze-rebalance-unfreeze' perspective on change.

In this chapter, we ground our discussion of strategic transition in three areas of change that are critical for international organizations and their continued ability to create value for stakeholders, i.e., organizational forms, managerial mindsets, and organizational boundaries. Following the contingency perspective on organizations, an organization can be described as an open system capable of processing and exchanging inputs and outputs with its surroundings, using the general conceptualization of open systems (Von Bertalanffy, 1972; Ashmos & Huber, 1987). According to general systems theory, a system is 'an assemblage or combination of parts whose relations make them interdependent' (Scott, 1992, p. 77). A system is delineated from its surroundings by a boundary that defines the system's domain. The boundary of an organization is a central design element, important for achieving the best fit with the organization's surroundings (Mintzberg, 1993/1979). System parts, however, vary in their degree of interdependence. Compared with biological systems, such as the human body, social systems such as organizations are 'loose', meaning that the coupling and configuration of the parts constituting the whole are changeable and subject to managerial discretion (Weick, 1976).

We refer to these central elements of contingency theory as organizational forms, managerial mindsets, and firm boundaries. *Organizational forms* are the organizational structures and processes that underpin the ability of the organization to be strategically resilient. *Managerial mindsets* arise from how managers view the roles of the actors, resources, and activities they can access through their current position in an international company and how this can create value. Finally, *firm boundaries* are formed by how international organizations engage in (re)defining boundaries in order to access and marshal actors, resources, and activities beyond their formal boundaries. We see these three aspects of change as interdependent and systemic in the transition process. As such, changes in any one of them will affect the other two areas, so transition within only one area seldom succeeds.

One approach to depicting our understanding of the international organization and the transition challenges it faces is through the Porterian value-chain template. Porter's model provides a widely recognized way of looking at an organizational system and how it processes and organizes exchange with its surroundings (Stabell & Fjeldstad, 1998). According to Porter, firms can generically be understood as aggregations of activities that aim to obtain inputs, developing and processing these into marketable outputs, and supporting these through (indirect) administrative activities. A value-chain 'disaggregates a firm into its strategically relevant activities' (Porter 1985, 33). The value-chain of a firm is embedded in a larger stream of activities called a value system, which plays a role in an industry-wide division of work among organizations. The generic value-chain template and the value system are shown in Figure 8.1.

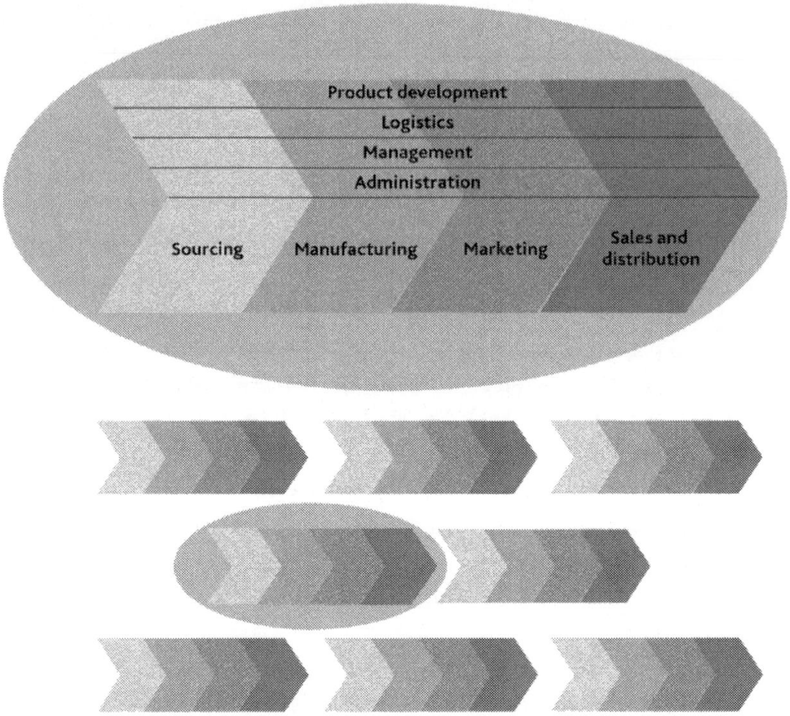

Figure 8.1. The value-chain and value system.

Inherent in the value-chain template is the sense of an assembly line transforming inputs into outputs (Stabell & Fjeldstad, 1998). The corresponding managerial mindset is one of understanding the competitive scope of the firm and the value-creating activities from this position in the wider industrial context (i.e., the value system). The organizational boundaries, which may be redefined and thus alter the competitive scope of the firm, are defined by the contingencies of the surrounding value system and the opportunities to generate better margins by resetting these. The value-chain represents a state of systemic balance for a firm. In many ways, this system represents a self-enforcing reality, as firms help maintain and stabilize the underlying rationale of the business system by performing their roles (Mathews, 2006b).

Managers are also engaged in strategic thought patterns that rely on unexamined assumptions concerning how firms are to be managed, critical success factors within an industry, etc. However, the combined effects of digitalization, globalization, and transportation costs disrupt many of these unexamined assumptions, leading to a process of radical disruption. The disintegration of entire industries, such as the personal computer and bank service industries, exemplifies the upheaval of seemingly stable value systems. For a long period, both these industries seemed – at least to outsiders – to present a stable assemblage of business activities with given roles and positions, defining the competitive scope of a value-chain, setting boundaries, designing organizational forms, and defining what management should be concerned with. Yet, in a study of the disintegration processes in the United States mortgage bank industry, Jacobides (2005) illustrated how established industry practices shifted from services to standardized make-or-buy decisions, making existing business practices and value-chain configurations obsolete. In the banking industry, the corresponding assumptions of managers regarding their managerial role and position, and how these related to the bank's overall raison d'être, tended to linger beyond the apparent breakdown of the existing system (Gerstrøm, 2013).

In a similar vein, information digitalization and the ability to process and reprocess information have challenged contemporary rationales for and ways of configuring both organizations and their marketable outputs in a broad range of industries. Economies of scope gained from bundling activities have disappeared in many instances owing to digitalization. This development is reinforced by globalization, which makes it possible to develop a sufficiently large global market mass to justify the development of specialized services while enabling firms based in mature, developed economies to exploit their beneficial economic conditions without actually being located there. The outsourcing of data management, call centres, and even accounting services to specialized intermediaries in India, Pakistan, and Malaysia exemplify how digitalization serves to disintegrate value-chains. Consequently, organizational scopes and the nature of organizational boundaries are changing. With less permanence in competitive realities, organizational boundaries must change more frequently and the very nature of what constitutes an organizational boundary is changing as well.

One case in point is the company Facebook. What principle should one use to draw boundaries around this organization in a way that effectively captures its value-adding activities? Physical assets and employee payrolls? What about the external providers of dedicated software for social media: are they simply suppliers of inputs or are they buyers of advertising space?

Or what about the users of the Facebook website, who coproduce the site's content by adding personal information, pictures, and votes and by clicking 'like' buttons? The users essentially fuel the activities on the website. Multiple, rather than single, boundaries may be relevant if we are to capture the value-adding activities of such an organization.

With this transition also follow changes in managerial mindsets. In the value-chain logic, managers' scope of activities is linked to optimizing their role and position in the value system. However, with emerging possibilities stemming from the globalization drivers mentioned above (e.g., digitalization, decreasing transportation costs, and trade liberalization), management not only must steer the enterprise but also attend to building and rebuilding processes such as those described above as 'continuous change' processes (Weick & Quinn, 1999). Configuration changes follow the temporary successes and failures of business projects, representing a dynamic process of rapid scaling and rapid withdrawal from unsuccessful activities (Eisenhardt, 1989). These recent developments in the nature of business activities necessitate the use of a template to capture organizational forms, boundaries, and managerial mindsets that differs greatly from that of the value-chain. Such a new template is illustrated in Figure 8.2.

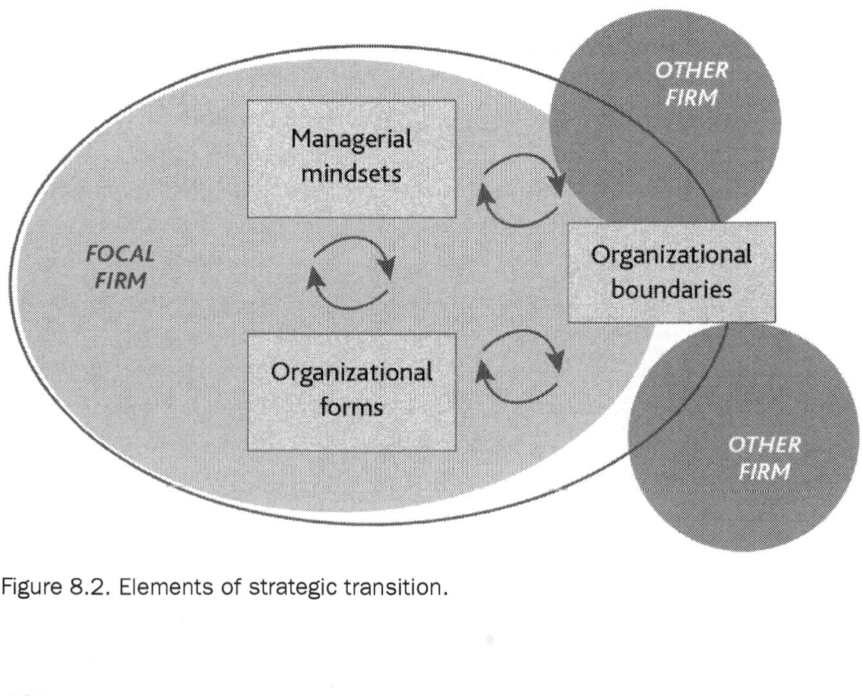

Figure 8.2. Elements of strategic transition.

The figure presents a more complex schema than that captured by the Porterian value-chain/value system template. More options are open for organizational reconfiguration and considerable complexity is added, as several assumptions regarding value drivers and key managerial focus areas are challenged (Stabell & Fjeldstad, 1998). Rather than starting from a given value-chain, Tapscott and Ticoll (2003) suggest that 'in the future, strategists will no longer look at the integrated corporation as the starting point for creating value, assigning functions and deciding what to manage inside and outside a firm's boundaries. Rather, strategists will start with a clean slate for the production and the delivery system'. Although not necessarily all firms in all industries face disruptions as radical as those suggested in the above quotation, the identified globalization drivers have a fundamental impact on the organization and management of value-creating activities and on the roles of organizations in most industries. The following cases illustrate the challenges of recognizing the impacts of this transition and the ensuing rebalancing effort.

Data and Methodology

We examine three Danish MNCs as cases for exploring the challenges of the transition outlined above. We apply a multiple case approach to convey some sense of the diversity of contexts and approaches. The case MNCs were selected based on one common criterion: all are manufacturing firms with international operations and considerable international experience. In addition, they all have been (and at least one still is) rooted in a value-creating logic akin to the value-chain mindset outlined in the previous section. Furthermore, they have all faced or expect to face major strategic disruption of their business context, driven by a combination of the globalization drivers discussed in the introduction to this chapter. Our rationale for conducting a multiple case study is not to look for similarities across the cases and make analytical generalizations, but rather to understand the cases as uniquely situated and as following quite different paths from their origins.

The case studies were not originally intended for presentation in this chapter but were developed for other purposes. The JAMO case was developed in collaboration with JAMO's then CEO in 2004 to serve as a teaching case for framing and discussing the strategic challenges faced by

JAMO at the time. The Modulex case was developed with managers from the firm in 2008 to serve as a teaching case for business students. The Grundfos case is the outgrowth of an ongoing research project. In all cases, issues of strategic transition came to the fore, which is why we think the case stories complement each other and help build a more nuanced representation of the transition challenges faced by established firms. Interviews with top management form the data backbone of all cases. In addition, internal materials, workshop participation, company visits, and other materials, such as newspaper clippings, have provided additional input when writing up the cases.

JAMO

JAMO was a highly internationally oriented producer of standalone loudspeakers. Two entrepreneurs and brothers-in-law established JAMO (JAcobsen & MOrtensen) in 1969. It developed its international market activities in the 1970s and 1980s, particularly in the Asian and Latin American markets. At one time, the company was the largest producer of standalone speakers in Europe and the fourth largest in the world. Several sales subsidiaries were established in the 1980s, when the company began importing components from Asian suppliers. In several countries, JAMO was, and still is, well known as a middle-range producer of well-designed, high-quality loudspeakers – typically framed in beautiful cabinets made of veneered wood or other high-quality materials.

In 2001, Audio Holding acquired JAMO. Its ambitious aim was to support the company with sufficient financial resources to boost its growth. However, market conditions were changing radically at the time. Although turnover had been fluctuating, JAMO had been able to maintain its performance until 2001, the first year in a long time when JAMO did not make a profit. Several interdependent factors contributed to this. First, new generations of customers with a very different approach to hi-fi equipment from that of their predecessors appeared. Customers increasingly regarded audio as an inexpensive and dispensable bulk good and bought integrated audio and electronic entertainment systems rather than standalone products. Retailers wanted fewer brands in their stores and key retail chain customers stopped carrying JAMO products. In several cases, speakers as a separate category ceased to exist in the purchasing planning systems of large retail chain specialists and discount stores. Another important factor was the distribution and sharing of music and video files, which meant that many newcomers were entering the market seeking speakers for computers.

Although these changes had long been underway, the market for standalone loudspeakers collapsed quite suddenly. Over a period of nine months, JAMO experienced flattening sales curves and started to lose money at an alarming rate. There was a general consensus that JAMO was facing a major disruption in its current business model. The market was simply no longer behaving according to the beliefs of JAMO managers: existing market knowledge was doubted and often regarded as obsolete. Simply reducing the current activity level and weathering the storm was an inadequate response; instead, there was a need for radical rethinking of current business practices. A general thrust of JAMO's turnaround strategy was to reduce complexity: rethink all elements of the current competence profile and organizational set-up, slough off those existing business practices that had grown obsolete, and reinvent the market presence of JAMO to meet changing market needs.

JAMO focused on renewing its market offerings. The ability to develop, produce, and market loudspeakers might still have a chance when combined with complementary products offered under the JAMO brand. Customers increasingly demanded integrated systems instead of standalone speakers, reducing the competitive space available for specialized producers of speakers as compared with producers such as Sony and Pioneer that offered entire home entertainment systems. Some of JAMO's most important competitors had already learned this lesson; for example, loudspeaker producers such as Bose had launched products combining speakers and DVD/CD players. Building partnerships with suppliers and OEM manufacturers and launching system solutions, such as home cinema systems, was believed to be the steppingstone to regain access to the large electronic chains.

JAMO developed a design and started searching for potential partners. First, it bought a bid option for flat-screen (plasma) displays from one of the largest producers in the world at that time. This was important, as flat screens had been a bottleneck technology since the early 2000s and everyone felt that the market was about to take off. Second, JAMO needed a partner to supply hardware, so it teamed up with Kiss Technology, a small but rapidly growing Danish firm. Kiss promised to offer JAMO leading-edge technology, including one of the world's first DVD players that could accommodate the Div-X format much used on P2P networks for exchanging video clips. JAMO had manufacturing ramp-up experience and was therefore not concerned that KISS lacked such experience.

Installing this new business plan necessitated radical organizational change. To cut costs, JAMO had to reduce its workforce considerably, cutting back in Denmark while increasing procurement activities in China. A few years earlier, JAMO had already established a working partnership with a reliable Chinese supplier and now it expanded this partnership. To strengthen its influence on production activities and ensure high quality, JAMO had already established a local sourcing unit in China at the premises of its main Chinese supplier, staffed with Danish engineers, responsible for local quality assurance and monitoring. More responsibility was handed over to this unit in the new manufacturing strategy.

The redirection of JAMO called for a prolonged process of freezing and rebalancing the organizational structure in order to accommodate new strategic realities. The process involved developing new operational targets and a much more open-ended, process-oriented approach, in which teamwork and continuous development in a flattened organizational structure replaced fixed responsibilities in a stable organization. The most challenging part was to abandon the thought of JAMO as a manufacturing company, since this had formerly been considered a core activity central to the JAMO identity. From being an independent company with a functional structure, JAMO had to assume a new role as leader of a coalition of partners, taking the initiative and coordinating a network of relationships. This called for the development of entirely new relationship management competences within the firm. Existing job descriptions were discarded and new job responsibilities reflecting the importance of maintaining effective exchange relationships with partners were created.

The turnaround turned out to be even more difficult than anticipated and the problems mounted. Internally, top managers left and were replaced in a relentless stream. Externally, the lack of manufacturing experience in KISS meant that it encountered problems delegating production tasks to external suppliers; JAMO had to step in and support this process. Likewise, problems emerged that JAMO managers had not thought of, as they were entering unknown territory. A central issue was that, by using the KISS technology and its ability to play a broad range of video formats,

JAMO was infringing on copyright laws. In 2005, the firm collapsed and Audio Holding decided to sell the remains of the company – the brand name in particular – to one of JAMO's former competitors.

Modulex

Modulex was established by Kirkbi, which also owns the LEGO Group, as an 'architectural developer of sign solutions'. Its customers were firms and organizations of all sizes with a need to provide directions to visitors and for brand communication/profiling. Its products were often sold through architects, design companies, and other services dealing with corporate brand communication and the interior design of new buildings. In the 1980s, Modulex became a world leader with a global range of customers. In the early 2000s, the company had 500 employees, sales subsidiaries in 15 markets, intermediaries in an additional 30 markets, and managed a franchise chain in the United States. Financial resources from the LEGO owners were abundant and management attention was set on long-term growth. Modulex followed the internationalization strategy of its parent company and developed an administrative structure worthy of a much larger company. In the early 2000s, Modulex started losing money but did not recognize this as indicating a serious problem. Gradually, however, management realized that more fundamental and structural change was occurring in the market, including a shift towards more individualized rather than global sign solutions. Local competition was becoming increasingly sophisticated and the competitive advantage of being a global firm with representation in the main world markets was shrinking rapidly.

The watershed change came as the LEGO Group faced financial trouble due to the poor performance of its parent company. Kirkbi wanted to eliminate activities that diverted attention from its core business and decided to sell Modulex, but soon realized that it was unsalable. In 2007, a consultancy report commissioned by Kirkbi concluded that Modulex needed to launch a new business model to regain its momentum while cutting costs. Modulex was saddled with a top-heavy sales organization and in addition, the franchise chain in the US generated a negative income due to high administrative costs.

In 2007, Modulex received a capital infusion of approximately EUR 18 million from Kirkbi with a clear mandate to trim the organization. Management immediately started to prune the organization's unprofitable products and liquidate most of the sales subsidiaries, some of which established themselves as Modulex dealers. Hence, although Modulex lost footholds in some of its key markets, it maintained a presence in most markets. Likewise, the United States franchise chain was sold off to a private investor who continued selling Modulex products. This change in the sales organization was almost completed in 2008. At the beginning of 2009, Modulex was sold to a business investor and developer, who bought Modulex with the present CEO as a minority owner. In strategic as well as management terms, the new ownership meant a fundamental change in governance. As an owner, Kirkbi had intervened little in Modulex operations. The new owners, in contrast, had clear ideas and a hands-on management approach. They continued the rationalization process outlined in the consultancy report, but at a faster pace and cutting deeper, in order not only to trim the organization but to convert it into a more market-oriented company.

As of 2014, Modulex employed fewer than 100 people compared with 500 in 2006, most senior managers had left the company, and the firm had outsourced various activities. The manufacturing of 80% and 90%, respectively, of all moulded parts and steel is being left to suppliers while Modulex builds its internal sourcing competences. The development of the Adriane software, a company platform for digital signs, has been taken over by Add-on, a Danish software developer. Flat-screens are delivered by the German company Altec, based on a Modulex design. Modulex assembles the screen solutions internally and is responsible for the controller managing the graphic display. The controller function has been developed jointly with Prevas, a Copenhagen-based producer of intelligent industrial control systems. So far, Prevas has developed a series of software tests that are run by Altec. Rationalization has also helped Modulex define which of its technologies are considered strategic and therefore kept in house until further notice. These include competences in aluminium, sign pretreatment and painting, text technologies, and knowledge of plastic injection moulding.

In 2007, about 80% of sales were generated by an internal sales force of 30 people in the sales subsidiaries and 120 in HQ. Clearly, the managerial focus was on Modulex's own sales organization, the dealer network not receiving the same level of attention. This way of servicing the market has changed radically. Today, Modulex has no sales subsidiaries; its focus is instead on the dealer network, which is being serviced by four new area sales managers responsible for sales in the USA, the UK, Central Europe, and Scandinavia. Modulex has developed a new set of competences for organizing and motivating a sales network instead of managing an internal sales organization. As part of this new, more network-based sales structure, Modulex must fight harder to maintain dealer focus by launching concepts and products faster and more in tune with changing market needs. One way to do this has been to involve the dealer network in new product development. Previously, Modulex had a strong 'inside-out' approach to new product development: R&D was a planned process, and products were only launched when they had been tested and new production schemes thoroughly implemented in the organization. In its new organizational form, Modulex has introduced a Product Management and Innovation Department as part of its marketing organization. This department is responsible for integrating dealers and innovation activities by co-launching new product ideas with dealers on an ongoing basis and by involving dealers in the creative process of developing new sign solutions. For example, Modulex hosts a dealer conference at which dealers are introduced to a range of new ideas not yet ready for full-scale production but that Modulex can deliver in small batches. The underlying idea is to induce dealers to introduce the new prototypes to customers and, based on customer reactions to these 'limited editions', to select new products. The aim is to reduce time-to-market from 24 to six months. This means that the production organization, which shares responsibility for new product implementation, must be able to react faster and increasingly develop and adapt to market conditions.

Strategically, Modulex has become a much more agile company. Break-even is at a turnover of DKK 120 million compared with DKK 340 million a few years ago. To support its reorientation, Modulex has undergone a major reorganization. Development activities are now the responsibility of the sales and marketing director, whereas all other activities (e.g., HR, finance, and production) are the responsibility of the CEO, who is one of the two owners. Compared with Modulex's previous organization, this is a major change of task structure and division of responsibilities. An important part of the change has been the substitution of sales and marketing employees for employees in upstream activities such as production, design, and technical functions. As in all organizational change, this has led to internal debate and conflict. Nevertheless, the company has succeeded in retaining several key characteristics, albeit in renewed versions. With the current activity level, the company is financially stable and able to react quickly to new market opportunities. Modulex is also increasingly adapted to the global competitive environment in terms of, for example, being able to more easily differentiate prices and individualize services. This has also allowed the company to dynamically integrate the internal and external competences of, for example, suppliers, customers, and partners.

Grundfos

Grundfos A/S is a multinational corporation headquartered in Bjerringbro, Denmark. The Poul Due Jensen Foundation owns most of the shares, followed by the Due Jensen family and Grundfos employees. The company specializes in designing and manufacturing pumps, controlling half of the world market for circulation pumps. It employs 18,000 people and is established in 45 countries in all regions of the world.

Grundfos has succeeded in its efforts to grow and continue to be an important player in the global pump industry. 'Be-Think-Innovate' is the slogan that Grundfos employs to articulate the company's values. Being willing to change, assume responsibility, and be innovative is crucial for meeting the challenges of the future. However, with increasing global competitive pressure, Grundfos also faces a competitive situation in which it will be increasingly squeezed in the pump market as new, lower-price pump suppliers gain footholds. For this reason, Grundfos has made a proactive move: It has reviewed its long-term business prospects by trying to look 15-20 years ahead, involving more than 900 Grundfos employees in developing a new vision. This led to the formulation of the Grundfos Innovation Intent in 2010,[3] which Grundfos internally describes as 'a guiding star that will bring focus to our long-term innovation efforts and make sure the company is heading in the right direction'. According

3. Carsten Bjerg, the architect of this goal-setting process, left Grundfos in December 2013. His replacement, Mads Nipper, was announced in March 2014.

to the Innovation Intent programme, every major concept Grundfos launches over the next 20-30 years must meet three criteria: first, it must deliver superior sustainable solutions and offerings; second, it must be based on technology that the world has not yet seen; finally, it must be aligned with Grundfos' core values, i.e., being responsible, thinking ahead, and innovating. The Innovation Intent is a bold clear statement of where and how Grundfos wants to develop its business. It also articulates the ambition that Grundfos will employ 75,000 people globally by 2025, and generate 50% of its growth from technology platforms that did not exist in 2007. In addition, one third of Grundfos' turnover is expected to come from products other than pumps. Grundfos aims to achieve this while maintaining its market leadership in circulators and being a specialist in sustainable solutions for housing. Furthermore, Grundfos has changed its market position and become a specialist in selling directly to end users in selected industrial segments and utilities. The company organizes activities around local centres of excellence, tapping into knowledge bases wherever they are. Moreover, Grundfos has become expert at translating user needs into new products and business concepts and at attracting world-class leadership talent in its field.

This is a tall order, but Grundfos is working determinedly towards these aims, mobilizing its entire organization to pursue them. Grundfos is well-known for its ability to manage by instilling corporate values in the minds of its employees and leading though them. There are several critical challenges in this process of growth and transition. A particularly important one concerns balancing a dual focus on developing a completely new line of non-pump-related business activities expected to account for one third of the company's entire future turnover, in effect exceeding Grundfos' current size, while maintaining a keen focus on remaining the world's number one supplier in its current core business.

An example that illustrates both the potential and competences of Grundfos is the development of Grundfos LIFELINK (GLL), an offshoot of the Innovation Intent strategy. GLL is a turnkey water solution that encompasses a solar-driven pump facility, a GPS-based monitoring system, and a payment system based on digital payments for water credits, which together represent the GLL business model. Since its cautious start in 2009, GLL has successfully expanded its operations. Today, 40 sites are working in Kenya and more are being established. Moreover, GLL has established a unit in Thailand and expects to enter several East African markets in the near future. GLL has demonstrated that it is possible to develop a market-based system that provides access to water for rural societies in so-called bottom-of-the-pyramid markets. This innovative system has gained Grundfos international recognition and contributed substantially to solving one of the biggest challenges facing rural communities in developing economies. In line with the Innovation Intent, pumps are not the centrepiece of the GLL offering. The core capability of GLL is to establish and manage an active network of local community partnerships in which each partner adds significant value to the product offered to the customer. Value is channelled back, allowing the technical system to be maintained and remain in operation. Grundfos is setting up a local service organization to take care of these services.

The new business model has also brought Grundfos into a novel business context. Meeting these novel market requirements has called for a stronger presence in the local market and a stronger global presence as well. This has led to the establishment of an organizational unit in Kenya acting as a sales subsidiary and the main organizer of the water facility's operation and payment system. In addition, Grundfos has developed an organizational unit to market the system to global seed-capital providers. The Grundfos LIFELINK development process foreshadows the challenges Grundfos will face in the future in pursuing its Innovation Intent. It is not effective for GLL to establish a parallel sales and service organization in every market it enters in the future. Instead, GLL should be able to benefit from Grundfos' existing infrastructure. Yet, because the GLL business model differs greatly from that of the company's main activities, GLL may be disruptive and therefore probably not be welcomed by a Grundfos country manager as an addition to his existing portfolio of activities. A manager explains:

> If anyone thinks that the same people who successfully sell our pumps will be equally successful in selling LIFELINK, I think they are mistaken. This business model differs from our conventional model in too many parameters. You create value in another way and work with different partners. There is no way you can ask a salesperson to devote 10% of his time to this type of business while using his remaining time on other business areas.

The model will probably entail using Grundfos' existing infrastructure as an incubator, sharing back-office functions with the main organization. Later, when some scale-up has been achieved, a functioning organization will be handed over to the country manager. As Grundfos develops more of these ideas, its sales subsidiary managers must develop competences for supporting business incubation activities.

Case Analysis

The three presented cases have several similarities, representing industrial contexts in which business practices have been disrupted or in which such disruptions are anticipated. In addition, realized or anticipated intensified globalization is causing these changes, compounding their complexity and unpredictability. For these reasons, the examples are suitable for illustrating the issues involved in the simultaneous transition of mindsets, organizational forms, and activity boundaries outlined at the beginning of the chapter. The cases also differ from each other in a number of key respects. One difference concerns the degree of anticipation of and preparedness for change. In our cases, the managerial stances range from frantic and reactive, as in the case of JAMO, to experimental and proactive, as in the Grundfos case. Another difference is the impact of digitalization – generally a major source of disruption – which affected business conditions and strategic responses quite differently in the three cases, ranging from a major shift in how music is purchased, stored, and consumed, as in the JAMO case, to providing the backbone for a new payment model, as in the case of Grundfos.

Table 8.1 summarizes the characteristics of each case and the key findings in relation to the transition of mindsets, organizational form, and activity boundaries experienced by the case companies. Next, the three types of transitions will be discussed across the case examples.

Table 8.1. Summary of key findings.

	JAMO	Modulex	Grundfos
Drivers of global market change	Digitalization of information (i.e., music formats) and market integration	Reduced transportation costs and virtualization of organizational communication	Market integration due to reduced transportation costs and increased information flow
Triggering event	Market disruption	Market change	Strategic foresight
Transition timing	Reactive	Reactive	Proactive
Mindset transition	Value creation logic: from production to brand management merchant	Value creation logic: from manufacturer to network architect	Value creation logic: from component to solution manufacturer
Transition of organizational form	From a functional to a market-oriented organization	From a mini multinational to a platform firm	From a more to a less integrated MNC
Boundary transition	From an internalized firm to a weak orchestrator	From an internalized firm to a strong orchestrator	From an internalized firm to a co-creator

Transition of Managerial Mindsets

An important part of an organizational transition is the mindset of the managers leading the change. Mindset refers to the cognitive filters that managers and employees use to select, absorb, and interpret the abundance of information that surrounds them (Gupta & Govindarajan, 2002). As such, our mindsets inform how we make sense of the world. From the perspective of established, international firms, managerial mindsets determine how managers interpret the roles of the actors, resources, and activities they can access through their current market positions and how they believe these can create value for their company. Their mindsets also determine the actors and resources managers are aware of in the first place. It is evident from all three cases that experience in the form of pre-existing organizational practices and priorities acts as a cognitive filter influencing managers' attempts to make sense of rapidly changing business contexts and concepts. Changing managerial mindsets is a slow process (Gupta & Govindarajan, 1991). Usually, organizational incentive schemes are designed to preserve existing practice, rather than endorsing behaviour that involves questioning the underlying rationale linking activities and capabilities with value creation (Weick, 1991). Transition from one mindset to another is a difficult and stressful process that is bound to meet internal resistance, as it questions the core identity and challenges the existing raison d'être of the managers (Argyris & Schön, 1978).

Arora et al. (2004) see a managerial mindset as comprising two elements: contextualization and conceptualization. Conceptualization refers to 'a person's way of thinking and his ability to comprehend oneself as a part of the global environment' (Arora et al., 2004, p. 399), whereas contextualization is 'a person's ability to act in a context and adapt his or her ideas to the local environment' (p. 400). Changing managers' mindsets to embrace the new realities (i.e., context) and value-creating role of the firm (i.e., conceptualization) in the global marketplace takes a primary role in the presented cases. In the case of Modulex, there was a tendency for managers to be unable to see the evolving change in business conditions, because their attention was on the functional performance targets set within a functional mindset. In a well-known case study of Facit – a Swedish producer of mechanical calculators – Starbuck (1983) demonstrated that managers strove to maintain their existing perspectives on the organization and, by keeping their focus on operational targets, were able to overlook more fundamental changes and challenges to their assumed business reality.

In the JAMO case, managers were unable to comprehend that the business context had been radically disrupted, and that customers were no longer found in the places where managerial attention was directed. Instead of searching for alternative ways to understand the conditions under which contemporary customers listened to music, managerial attention was largely directed towards the sales figures of the existing retail structure, overlooking that an important group of these retailers had in fact discontinued loudspeakers as a separate category in their shops. JAMO understood value creation as a matter of producing attractive speakers, so managerial attention was focused on this activity – even in the sales and marketing departments. Even in Grundfos, which is in fact proactively challenging current conceptualizations and contextualizations and trying to identify the current forces of transformation, it is still difficult to predict or imagine how the business context will be shaped by transformative forces and, consequently, how the alignment of existing and novel activities is to be managed.

Transition of Organizational Form

The mechanisms that preserve an organization's memory are not only found in the minds of managers; organizational forms also help preserve activities and worldviews. Organizational departmentalization (i.e., the internal division of tasks among departments), the degree of formalization, coordination routines and the like, all help stabilize a specific organizational identity for an organization's members and help determine their tasks in preserving this identity. By performing a specific task set, each manager contributes to stabilizing the organizational forms for other managers, helping to solidify the organizational system as a set of roles and responsibilities (Katz & Kahn, 1978; Weick, 1991). These role sets and how they are combined into a system for processing inputs into marketable outputs also reflect the organization's task boundaries with its surrounding business environment, i.e., what activities the organization performs and how activities are partitioned among organizations in a larger business system context (Porter, 1985). International firms face particular challenges in this, as they find themselves in multiple business realities and need to strike a balance between adapting to their idiosyncrasies and concurrently mustering economies of scale and scope through integration. The underlying principles of the current organizational form are challenged in step with the forces of globalization and the ensuing increased competitive pressure and complexity of the decreasingly 'local' and increasingly interdependent operating environments. When competitiveness is increasingly driven by the ability to innovate, international organizations with a conventional organizational design lose out to those with designs that allow them to collect, combine, and deploy ideas across the multiple business environments in which they operate. As pointed out by Birkinshaw and Hood (2001, p. 137), 'in an era in which new business ideas are as likely to come from Stockholm as from Silicon Valley, multinational companies cannot afford to limit their creative gene pools to corporate R&D labs or a few select outposts. They must find ways to tap into the diverse and multifaceted opportunities that exist in foreign operations'.

Once managers start to rethink how an organization can realign its role and thus change its position in a range of business environments, this has consequences for how task boundaries are drawn and how the internal organization can best accommodate effective change in line with taking on new roles in order to reposition itself. Beginning with the case of Grundfos, establishing a new business division, with the ensuing responsibilities, and freeing up resources from the existing organization is one way to achieve transition. The management of transition in an incoherent business context is sometimes referred to as ambidexterity, i.e., a way of maintaining the operational core of the firm while exploring new possibilities for strategic innovation. Such ambidexterity must be handled without having these possibly competing interests interfere too much with each other (Gibson & Birkinshaw, 2004). In the Grundfos LIFELINK case, the challenges of applying this principle in redesigning the organization are evident. There is an implicit incentive for the division responsible for innovative activities to deploy radical measures to differentiate themselves from the existing business model but without conflicting with its activities and priorities. However, new business ideas developed from this process, which display durability and offer true value to the firm, may be difficult to graft onto the existing organization as the two business models start struggling for resources. In the cases of both Modulex and JAMO, aligning the need for new organizational forms with the existing business did not cause serious problems, as their original businesses were already declining and internal resources were redundant. However, in both organizations, radical changes in form were made in order to orient the firms away from viewing manufacturing as the core activity and to emphasize market orientation and the ability to manage new interfaces with external partners. In the case of JAMO, refocusing on partners and re-establishing relationships with distribution channels, while radically shrinking existing production activities, led to several successive changes in the organization over a very short period. In the case of Modulex, the new owners turned the organizational form upside down: from being focused on the ability to manage and control production quality, the emphasis shifted to the ability to scale up new ideas rapidly and to aligning with market intermediaries.

Transition of Boundaries

A third fundamental driver of the transition process faced by established multinationals is the increased reliance of international organizations on relationships with external business actors such as suppliers, customers, and alliance partners (Gulati & Kletter, 2005). It seems as though companies in an increasing number of industries in Denmark are realizing that to cope with the demands for strategic resilience in the face of unpredictability, there is a need to continually and dynamically involve external resources and capabilities. This observation is supported by a survey of sources of novel ideas among innovative Danish manufacturers. Here, the number of firms collaborating with external knowledge sources (e.g., suppliers, customers, universities, and partners) increased from roughly one out of four in 2007 to roughly two out of five in 2010 (Danmarks Statistik, 2012). The emerging understanding of collaboration as the key to sustained competitive advantage has implications for our understanding of how MNCs enact boundaries. Managers are increasingly recognizing that they cannot sustain their growth targets based solely on internally developed innovations and knowledge, but instead must also look outside their boundaries for knowledge and resources. This shift has drawn attention to the increased importance of relational capital, i.e., the value of a company's network of relationships with customers, suppliers, and other alliance partners, as well as with and between internal units such as subsidiaries (Gulati & Kletter, 2005).

This development, described by Gulati and Kletter (2005) as a shift from managing physical and intellectual assets to managing relational assets, has serious implications for the structure and management of MNCs and for the competences needed by their managers. Procter & Gamble provides an example: through increased leverage of external R&D resources, it was able to improve its innovation success rate and reduce the cost and time-to-market of innovations (Huston & Sakkab, 2006). Shifts towards increased reliance on relational assets, and the changing nature of these assets, are evident in the case examples as well. In the case of Grundfos, the increased involvement in new business areas called for mobilizing and enrolling external resources in a range of areas and using various skills in order to develop a market proposal. Similar examples are found in the case of Modulex, which drastically reduced its sales subsidiary structure and replaced it with a network of international intermediaries. It also reduced its development activities in exchange for a focused partnership with providers of hardware and software for digital signage systems. In the case of JAMO, the development of a home cinema solution for the market also required the expansion of its partner network – by providing new external assets closer to JAMO and, not least, by supplementing internal knowledge with external capabilities necessary for developing a marketable product.

Rather than coordinating a vast range of value-chain activities internally, the main task of the network organization is to bring together the right set of business actors – for example, suppliers, manufacturers, and logistics providers – to meet the exact needs of the customer. The resulting network then comprises the capabilities of several firms assembled for a specific purpose. An organization may participate in several networks, possibly serving as the key organizer of some or playing less prominent roles in others (Shuman & Twombly, 2010). When network organizations focus on providing solutions for particular customers, they must include customers, suppliers, and other partners in developing these solutions. The ability to form and develop appropriate relationships is therefore becoming increasingly important (Birkinshaw, Bessant et al., 2007). The shift in the importance of intellectual assets challenges traditional notions of organizational boundaries as well. Whereas boundaries have traditionally implicitly been defined in terms of control – through ownership of physical assets or contractual control of employees – other forms of boundaries, such as boundaries of competence or even identity, now take primacy (Santos & Eisenhardt, 2005). For the organization, this means more subtle ways of managing activities.

According to Snow, Miles, and Coleman (1992), the fundamental role of management in network organizations has changed from the planning, organizing, and controlling of internal resources associated with the traditional hierarchy to creating and assembling resources located outside the MNC. In other words, the MNC assumes a brokering role, which the authors divide into three different types of brokers, i.e., architect, lead operator, and caretaker. In a similar vein, Shuman and Twombly (2010) refer to the leadership role in a network as that of a choreographer. A network choreographer is the individual or firm responsible for designing the collaborative network. The legitimate means for co-mediating or co-choreographing an activity network depends on the boundary-setting context. In the case of JAMO, legitimate co-mediation means were clearly limited: JAMO had little influence over its partners and held – besides its control of a brand – very little influence. Rather than collaborating with suppliers of flat-screen displays to share the risk and gain access to knowledge, JAMO internalized the risk and bought an extremely risky option for a standard display. Likewise, rather than partnering with an existing player – an arrangement in which it believed it would have no influence – it teamed up with a newcomer with no manufacturing experience. In the case of Modulex, the new partnership role of its intermediaries also means that Modulex, rather than rolling out a signage programme for distribution, finds itself in a community of partners sharing identity and cognition. The legitimate means for orchestration in this case is dialogue and co-creative activities rather than command and control.

Concluding Discussion

With this chapter, we hope to have addressed what we believe is an important issue: the strategic transition of firms that need to leave behind established mindsets in order to grasp emerging possibilities. Our intent was to approach these challenges in a holistic rather than piecemeal fashion; in doing so, we deployed a framework inspired by contingency theory. We think that our focus on strategic transition as rebalancing could help managers better understand the challenges they face. In addition, we hope that our framework can address the limitations of existing analytical models and advance the discussion of how such frameworks can help managers address strategic issues and transition challenges.

With the advent of less stable competitive conditions, managers must accept that they – for the coming decades at least – will find themselves in a space where few assumptions concerning the nature of market value and how to effectively organize the firm in order to reap it will remain stable. For this matter, rather than searching for an optimal fit with a stable set of market conditions, firms must develop their abilities to stitch together workable ways of organizing, which may look more like organizations of loosely patched teams and units than finely tuned organizational charts. The existing notion of organizational change as a process of 'unfreezing', 'moving', and 'refreezing' the organization so as to stabilize and hone organizational performance may have to give way to a concept of the organization as constantly balancing existing activities with new ones, constantly both dismantling old processes and inventing new ones, and constantly questioning existing beliefs while still acting on them as if they were true. According to Tsoukas and Chia (2002, p. 567), change is 'the reweaving of actors' webs of beliefs and habits of action to accommodate new experiences obtained through interactions ... change is inherent in human action, and organizations are sites of continuously evolving human action'. The underlying assumption is that reality is in a steady state of flow, rather than one in which constants should be sought. Rather than seeking the manifestation of such flows, in the form of products or even competences around which to build strategies, managers must embrace the processes that have led to the creation of such manifestations in the first place.

In research, the transition towards understanding change as a continuous process is already well underway in some parts of the literature. However, this development has not really established itself in International Business research, in which theoretical perspectives that assume organizational stability dominate. Institutional theory and transaction cost analysis are dominant modes of theoretical inquiry and both have organizational permanence as their default assumption. From this perspective follows rather specific notions regarding organizational design, management, etc. Yet, when these epistemic assumptions are loosened, we encounter issues in the International Business area that merit further scrutiny. This paper attempts to expose some of these issues, though much more research is clearly required. For example, if the notion of organizations as semi-permanent stabilizers is taken seriously, an interesting question arises with respect to the notion of the competences of managerial teams in international ventures. In addition, issues such as the ability to interconnect activities and resources across business actors and sociocultural contexts in order to assemble value proposals come to the fore. Finally, how such activities are stitched together and the practices through which performance is at all possible in a complex pattern of actors and activities emerge as interesting research questions, rather than matters simply seen as derived from a given role and position in an organizational complex. We hope to address some of these questions in the future and certainly invite others to join us in this effort.

References

Andersen, P.H. (2008). Knowledge versus learning in internationalization of offshoring activities in China: A case study. *Journal of Engineering and Technology Management 25*(3), 184-199.

Argyris, C. & Schön, D.A. (1978). *Organizational learning: a theory of action perspective.* London, Addison-Wesley.

Arora, A., Jaju, A., Kefalas, A.G. & Perenich, T. (2004). An exploratory analysis of global managerial mindsets: a case of US textile and apparel industry. *Journal of International Management, 10*(3), 393-411.

Ashmos, D.P. & Hubert, G.P. (1987). The systems paradigm in organization theory: Correcting the record and suggesting the future. *Academy of Management Review*, 607-621.

Birkinshaw, J. (2006). *Finding, forming, and performing: creating networks for discontinuous innovation* (Doctoral dissertation, Institute of Management Research Tanaka Business School, Imperial College London).

Birkinshaw, J. & Hood, N. (2001). Unleash Innovation in Foreign Subsidiaries. *Harvard Business Review* (March), 131-137.

Cule, P.E. & Robey, D. (2004). A Dual-Motor, Constructive Process Model of Organizational Transition, *Organization studies 25*(2), 229-260.

Danmarks Statistik (2012): *Innovation og forskning* (Innovation and research) available at www.dst.dk.

Eisenhardt, K.M. (1989). Making Fast Strategic Decisions in High-Velocity Environments. *Academy of Management Journal 32*(3), 543-576.

Eisenhardt, K.M. & Brown, S.L. (1998). Time pacing: Competing in markets that won't stand still. *Harvard Business Review 76*(2), 59-69.

Gerstrøm, A. (2013): *World Disruption*, PhD Thesis, Aarhus University.

Gibson, C. & Birkinshaw, J. (2004). The antecedents, consequences, and mediating role of organizational ambidexterity. *Academy of Management Journal 47*, 209-226.

Greiner, L.E. (1998). Evolution and revolution as organizations grow. (original 1972). *Harvard Business Review 76*(3), 55.

Gulati, R. & Kletter, D (2005). Shrinking Core, expanding periphery: The relational architecture of High-Performing organizations. *California Management Review 47*(3), 77-104.

Gupta, A.K. & Govindarajan, V. (1991). Knowledge flows and the structure of control within multinational corporations. *Academy of Management Review*, 768-792.

Gupta, A.K. & Govindarajan, V. (2002). Cultivating a global mindset. *Academy of Management Executive 16*(1), 116-126.

Huston, L. & Sakkab, N. (2006). Connect and develop, *Harvard Business Review 84*(3), 58-66.

Jacobides, M.G. (2005). Industry change through vertical disintegration: How and why markets emerged in mortgage banking. *Academy of Management Journal 48*(3), 465-498.

Katz, D. & Kahn, R. (1978). *The Social Psychology of Organizations, 2nd ed.* New York, Wiley & Sons.

Kotter, J.P. & Cohen, D.S. (2002). *The heart of change: Real-life stories of how people change their organizations*, Harvard Business Press.

Kristensen, P.H. & Zeitlin, J. (2005). *Local players in global games: The strategic constitution of a multinational corporation*, Oxford University Press, USA.

Leamer, E., E. & Storper, M. (2001). The Economic Geography of the Internet Age. *Journal of International Business Studies 32*(4), 641-665.

Leonard-Barton, D. (1992). Core Capabilities and Core Rigidities – A Paradox in Managing New Product Development. *Strategic Management Journal 13*(8), 111-125.

Mathews, J.A. (2006a). Dragon multinationals: New players in 21st century globalization. *Asia Pacific Journal of Management 23*(1), 5-27.

Mathews, J.A. (2006b). *Strategizing, Disequilibrium and Profit*, Stanford Business Books, Stanford University, USA.

Miller, D. & Friesen, P. (1980). Archetypes of Organizational Transition. *Administrative Science Quarterly 25*, 268-299.

Porter, M.E. (1985). *Competitive advantage: creating and sustaining superior performance.* New York, Free Press.

Quah, D. (2011). The Global Economy's Shifting Centre of Gravity. *Global Policy 2*, 3-9.

Santos, F.M. & Eisenhardt, K. (2005). Organizational Boundaries and Theories of Organization. *Organization Science 16*(5), 491-508.

Schumpeter, J.A. (1934). *The Theory of Economic Development.* Cambridge, MA, Harvard University Press.

Scott, R.W. (1992). *Organizations – rational, natural and open systems, 3rd ed.* Englewood Cliffs, NJ, Prentice-Hall International.

Shuman, J. & Twombly, J. (2010). Collaborative networks are the organization: An innovation in organization design and management. *Vikalpa 35*(1), 1-13.

Snow, C., Miles, R. & Coleman Jr, H.J. (2000). Managing 21st century network organizations In: Ian McLoughlin, David Preece, Patrick Dawson *Technology, Organizations and Innovation: Towards 'Real Virtuality'*, 1621-1638.

Stabell, C. & Fjeldstad, Ø. (1998). Configuring value for competitive advantage: on chains, shops, and networks. *Strategic Management Journal*, 413-437.

Tapscott, D. & Ticoll; D. (2003). *The Naked Corporation: How the age of Transparency will Revolutionalize Business.* New York, Free Press.

Tsoukas, H. & R. Chia (2002). On Organizational Becoming: Rethinking Organizational Change, *Organization Science*, 13(5), 567-582.

Von Bertalanffy, L. (1972).The History and Status of General Systems Theory. *Academy of Management Journal 15*(4), 407-426.

Weick, K.E. (1976). Educational organizations as loosely coupled systems. *Administrative Science Quarterly* (March), 1-11.

Weick, K.E. (1991). The nontraditional quality of Organizational Learning. *Organization Science 2*(1), 116-124.

Weick, K.E. & Quinn, R.E. (1999). Organizational change and development. *Annual Review of Psychology* 50, 361-386.

WTO (2012). *World Trade Statistics*, World Trade Organization.

CHAPTER 9

Collaboration in the Dynamic Organizing of Global Business Networks: CSR in Commons, Protocols, and Infrastructures

Mai S. Linneberg and Poul Houman Andersen

As discussed in chapter one, fierce competition, a high level of activity, resource interconnectivity, and the unbundling of value-chains resulting in increased dependence on sourcing all require that both small and large companies adjust and explore novel ways to organize and arrange resources in order to exploit business opportunities and create value. Increased access to sourcing and collaboration for smaller companies and start-up firms in general opens up new business opportunities previously accessible only to large, integrated firms with sufficient resources to project their organizational power across national boundaries. However, in seeking to orchestrate international activities, using a global network of resource providers comes with a new set of managerial and organizational challenges. While collaborative forms of organizing can mobilize resources and activities from the stakeholder network to create value (Jiang, 2009; Ritter et al., 2004), to be effective, a collaborative organization relies less on hierarchy and more on shared values, processes, and infrastructures (Fjeldstad et al., 2012). A relevant example of a governing set of value infused practices is that of corporate social responsibility (CSR) standards, which, besides providing companies with a set of guidelines for behaving in an ethically or socially responsible manner, can have a secondary function of aligning and coordinating global business actors.

This chapter seeks a better understanding of the role CSR plays in supporting inter-firm collaboration. To do so, we investigate how the implementation of CSR policies and practices relates to establishing shared *values, commons, protocols, processes,* and *infrastructures.* The chapter provides insights into the characteristics of dynamic organizing and the role CSR can play in realizing business opportunities through inter-firm collaboration. We take steps to respond to a standing criticism of earlier marketing literature, namely, that it is unable to 'address the challenges inherent in a world moving quickly toward competition among networks of firms that can be referred to as global supply chains' (Flint, 2004, p. 45). Such challenges include an extension of the conceptualization of marketing strategy and planning to encompass more than one business enterprise, entailing the practical challenge of aligning value propositions at the multi-firm level. At the same time, the findings articulate some of the actual strategies and practices actors use at the micro level so that multi-firm collaborations can arise and endure. The study of such challenges can teach us about the creation of competitive advantages in a globalized world where hierarchies are increasingly complemented or replaced by more dynamic organizational forms.

The chapter is organized as follows. First, we address the main theme of the book: the organizational design challenges that globalization imposes on the organization and management of a Danish business enterprise. We address the issue of boundary setting and point out that differentiated organizational forms are required, noting that collaborative forms constitute an important addition to more traditional forms of organization. We use a collaborative actor approach (Fjeldstad, Snow, Miles, & Lettl, 2012), partly to frame our analysis of CSR's role in collaboration, which allows us to understand how collaboration actually works at the micro level. Similar to the practice perspective, this approach emphasizes the role of individual actors in reinforcing collaboration through CSR practices. We also revisit the CSR literature, focusing on the strategic view of CSR and on extant knowledge of CSR and collaboration. Before presenting the findings, this chapter elaborates on the methodology of the single-case study and describes the chosen case. The chapter closes with a discussion and conclusion.

Globalization and Organizational Reconfiguration

Globalization increases the task complexity of business enterprises, primarily through intensifying competition. As competition increases, still more companies seek to leverage their competitive advantage through externalizing and unbundling activities, typically by replacing some, or most, of the company's manufacturing activities with internationally sourced components and services, and by offshoring other activities. On average in Denmark, 25% of all manufacturing firms and 30% of all firms in communication and information services engaged in international outsourcing in 2011 (Statistics, 2011).

Externalizing activities internationally and increasingly relying on market exchange make for a more agile business enterprise that is less bound to capital investment in production equipment and thus better able to shed existing activities to seize new opportunities, exploit cost differentials, and arbitrage possibilities in the global marketplace. An unintended, negative consequence of this unbundling, however, is that managing global activities becomes increasingly complex and the business of the unbundled company becomes increasingly vulnerable to disruption from operating in multiple supply and customer markets (KPMG, 2012). Moreover, operating under these new business circumstances calls for organizational transition (see Andersen and Kragh, this volume). Existing organizational forms crafted to fit other task environments often struggle to meet these new challenges. In the typical Danish organization, management is still largely compartmentalized into functional areas, each endeavouring to optimize its part of an expected activity flow reflecting a given position in an industry (Det Danske Ledelsesbarometer, 2011a). Although Danish organizations exposed to intensifying internationalization have increasingly decentralized their decision making over the past decade (see Figure 9.1), other indicators in combination suggest that the hierarchical organizational form remains dominant in Danish business enterprises (Det Danske Ledelsesbarometer, 2011b).

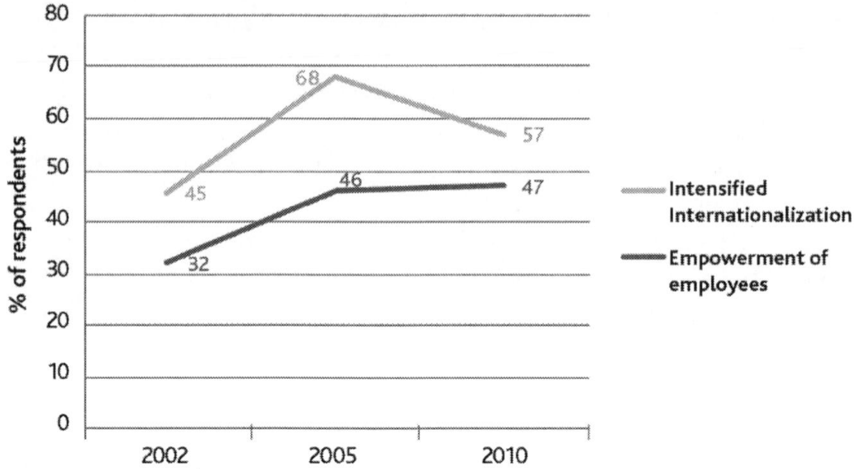

Figure 9.1. Internationalization and organizational development (Source: Dansk Ledelsesbarometer, 2011, 2006, 2003).

However, with the disruptive changes in business and competitive scope that follow from the globalization of customers, technologies, and supply sources, the task environment becomes increasingly complex. From an organizational design perspective, a powerful way to understand these organizational challenges is to explore the dynamic fitting processes between task complexity and activity design (Miles & Snow, 1978). Managers of business organizations in dynamic task environments must constantly realign organizational form to hedge the unpredictability of the task environment and maintain market exchange effectiveness. Organizational theorists treat these uncertainties as contingencies, i.e., future possibilities or states of the task environment that may or may not occur (Drazin & Van de Ven, 1985). According to behavioural approaches to decision making, decision makers have limited abilities to process information and make optimal choices to prepare for contingencies (Sarasvathy, 2001). The more information decision makers must take into account, the more unpredictable the possible contingencies and the greater the task uncertainty.

Two overall dimensions of contingencies determine the (un)predictability of the task environment (Duncan, 1972). The first dimension is the variability of the task environment, which ranges from static to dynamic. This dimension captures the degree to which critical factors in the task environment remain essentially the same over a considerable period or are better described as in a process of constant change. The second dimension determining the level of (un)predictability in a task environment concerns its tendency towards simplicity or complexity. In a simple task environment, only a few contingencies influence the decision maker's options, and interaction between these contingencies is restricted. As the number of contingencies and their interrelationships grows, the complexity of the task environment grows as well. Developments along these two dimensions drive complexity with respect to organizational design alignment and pose different challenges to the organization and coordination of the activities of an international business enterprise (Miles & Snow, 1986, 1992).

This is described in the organizational design literature as the organizational form or architecture. Fjeldstad et al. (2012, p. 735) quote a useful definition of organizational architecture: '[the] fundamental organization of a system embodied in its components, their relationships to each other and to the environment, and the principles guiding its design and evolution'. This definition implies the architectural axiom that an organizational system in its design must discharge a specific function in order to fulfil its purpose effectively. As this purpose becomes increasingly unpredictable, the ability to reconfigure the components and their relationships takes primacy over the ability to perform a set activity procedure expediently. Figure 9.2 outlines these dimensions and identifies organizational forms aligned with them.

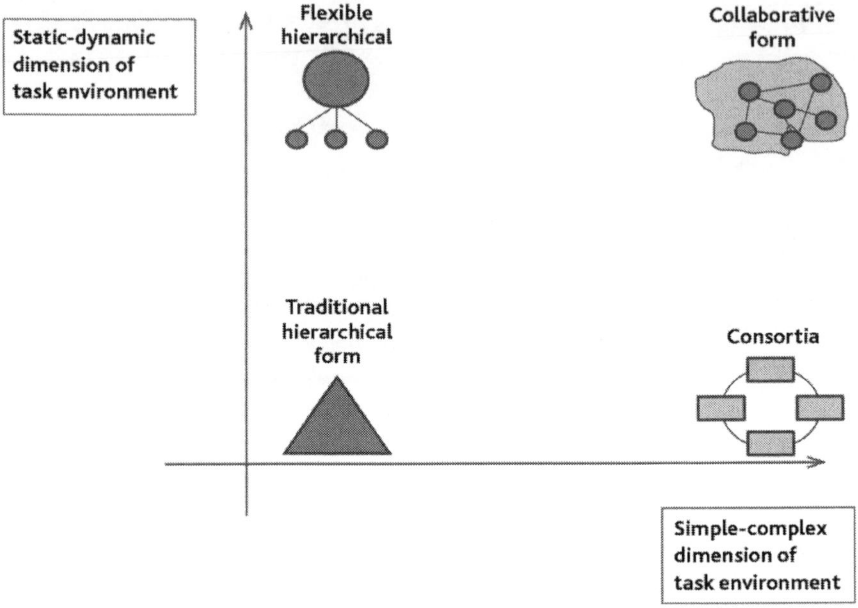

Figure 9.2. Task unpredictability and organizational form.

Starting at the bottom left in the figure, the traditional hierarchical form refers to what others describe as a simple hierarchy with a reasonably defined compartmentalization of tasks coupled in a fairly linear fashion. It is a form well suited for repetitive tasks and for honing organizational efficiency through stable task portioning and increased specialization. In the upper left corner, the level of change increases, necessitating more flexible organizational responses to cope with increasing task dissimilarity. This includes responding to seasonal and other forms of cyclic changes in demand. To this end, organizational designs accommodating organizational flexibility have emerged that can quickly respond to changes in demand (Peters & Waterman, 1982; Piore & Sabel, 1984). In the bottom right corner, the task complexity is high, meaning that organizations must be able to hedge uncertainties in the activities needed to ensure effective exchange relationships with customers, suppliers, and other partners. In these situations, different types of project-by-project consortia of independent business actors are seen as effective for configuring organizational responses in different parts of the literature on organizational configuration (Storper & Harrison, 1991). The upper right corner, the collaborative form of organization, simultaneously copes with high degrees of both variability and unpredictability. The internal coupling of activities must correspond to the external dynamics (Weick, 1976). More complex tasks call for flexible organizational designs with a wide degree of freedom to configure the organizational elements and the relationships among them. This extends to a point at which it becomes increasingly difficult to draw a clear boundary separating the organizational system from its context.

Unlike the other three organizational forms shown in Figure 9.2, the collaborative mode of organization is loose and indeterminate. It does not spring from a specific centre of control; rather, influence is distributed among actors in the collaborative context of the company. Much as in web-based communities, many actors seem to be governing at the same time. Moreover, unlike the flexible hierarchical and the consortium forms, which also challenge the static organizational design principles of the hierarchy, community-based coordination mechanisms take precedence over other mechanisms in collaborative organizational forms (Fjeldstad et al., 2012). In this sense, a collaborative community permits more active participation of member actors in organizing activities. To conceptualize this further, we find inspiration in the approach of Fjeldstad et al. (2012), who propose an actor-oriented scheme to support the analysis of collaborative infrastructures across organizational boundaries. The main conceptual foundations of their actor-oriented scheme are: '(1) actors who have the capabilities and values to self-organize; (2) commons where the actors accumulate and share resources; and (3) protocols, processes, and infrastructures that enable multi-actor collaboration' (Fjeldstad et al., 2012, p. 739). The collaborative community supports or hosts organizing features on which members can draw, and provides a repertoire of routine actions for members of the community. The elements of the scheme, presented as universally applicable and similar to an administrative technology (Thompson, 1967), are used in organizing various activities within organizations. 'Commons' refers to resources that are collectively owned and available to all the actors, such as a shared situational awareness (Fjeldstad et al., 2012). This situational awareness constitutes a current understanding of problems and opportunities in the organization's environment and of how these can be approached, or relevant shared knowledge that is collaboratively assembled and used (Hess & Ostrom, 2006). Protocol and process categories concern shared and recognizable schemes for interaction and inter-actor coordination within the resulting network. Collaborative infrastructures are the systems that connect actors and allow them to access the same pool of resources, for example, knowledge or information. Examples of infrastructures and protocols include designated IT systems (e.g., wide distribution of the software system AutoCAD among members of a collaborative community) and codes of conduct used by organizational actors in their exchange and collaboration activities. Collectively, the above elements enable actors to collaborate in a goal-oriented fashion (Fjeldstad et al., 2012).

Increasingly, field studies of organizations have uncovered organizational outliers that have left behind traditional organizational forms and now rely on modes of self-organization as well as local decision making based on shared protocols, commons, and infrastructures. Despite their small size, these entities are often thriving on a global scale, interacting in a complex and intricate web of relationships. To some extent, they confirm William Gibson's famous words: 'The future is already here – it's just not very evenly distributed'. Examples are found among small, but global, developers of games and other apps, who draw on specific IT protocols but also rely on norms and resources such as virtual communities, game festivals, and followers as resources to be mobilized and used for certain purposes. These and other avant-garde companies dynamically reorganize and rearrange resources to create value and hedge risks while realizing new business opportunities. This means an increasing diversity of organizational forms or principles for organizationally linking activities in a particular design.

An important but somewhat overlooked lever for organizing collaboration that combines several coordination elements are CSR standards. We believe that these standards reflect many of the characteristics that enhance spontaneous self-organization in actor communities, as identified by Fjeldstad et al. (2012). Their study of actor schemes in various sectors, such as coordination among military units and software developers, presents a wide range of protocols and commons. However, compared with the cases and examples they cite, little emphasis is placed on the role of shared values in collaboration or on how these values infuse infrastructures and protocols with meaning. As pointed out by other researchers into complex, global organizational schemes, shared value sets can help align viewpoints and help organizational elements to interrelate purposefully (Nohria & Ghoshal, 1994). In the following section, we elaborate on CSR as a shared set of values and consider how it can provide an actor-oriented collaborative structure for global organizing.

Corporate Social Responsibility

A classic definition of CSR conceptualizes the firm's social responsibility as a combination of economic, legal, ethical, and discretionary responsibilities (Carroll, 1979). In recent years, the literature has emphasized a strategic approach to CSR as guiding practice: 'the effective alignment of philanthropic contributions with business goals and strategies ... [allows] the reconciliation of social and economic benefits' (Jamali, 2007, p. 8). From a strategic perspective, it is argued that CSR is compatible with profitability and should be coupled with the overall strategy of a business enterprise (Drucker, 1984; Lantos, 2001; Porter & Kramer, 2006). CSR is expected to facilitate long-term strategic value creation (cf. Hart, 1995; Lantos, 2001; Nidumolu et al., 2009). CSR standards are here defined as the ethical claims made by a corporation with respect to the impact of a business activity on one or several relevant stakeholders or dimensions. It signals that a certain set of interests are promoted by the company and those engaging in exchange activities with it (McGuire et al., 1988). For this reason, a CSR standard is an important market asset. In a global supply chain context, a CSR standard expresses particular values upheld not only by the sourcing company but ideally also by the entire community, forming a backdrop for supplier certification, negotiation, etc. For this and related reasons, CSR standards are provided as management systems and tools that can help companies structure their collaborative efforts with suppliers.

The potential benefits of integrating CSR considerations into corporate activities have become more evident in recent years (Ayuso et al., 2012; Vurro et al., 2009). A recent unrepresentative survey of Nordic firms regarding their use of the ISO 26000 CSR standard found that almost 60% of the respondents had implemented CSR strategies. In addition, companies had strong knowledge of and were inspired by the ISO 26000 or other CSR-related standards. Moreover, when asked about their primary reason for implementing CSR strategies, almost half of the respondents attributed it to 'ensuring that all essential CSR elements of relevance for their company were considered' (Nordic Council of Ministers, 2006, p. 3).

CSR as a Collaborative Infrastructure

Though the literature recognizes the role that the corporate implementation of CSR standards and policies plays in market differentiation (Paine, 2003), the role CSR standards may play in advancing collaborative organizational design has hardly been investigated (Jamali, Yianni & Abdallah, 2011). While the complexity of CSR-related issues can motivate collaboration with stakeholders on CSR issues (Jamali et al., 2011), the fact that pressure groups and other constituents regard CSR as extending organizational boundaries (Amaeshi, Osuji & Nnodim, 2008) provides further impetus to pursue collaboration with business partners, particularly those contributing to product value. In the general discussion of whether each business enterprise is responsible only for its own actions or whether firms are eligible for extended responsibility, we sympathize with Emmelhainz and Adams (1999) who advocate an extended chain of responsibility on the part of the individual business enterprise. By analogy, in a world where the network organization is increasingly required to accommodate the growing complexity of the environment, engaging in CSR activities presents an opportunity for shared value creation in stakeholder relations if CSR is approached collaboratively across the value-chain. It can therefore be assumed that the strategic benefits of implementing CSR policies extend to the entire supply chain. In line with this notion, Pagell (2010) suggests that forming collaborative relationships around creating socially responsible supply chains can result in sustainable advantages (Pagell, Wu & Wasserman, 2010).

The use of CSR standards and policies can be considered a way to counteract the loss of hierarchical control over the stages of production and distribution resulting from the ongoing outsourcing trend (Vurro, Russo & Perrini, 2010). This trend particularly favours the implementation of CSR practices across the value-chain when customers have concerns about how suppliers' possible transgression of environmental or ethical boundaries may affect legitimacy. Applying CSR standards to suppliers and other partners in the global value-chain entails specifying how to handle decisions involving potential ethical, social, or environmental dilemmas. Agreeing on a CSR standard signifies collaborative intent and the alignment of partners in the value-chain. Shared codes of conduct can help establish cohesion, meaning that they can also serve as a coordination and control mechanism in place of or complementing hierarchical mechanisms.

Starting with the environmental impact of purchasing decisions and the implementation of green practices, discussions of the integration of sustainability issues and supply chain management practices have broadened to encompass environmental issues related to supply (Vurro et al., 2010). While most studies of this matter consider environmental practices and representations, similar studies of CSR have only begun to appear in the last decade as such practices have begun to spread (Gimenez & Tachizawa, 2012; Jamali et al., 2011).

The study of the extension of CSR practices to suppliers through collaboration or collaborative forms of governance has so far focused largely on companies' motives for engaging in such practices. Typical motives, such as strengthening trust and reducing the abuse of power among firms in the supply chain, have been emphasized (Ayuso, Roca & Colomé, 2013; Drake & Schlachter, 2008). The impact of assessment and collaboration on CSR performance (Gimenez & Tachizawa, 2012), i.e., how do such interactions translate into changed action regarding social and environmental issues, has also been studied. In the present analysis, we will concentrate on the infrastructural role CSR standards have played by providing protocols and commons for combining business actors in collaborative architectures in a concrete case. Our analysis considers elements of collaboration, helping us construct an in-depth micro portrait of how CSR influences collaborative activities as it crosses organizational boundaries.

Methodology

The Research

To gain a deeper understanding of the role of CSR standards in organizing collaboration, we rely on a single critical case study. We analyze a case of CSR collaboration, which we would characterize as an outlier, far from the mean in the normally distributed population of Danish business enterprises. An important function of in-depth studies of single cases is precisely to scrutinize exceptions and understand how a single case can challenge or extend what is already known. We believe that the present case involves central elements of the actor-oriented scheme (Fjeldstad et al., 2012); we also believe that it extends the scheme in several ways by emphasizing shared values as the community 'glue' that binds organizations together.

The case company is a provider of graphic solutions located in Denmark. We have anonymized the studied company, referring to it simply as GRAPHICS. We selected this case company for the following reasons: 1) it engages in a high level of CSR implementation and standards usage across the value-chain; 2) the case company partners with other stakeholders in its value-chain; and 3) it is facing global competitive challenges stemming from customer base globalization, increased global competition, and the advent of new market practices, automation, and rationalizations with the increasing digitalization of information.

The data for the current study come from a combination of several sources: interview, observation, and archival data. A series of ten extended in-depth interviews with various representatives of the firm and from workshops attended by both GRAPHICS representatives and the first author. Most of the formal interviews were conducted at GRAPHICS premises during three full days of observation in fall 2013. On these three days, we obtained knowledge of the work context and, in particular, of practices relating to suppliers and customers. During the observation period, the first author attended a weekly information meeting at which information on the overall pipeline and the progress of individual projects was discussed. The meeting also included a discussion of project turnover and overall focus areas, such as the importance of suppliers' prices vis-à-vis competitors' prices, contacts in the customer base, and the ability to bring in jobs in the fourth quarter of the year. Concurrent with the observational study, a series of brief unstructured in situ interviews was carried out, having conversation rather than data mining as the research ideal (Kvale & Brinkmann, 2007). The first author subsequently communicated with informants via e-mail and telephone for further clarification. All interviews were audio-recorded, transcribed, and, for analytical purposes, combined into a case narrative, which was based on observation notes and the in situ interviews. Quotations used in the analysis have all been verified with the relevant informants from GRAPHICS, which led to minor revisions, including the addition of further detail.

In support of the interviews and following Yin's (2009) notion of triangulating data from multiple sources to establish a deeper understanding of a case in its context, the following archival data have been studied: the personnel handbook, which covers core values; progress reports to the UN Global Compact; the code of conduct for suppliers, i.e., the integrated management system (which combines all certifications); examples of printed works from GRAPHICS; examples of competitive bids drafted by the company; the company website; and a logbook of all CSR communications produced by the company.

GRAPHICS

The owner and current CEO established the company in the late 1990s. GRAPHICS presents itself as a total solution provider with expertise in graphics solutions including web publishing, concept development, and printing.

A combination of three core values is central to company management: *partnerships* with customers and suppliers; *sustainability*, as manifested in products and processes; and *innovation*, specifically regarding technological solutions related to products and the production process. The company helps its customers with artwork and printing for all kinds of graphic communication material, managing the entire process up to delivery by offering the following services: design concepts, editing and translation, pre-press services, printing and binding, delivery and distribution, e-Books, online promotion and sale of publications, and production of films, trade exhibition stands, and merchandise.

GRAPHICS caters particularly to the graphic needs of international humanitarian and development organizations, such as the UN and WWF, for which it develops graphic materials on a project-by-project basis. Given that most of these organizations are sponsored by public funds, new projects are often subject to public tender policies and are globally announced to potential suppliers. This makes for fierce global competition among capable graphic design companies. Over the years, GRAPHICS has focused on acquiring and using certifications as a means to attract, organize, and cooperate with clients. To this end, GRAPHICS has focused on developing a strong CSR profile with an increasing focus on suppliers. The company is certified as CO_2 neutral and adheres to the UN's well-known Global Compact standard. The company takes pride in being one of the few Danish companies to belong to the UN Global Compact Advanced Level. In terms of other standards, GRAPHICS has, as a first mover in the industry, embarked on an ambitious endeavour to certify a series of practices. The main certifications held by GRAPHICS include: quality

(ISO 9001); environment (ISO 14001); health and safety management (OHSAS 18001); and social responsibility (DS 49001), building on ISO 26000 on social responsibility. In a rather unorthodox fashion, these management systems have all been integrated into one certified management system organized around the CSR certification.

Overall, much of GRAPHICS' development has been directed by a desire to serve the UN as a main client:

> We have competitors in the industry who deliver the same products as we do. They do not deliver to the UN, but they would give their right arm to be able to do so ... Over the past ten to fifteen years, GRAPHICS and our CEO have put a great deal of effort into looking attractive to the UN and we have done that very well. Adherence to the UN Global Compact is an obvious example of our efforts to meet the strict requirements of the industry in which we now operate. If the UN says jump – we jump.
> (GRAPHICS HR Responsible)

GRAPHICS' micro-level adjustments relate mainly to two overall traits of the organization: organizing through external partnerships and continuously upgrading employee skills through education and recruitment.

GRAPHICS relies strongly on its organizational ability to mobilize, configure, and internally match a project-based network of partners. Although partnerships are long-term, specific arrangements are project based and close cooperation is dismantled once a job is finished. For this reason, GRAPHICS' activities are organized largely through collaborative partnerships. The company retains about ten full-time permanent employees in Denmark and relies on contracted partners/freelancers for the actual production. GRAPHICS describes this web of partners as follows:

> The contracted partners of GRAPHICS are highly qualified and hold a wide variety of resources and expertise. Partners are local and international and include translators, graphic designers, logistic and transportation companies as well as editors.

GRAPHICS outsources all its graphic work, translation, printing, and transportation services. The seasonal structure of demand in the global humanitarian organization market is also attributed some significance as an explanation of the dynamic organizational set-up: 'when tied up to the UN system, we cannot carry too many permanent employees' (GRAPHICS CEO). The tenders run in specific periods followed by periods of production. During production peaks, GRAPHICS may work with up to 30-40 partners. Equally relevant, the number of employees is based on the ability to scale up and down:

> We can scale up and down depending on the needs of the customers. At the same time, our customers have a wider palette of competences available through one-stop shopping. (GRAPHICS CEO)

GRAPHICS' business model relies on the flexible assembly of partners with specialized abilities to achieve economies of scale, capability, and experience. Sourcing is therefore a collaborative rather than an arm's-length venture. However, partners are still contracted on an order-to-order basis. Specific partners are chosen from the larger pool of potential suppliers with an eye to the job at hand. The description of suppliers as partners emphasizes a desire to link suppliers closely to GRAPHICS.

Creating CSR through Collaboration

Collaborative Practices

The project manager assembles a relevant team of partners to take on a particular job, coordinating the process from start to delivery. In most cases, the project manager maintains the customer contact and liaises among the contracted partners. From formulating the competitive bid to the final product, project managers work independently and handle exchanges with the suppliers on a particular job. Throughout this process, it is particularly valuable that employees be flexible enough to adjust to the multiple nationalities for which they are working. Capacity and competences are likewise adjustable and the organization grows and shrinks according to market flux and specific customer requirements.

A web-based communication platform, WebProof, allows customers and partners to view proofs and amend designs online in real time. Interaction among all project stakeholders may also involve sharing ideas, requesting versions, and project approval. Dependence on a real-time online tool such as WebProof highlights the collaborative approach taken with customers and suppliers, as such tools induce transparency and openness towards value-chain partners. This web-based platform mirrors similar platforms found in other studies of actor-oriented organization schemes (Fjeldstad et al., 2012). Besides being a tool, it actively mediates and funnels activities in a certain direction and sequence, contributing to alignment across organizational boundaries in the value-chain.

The Role of CSR in Commons, Infrastructures, and Protocols

Internally, GRAPHICS is an ambitious collaborative effort. Engaging in a stakeholder approach to CSR requires that all employees have collaborative values and capabilities, because such an approach entails collaborating on possibly sensitive issues regarding suppliers' decisions that may have environmental, social, and economic impacts on the firm's processes.

Commons: A Situational Awareness

The current understanding of problems and opportunities in the environment of GRAPHICS, and how these can be approached, exemplifies a common resource that has come to be shared with partners in the wider ecosystem. It represents a shared situational awareness (Fjeldstad et al., 2012) of the requirements of focal customers, of the content of CSR, and of the market opportunities tied to CSR performance. The significance of CSR in this collaborative community is not related just to how communication is handled but also to how tasks are executed, notably, in terms of project managers' affecting suppliers:

> It is important that we be aligned internally – the internal dialogue is pivotal. It is useless for communication and management to do something [i.e., regarding CSR] if the rest of us do not get involved. Hence, it is the project manager who deals with the supplier ... Notably, it is important that we know our values ... also, we are able to make a point to suppliers and, at the same time, try to affect them. I think that is a natural thing. (GRAPHICS Project Manager)

CSR is well internalized in the company, not least because it is a core value for employees. Accordingly, CSR procedures have been implemented in the management system, in supplier selection, and in associated supplier evaluation. Externally, CSR is central to dialogue with suppliers from the inception of a partnership. GRAPHICS strives to align partners regarding specific aspects of CSR through dialogue and education. As pointed out by one project manager, 'once the suppliers are to become partners, they have been through our CEO's treatment [i.e., CSR presentation and briefing] many times'. All suppliers are thoroughly investigated before becoming partners and, in particular, GRAPHICS attempts to extend the internal dialogue on CSR to suppliers as well. Having the UN as a main customer, with its demand for CSR, legitimizes dialogue on related practices and facilitates the process of creating a common situational awareness with suppliers: 'Our suppliers know very well that having the UN as a customer entails certain ethical commitments. There are simply don'ts' (GRAPHICS Project Manager). Having organizations in the network with especially strong values eases the creation of commons, as a project manager at GRAPHICS explains:

> CSR is not just writing everything down ... you have to act on it ... I actually think that is really easy when working with the UN. They have clear values themselves and therefore there are some clear rules of the game. (GRAPHICS Project Manager)

As such, understanding the nature of the main end customer's demands is part of the situational awareness and is an important aspect of understanding the particular challenges in the global marketplace for humanitarian organization clients: 'It is special to work with the UN ... Everything happens at the last minute and it requires know-how, flexibility, and devotion. Our experience with the UN system has taught us which approach to choose – and our partners appreciate this as well' (GRAPHICS CEO).

In a similar vein, dialogue sometimes results in suppliers' committing to certifications similar to those GRAPHICS possesses. Knowledge sharing is a key to choosing suppliers with similar values, but even more so when pushing for certification:

> We have ongoing dialogue with our suppliers about certification, its content and how to ... We would like to educate them, and communication of our values is a continuous effort for us. (GRAPHICS Communications Manager)

In particular, project managers must make a collaborative effort in mobilizing partners to undertake projects and in communicating with the diverse customer base. To support this wide range of collaboration, GRAPHICS continuously seeks employees who are flexible and highly skilled in collaboration.

Protocols, Processes, and Infrastructures

Alongside communication about GRAPHICS' CSR values and expectations to suppliers, protocols are used to admit specific suppliers into the value-chain. GRAPHICS employees engage in a preparatory process to motivate partners to understand the implementation of CSR-related practices, meaning that potential suppliers are not ruled out if they cannot immediately comply. GRAPHICS' code of conduct concerning CSR is based on the UN Global Compact and sets an example of both a contract and a shared protocol that partners accept before engaging with GRAPHICS.

GRAPHICS not only meets the demands of its UN client, including upholding the UN Global Compact, supplying products on environmentally certified papers, and using environmentally friendly inks, but also seeks third-party certifications. CSR certification according to a management system, for example, ISO 26000, exemplifies a collaborative protocol. However, GRAPHICS is well aware of the alluring pitfalls of certification in terms of window-dressing:

> The certification is sort of skeleton, but that is not enough ... You need to be committed and act upon what has been written down ... Here, the CSR [certification] is the culmination of everything in our history and, at the same time, it extends to our suppliers and partners ... It is so challenging it makes you go further than your own desk. (GRAPHICS Project Manager)

When customers' CSR demands are passed on to suppliers, this process is not handled as a simple certification process per se, as would be expected in a flexible organization; rather, there is a large element of direct interaction, knowledge transfer, and negotiation about what road to take. In some instances, such interaction with suppliers will lead to the third-party certification of suppliers, as the GRAPHICS CEO describes:

> We take pride in sharing our experience with certification procedures with our partners. It is essential to us that our partners share our approach to CSR matters, and any CSR-related steps taken on their behalf entail benefits ... they have paid for the certification themselves. But I have done the homework and shared it with them – and told them about the advantages for them ... We share our system with them and tell them how we do it so that they can also see the benefits.
>
> We communicate about the requirements of the UN, and therefore we do not encounter resistance over the fact that we ask suppliers to sign a code of conduct and comply with it. (GRAPHICS CEO)

Having a specific infrastructure, i.e., certain ways of working with CSR, such as certification, facilitates interaction with current partners. At the same time, it allows partners to focus on the core product, as the risk of suppliers' transgressing ethical or environmental boundaries is likely limited. However, a fixed infrastructure complicates the initiation of work with new suppliers. It can take a long time to educate suppliers on CSR, especially when suppliers are international and do not share the same values/ethical considerations:

> Whether the printing house is located in Ireland, Bangladesh, or Denmark I could not care less ... there is a lot of dialogue concerning specifications and delivery times, but all that is taken care of via the telephone and e-mail. And the file is sent off from my e-mail ... But it has to do with locating someone – they are out there of course – but it has to do with the resources [needed] to locate them and to uncover whether they can live up to our demands ... If we take the example of a Middle Eastern printing house, it took years to get to a point where we could actually start something up. (GRAPHICS Project Manager)

Being located in the same geographical region simplifies collaboration as it provides a common context for the actors involved. A project manager describing a situation in which the pool of suppliers could not deliver a specific product item, which was part of a larger tender, elaborates on the challenge:

> Suppliers have been scrutinized, but I just had an incident with some bucket bags. ... At the last minute, I needed a price for some printed bucket bags as part of a larger bid, and as this is quite far from our regular product, I needed a new supplier. I have a Danish supplier and I asked, 'Claus, can you handle this?' 'Well yes, I know a *sewing shed'. And I asked, 'Hmm, what kind of a sewing shed is that then?' As* it turned out, it was here in Denmark, so I was not concerned ... I can find a bucket bag in China without problems ... but what's behind it, you really have to check that out ... If you are looking for continuous collaboration, you'll have to go down there! (GRAPHICS Project Manager)

On the other hand, involving suppliers from other geographical regions is attractive, partly due to the locations themselves and partly due to competences not found locally. These two factors can differentiate a new supplier from the existing supplier portfolio and allow catering to novel customer preferences. Referring to the partnering printing house in the Middle East, the project manager explains:

> That supplier holds a golden egg. He is able to provide something different from our supplier in Denmark ... They practice different techniques where he can deliver the volume at a different price and his location possibly results in lower transportation costs. (GRAPHICS Project Manager)

In the collaboration described in this quotation, CSR is used as a common language, a semi-shared technology, and certification is used as an infrastructure according to which decisions are made and actions guided. A collaborative infrastructure is not a given and is not particularly stable with respect to the actors and resources it includes; instead, it must constantly be realigned if it is not to fall apart. Balancing the need to constantly realign suppliers with the need to expand and change the current portfolio of suppliers is at the heart of managing the GRAPHICS network. As described by Li Fung, a Hong Kong-based network mediator in the apparel industry, balancing these contradictory needs is a critical relational skill needed in order to maintain exchange efficiency in the type of global business context discussed here (Magretta, 1998).

GRAPHICS' paradoxical dependence on its suppliers is the result of its ongoing arms-length relationship with them. On one hand, GRAPHICS depends almost entirely on suppliers because virtually no actual production is internalized. On the other hand, GRAPHICS has created close relationships with a specific pool of suppliers sharing at least some CSR values and protocols, so suppliers are not considered entirely fungible commodities. Due to the significance of its suppliers, GRAPHICS is preoccupied with the risk that suppliers may abrogate their ethical or environmental responsibilities. Therefore, for suppliers to become accepted in its pool of suppliers or partners, GRAPHICS needs to cooperate with suppliers in their CSR work.

In terms of infrastructures that enable collaboration and support the dynamic elements of organizing, the web-based communication platform WebProof permits the effective management of a project with partners located in different places and time zones. As an infrastructure, it provides a mechanism for coordination and control. Whereas CSR-related issues are the basis for collaboration in constructing a shared understanding of the opportunities and challenges in a particular market, focusing collaboration on what CSR represents in the GRAPHICS value-chain and how to realize it, WebProof is an infrastructure that allows for collaborative efforts concerning the end product. In this sense, we think that CSR conforms to Fjeldstad et al.'s (2012) notion of the elements that form the collaborative architecture. However, we also believe that CSR extends the scheme in several ways, as it emphasizes shared values as the communal 'glue' that binds organizations together.

Discussion and Conclusion

In this chapter, we set out to improve our understanding of how CSR standards and certification can support inter-firm collaboration. We have illustrated how implementing CSR policies and practices relates to establishing shared *values*, *commons*, *protocols*, *processes*, and *infrastructures*. The chapter offers insights into the characteristics of dynamic organizing and the role CSR can play in realizing business opportunities through inter-firm collaboration.

GRAPHICS serves as a good case for examining the versatility of the forms of inter-firm governance emerging in recent years. In itself GRAPHICS is an ambitious collaborative effort, a trait which can be regarded a prerequisite for the level of flexibility of the organizational responses that can be supplied (cf. Piore & Sabel, 1984). GRAPHICS faces a high degree of task dissimilarity: It has gone from providing only graphic solutions to being a total graphic communication solution provider with a much broader product portfolio, while facing considerable seasonality in demand. GRAPHICS is motivated to retain just a few permanent employees, who collaborate with a large number of contracted partners to undertake global projects. GRAPHICS as a multi-firm network relies on the flexible assembly of firms with specialized capabilities to achieve economies of scale and experience (cf. Fjeldstad et al., 2008). As well as collaborating with a diverse set of suppliers, GRAPHICS' project managers have cross-cultural capabilities that enable them to serve customers from various cultures.

Applying a stakeholder's approach to CSR requires that employees have collaborative values and capabilities: project managers must make collaborative efforts in mobilizing partners to complete projects and in communicating with the diverse customer base; systems must be networked to allow shared access to products during the production process; and all partners must share an awareness of what it takes to work with the UN as a customer. To support these collaboration issues, GRAPHICS continuously seeks employees who are both flexible and highly skilled in collaboration. The company engages in educating suppliers and shares knowledge about how CSR can be implemented. In terms of CSR, GRAPHICS is a leading-edge firm, well ahead of the rest of its industry. While maintaining economic viability, GRAPHICS keeps CSR a priority, and educating suppliers and sharing knowledge are cornerstones of its supplier communication. Moreover, knowledge sharing and communication regarding CSR help promote a common understanding of the challenges and opportunities of serving this particular market and of implementing CSR in work practices (cf. Fjeldstad et al., 2012). Creating such a commons, as well as embedding CSR processes via certification and selected work processes, helps create closer collaboration as the means and the ends become more similar. Because of the formal organization of GRAPHICS, the firm is dependent on its suppliers. The success of GRAPHICS' CSR effort therefore relies on the actions of its suppliers, rendering effective governance of these inter-organizational relationships essential. Failure to manage and control the social and environmental impacts of the supply chain will increase the risk of non-compliance, which in turn may damage the reputation of the company that developed the code. This explains GRAPHICS' efforts to make CSR an important process and protocol in collaboration with suppliers (Pedersen & Andersen, 2006).

Through its explorative questions, this chapter has contributed detailed knowledge of what may constitute the commons, protocols, and infrastructures employed by firms as collaboration tools. Due to the nature of the case, in which CSR was a prevalent tool, the chapter clearly demonstrates the significance of CSR in a business-to-business context. Although consumer research may be the prevalent approach to CSR, we note the relevance of CSR in the studied business-to-business setting. The current findings illustrate how CSR is an issue in relation to all business partners and has particular relevance in the business-to-business market (cf. Homburg, Stierl & Bornemann, 2013).

Despite some research questioning the merits of working collaboratively on CSR (Hollos, Blome & Foerstl, 2012), the literature on this subject converges on the notion that, in promoting CSR, a collaborative approach to supply chains is essential (e.g., Tencati & Zsolnai, 2008). In general, certification and collaboration are the two best practices that have received particular attention with regard to promoting CSR in the supply chain (Pagell & Wu, 2009). In terms of collaboration, shared knowledge and its development are key (Maignan, Hellebrand & McAlister, 2002); in this vein, CSR processes may be integrated and managed along the supply chain (Vurro et al., 2010). This chapter confirms that these practices are prevalent, and that they also appear to be interlinked and mutually complementary. While certification might have been the end goal for suppliers, knowledge transfer from GRAPHICS to its partners was a prerequisite for certification even to occur. As in the case of implementing environmental practices and greening suppliers (Rao & Holt, 2005), education in CSR content and practices may also be achieved through collaboration. However, the current CSR literature has little to say about the properties of CSR collaboration except that CSR entails knowledge sharing and education. The case study extends this perspective and illustrates how CSR is used as a structuring device for collaboration in terms of, for example, the infrastructural characteristics of CSR that make it an enabler of some collaborations while avoiding others. CSR and collaboration exist in a two-sided relationship in which CSR practices can emerge from collaboration, as exemplified by GRAPHICS' ongoing learning-by-doing followed by teaching suppliers about implementation. GRAPHICS remains a driving force in its business networks, striving to raise its customers' CSR standards and, in turn, raise the CSR level of its suppliers. For an organization to take this leading position suggests that the organization is functioning well in terms of CSR, as not only communication, but also having employees that understand and have internalised practices aligning with CSR strategies and communication.

References

Amaeshi, K.M., Osuji, O.K. & Nnodim, P. (2008). Corporate Social Responsibility in Supply Chains of Global Brands: a Boundaryless Responsibility? Clarifications, Exceptions and Implications. *Journal of Business Ethics, 81*(1), 223-234.

Ayuso, S., Roca, M. & Colomé, R. (2013). SMEs as 'Transmitters' of CSR Requirements in the Supply Chain. *Supply Chain Management, 18*(5), 497-508.

Carroll, A.B. (1979). A Three-Dimensional Conceptual Model of Corporate Performance. *The Academy of Management Review, 4*(4), 497-505.

Carroll, A.B. (1999). Corporate Social Responsibility Evolution of a Definitional Construct. *Business & Society, 38*(3), 268-295.

Det Danske Ledelsesbarometer. (2011a). Dokumentationsrapport (Lederne). Retrieved 010114, 2014, from http://www.lederne.dk/lho/publikationer/undersoegelserogudgivelser/detdanskeledelsesbarometer/detdanskeledelsesbarometer2011dokumentationsrapport.htm

Det Danske Ledelsesbarometer. (2011b). Udviklingsrapport (Lederne). Retrieved 010114, 2014, from http://www.lederne.dk/lho/publikationer/undersoegelserogudgivelser/detdanskeledelsesbarometer/Detdanskeledelsesbarometer2011udviklingsrapport.htm

Drake, M.J. & Schlachter, J.T. (2008). A Virtue-Ethics Analysis of Supply Chain Collaboration. *Journal of Business Ethics, 82*(4), 851-864.

Drucker, P. (1984). The New Meaning of Corporate Social Responsibility. *California Management Review*, (26), 53-63.

Duncan, R.B. (1972). Characteristics of Organizational Environments and Perceived Environmental Uncertainty. *Administrative Science Quarterly*, 313-327.

Emmelhainz, M.A. & Adams, R.J. (1999). The Apparel Industry Response to Sweatshop Concerns: a Review and Analysis of Codes of Conduct. *Journal of Supply Chain Management*, summer *51*(7).

Fjeldstad, O.D., Snow, C.C., Miles, R.E. & Lettl, C. (2012). The Architecture of Collaboration. *Strategic Management Journal*, *33*(6), 734-750.

Gimenez, C. & Tachizawa, E.M. (2012). Extending Sustainability to Suppliers: a Systematic Literature Review. *Supply Chain Management: an International Journal*, *17*(5), 531-543.

Hess, C. & Ostrom, E. (2006). A Framework for Analysing the Microbiological Commons. *International Social Science Journal*, *58*(188), 335.

Hollos, D., Blome, C. & Foerstl, K. (2012). Does Sustainable Supplier Co-operation Affect Performance? Examining Implications for the Triple Bottom Line. *International Journal of Production Research*, *50*(11), 2968-2986.

Homburg, C., Stierl, M. & Bornemann, T. (2013). Corporate Social Responsibility in Business-to-Business Markets: How Organizational Customers Account for Supplier Corporate Social Responsibility Engagement. *Journal of Marketing*, *77*(6), 54-72.

Jamali, D., Yianni, M. & Abdallah, H. (2011). Strategic Partnerships. Social Capital and Innovation: Accounting for Social Alliance Innovation. *Business Ethics: a European Review*, *20*(4), 375-391.

KPMG. (2012). Expect the Unexpected: Building Business Value in a Changing World. In K. International (Ed.).

Lantos, G.P. (2001). The Boundaries of Strategic Corporate Social Responsibility. *Journal of Consumer Marketing*, *18*(7), 595-630.

Magretta, J. (1998). Fast, Global, and Entrepreneurial: Supply Chain Management, Hong Kong Style-an Interview with Victor Fung. *Harvard Business Review*, 76, 102-115.

Maignan, I., Hellebrand, B. & McAlister, D. (2002). Managing Socially-Responsible Buying: How to Integrate Non-economic Criteria into the Purchasing Process. *European Management Journal*, 20, 641-648.

Miles, R. & Snow, C. (1986). Organizations: New Concepts for New Forms. *California Management Review*, *28*(2), 68-73.

Miles, R. & Snow, C. (1992). Causes of Failure in Network Organizations. *California Management Review*, 53-72.

Nohria, N. & Ghoshal, S. (1994). Differentiated Fit and Shared Values: Alternatives for Managing Headquarters-Subsidiary Relations. *Strategic Management Journal*, *15*(6), 491-502.

Nordic Council of Ministers. (2006). Survey Report on Nordic Initiative for Social Responsibility Using ISO 26000.

Pagell, M. & Wu, X. (2009). Building a More Complete Theory of Sustainable Supply Chain Management Using Case Studies of 10 Examplars. *Journal of Supply Chain Management*, *45*(2), 37-56.

Pagell, M., Wu, Z. & Wasserman, M.E. (2010). Thinking Differently About Purchasing Portfolios: an Assessment of Sustainable Sourcing. *Journal of Supply Chain Management, 46*(1), 57-73.

Paine, L.S. (2003). *Value Shift: Why Companies Must Merge Social and Financial Imperatives to Achieve Superior Performance*. New York: McGraw-Hill.

Pedersen, E.R. & Andersen, M. (2006). Safeguarding Corporate Social Responsibility (CSR) in Global Supply Chains: How Codes of Conduct are Managed in Buyer-Supplier Relationships. *Journal of Public Affairs, 6*(3/4), 228-240.

Peters, T. & Waterman, R. (1982). *In Search of Excellence: Lessons from America's Best-Run Corporations*. New York: Warner.

Piore, M.J. & Sabel, C. (1984). *The Second Industrial Divide: Possibilities for Prosperity*: Basic Books.

Porter, M.E. & Kramer, M.A. (2006). Strategy and Society: the Link between Competitive Advantage and Corporate Social Responsibility. *Harvard Business Review* (78-92).

Rao, P. & Holt, D. (2005). Do Green Supply Chains Lead to Competitiveness and Economic Performance? *International Journal of Operations & Production Management, 25*(9), 898-916.

Sarasvathy, S.D. (2001). Causation and Effectuation: toward a Theoretical Shift from Economic Inevitability to Entrepreneurial Contingency. *Academy of Management Review, 26*(2), 243-263.

Statistics, D. (2011). International Outsourcing. Retrieved 010114, 2014, from http://www.dst.dk/da/Statistik/emner/globalisering/outsourcing.aspx?tab=nog

Storper, M. & Harrison, B. (1991). Flexibility, Hierarchy and Regional Development: the Changing Structure of Industrial Production Systems and Their Forms of Governance in the 1990s. *Research Policy, 20*(5), 407-422.

Tencati, A. & Zsolnai. (2008). The Collaborative Enterprise. *Journal of Business Ethics*.

Thompson, J.D. (1967). *Organizations in Action*. New York: McGraw-Hill.

Vogel, D. (2008). Private Global Business Regulation. *Annual Review of Political Science, 11*, 261-282.

Vurro, C., Russo, A. & Perrini, F. (2010). Shaping Suistainable Value-chains: Network Determinants of Supply Chain Governance Models. *Journal of Business Ethics*, 90, 607-621.

CHAPTER 10

Sourcing Intermediary Profiles in the Global Clothing Industry

Chris Ellegaard and Mette Vedel

The clothing industry, though in many ways a traditional industry characterized by labour-intensive manufacturing, is also one of the most globalized industries. Since the early 1990s, the Danish clothing industry has changed from a low-tech manufacturing industry into a globalized design and fashion industry highly dependent on global sourcing. The industry survived as a competitive domestic manufacturing industry for many years despite the increased competition resulting from Denmark's decision to join the EU in 1972. However, the fall of the Berlin wall in 1989 signalled the beginning of a new era. As a first step, a number of manufacturers offshored production to Poland. During the 1990s, production gradually moved farther away, first from Poland to the Baltic states, Ukraine, and other Eastern European countries, and later to Asia. This development was accompanied by an equally important change in which sourcing from independent foreign suppliers increasingly replaced production in offshore manufacturing facilities. Today, Danish clothing companies today source around the world, and China has become a major supply market.

The capabilities needed to source successfully from Asia have developed over a long period. Some Danish clothing companies have sourced in Asia since the early 1960s and therefore possess considerable experience and knowledge of efficient and effective global supply network set-ups. The industry is now characterized by a willingness and capacity to restructure activities in response to new challenges and opportunities. Consequently, many specialized sourcing set-ups, involving highly specialized sourcing intermediaries, have developed through unbundling and rebundling of sourcing functions. We believe that these specialized sourcing intermediary profiles offer inspiring examples for purchasing and sourcing managers in other industries, too. Their existence in a mature global industry challenges best practice sourcing, which in some industries is equated with 'avoiding the middleman', and indicates that sourcing intermediaries may serve an important purpose in global sourcing. Our aim in this chapter is therefore to learn why and in what contexts buying companies rely on sourcing intermediaries as an alternative or supplement to direct sourcing. Ultimately, we seek to identify specific contemporary value-adding sourcing intermediary profiles in the clothing industry.

To learn about sourcing intermediaries, we interviewed 20 sourcing specialists occupying central positions in 20 companies covering a broad range of the supply network in the Danish clothing industry. Respondents included retailers, brand marketers, wholesalers, and sourcing intermediaries. We asked the sourcing intermediaries, who constituted half of the informants, to describe the services they offer and the customers they serve. The remaining informants, who had significant insights into the clothing supply network, all bought from sourcing intermediaries to some extent. We asked them to describe what sourcing intermediary services they relied on, the strengths of sourcing through intermediaries versus sourcing directly, and how sourcing strategies supported their overall corporate strategies and consumer markets.

The chapter is structured as follows. We first present background to the study and an overview of the services traditionally offered by sourcing intermediaries as outlined in the relevant literature. We then describe the major changes that have occurred in the clothing industry and present the findings of our study. Finally, we summarize the study, discussing its implications for managers inside and outside the clothing industry, before presenting our conclusions.

Background

The most desired global sourcing incentive has always been low purchase prices caused by the low factor costs of less-developed or emerging supply markets (Cho & Kang, 2001). Nevertheless, entering and establishing a presence in global sourcing markets, characterized by considerable uncertainty and large distances between buyer and seller, is perceived as risky. This is particularly the case among micro enterprises or SMEs, which have limited resources and therefore find it difficult to enter distant supply markets and maintain a global presence. One option is to rely on sourcing intermediaries that have already established a presence globally, in the hope of benefitting from low factor costs in less-developed locations. Sourcing intermediaries have encountered harsh criticism and been accused of taking an excessive share of supply network profits without adding enough value. In the transition towards a new global division of work, sourcing intermediaries have increasingly been regarded as lacking legitimacy, as buying companies have globalized their own sourcing, production, and marketing/sales activities.

Increasing criticism has attacked the feasibility of global sourcing. First, authors taking a total cost perspective are questioning whether global sourcing really is cheaper when all costs related to acquiring a product are taken into consideration. For example, costs related to product quality, delivery performance, and inventories tend to increase significantly with higher levels of global sourcing (Horn, Schiele & Werner, 2013). These increased costs reflect the greater distances and uncertainties of various kinds that appear when sourcing globally. Somehow, many companies seem to ignore these changed circumstances when calculating sourcing costs. At least three observed and/or reported reasons for this phenomenon should be mentioned: 1) companies are simply *not* applying a total cost perspective in their accounting, taking the quoted purchase price (Weber et al., 2010) and perhaps adding a few per cent as a rule of thumb to cover unforeseen costs; 2) even if companies would like to apply a total cost perspective, they often lack the data and systems required to make accurate total cost calculations within reasonable limits of resources and time (Song, Platts & Bance, 2007); or 3) they are blindly going global because they are subject to a follow-the-leader effect, automatically assuming that global sourcing is cheaper (Horn, Schiele & Werner, 2013). These studies indicate that sourcing organizations frequently make suboptimal global sourcing decisions, which may also affect their ability to recognize the sourcing intermediary as a viable option.

Traditional Sourcing Intermediary Services

We first describe the traditional role of the sourcing intermediary. Sourcing intermediaries do not carry out manufacturing activities, but profit from bridging distances and coordinating trade between buying and selling companies on the global stage. They source for a large group of buying companies (Ferber & McVey, 1960), helping them gain an overview of possible suppliers and providing information that can help in supplier selection decisions. They compile and generate information and are involved in search and match activities (Balderston, 1958). Another way to characterize intermediaries is based on the risk they take. They may either source and negotiate on behalf of the buying company or take ownership of the traded goods themselves (Mallen, 1976). They have traditionally been involved in the logistics of creating assortments of heterogeneous resources and aggregating homogeneous bulk supplies from a variety of sources (Alderson & Martin, 1965), and some intermediaries have even absorbed the risk of speculative inventories (Bucklin, 1965). In other words, sourcing intermediaries solve customer problems (Anderson & Anderson, 2002). Overall, the management literature has devoted surprisingly little attention to the sourcing intermediary, including those parts of the literature concerned with global sourcing, strategic purchasing, supply chain management, B2B marketing, and international business. Those few writers that have studies the intermediary, split the services of sourcing intermediaries into three types: establishment, operational, and relational. First, the sourcing intermediary helps companies reduce the time, resources, and difficulties associated with entering a new sourcing market (Casson, 1997; Ellis, 2003, 2006). Moreover, some Western companies possess less knowledge than the intermediary of the many possible global sourcing markets and supplier opportunities (Magretta, 1998). Reducing information asymmetries in general, in both new and established exchanges, has historically been among the core services of sourcing intermediaries (Casson, 1997). Second, the sourcing intermediary has traditionally played an operational coordination role between buyers and sellers in international trade (Ellis, 2006; Fung, Chen & Yip, 2007; Peng and York, 2001). The intermediary serves as a buffer between buyer and supplier by holding inventories, ensuring delivery performance for the buying company (Bucklin, 1965; Casson, 1997; Nassimbeni & Sartor, 2007). By consolidating demand from many customers, the sourcing intermediary reduces inventory risks while representing a large and important customer account for clothing producers used to dealing in very large order sizes, making them prioritize the intermediary (Belevina & Girotra, 2012; Ellis, 2003; Mallen, 1976). In other cases, the sourcing intermediary takes responsibility for coordinating upstream logistics and production in networks of small producers, thereby securing deliveries at low price (Fung & Chen, 2010; Magretta, 1998; Popp, 2000).

Finally, the sourcing intermediary limits opportunistic behaviour and improves communication and coordination by maintaining close relationships with suppliers. By being located near the supplier's facilities, and by visiting and meeting the supplier relatively often, the intermediary can keep an eye on work progress. In addition, the intermediary can develop and maintain close relationships with decision makers in suppliers' organizations on whom the buying company can rely in suppliers' organizations (Belevina & Girotra, 2010; Casson, 1997; Popp, 2000). Suppliers that perceive the intermediary as part of their network tend to refrain, for example, from cheating on production processes and materials or from copying products and drawings (Belevina & Girotra, 2010; Ellis, 2003; Magretta, 1998). This presence also allows the intermediary to follow up on agreements and communicate regularly regarding deliveries and potential problems, which occur at higher frequencies when sourcing internationally rather than locally. Generally, the sourcing intermediary has been known to build bridges between cultures, an ability born of the intermediary's knowledge and experience of acting in more than one national culture (Casson, 1997; Ellis, 2003). The above description sketches the services of the traditional generic sourcing intermediary. Our findings, however, indicate that these services have changed.

The Clothing Industry Today: Different Ways of Meeting Consumer Demands

Before delving into the services and profiles of sourcing intermediaries, we briefly review the clothing industry anno 2014. The clothing industry is a mature globalized industry. The export of silk fabrics from China has been going on for more than two thousand years and has always depended on intermediaries, initially traders who were willing to risk speculative investments in fabrics and transport from China to Europe along the Silk

Road. The present globalized clothing industry still depends on intermediaries, but their roles and functions have changed as the industry has developed. Over the past two decades, three major developments have significantly influenced the clothing industry:

1. The expiration of the Multi-Fibre Arrangement (MFA; 1974-1994) and the subsequent Agreement on Textiles and Clothing (ATC; 1995-2004),[4] which allowed developed countries to restrict imports of clothing from 1974 to 2005, has resulted in widespread globalization of the clothing supply networks.[5]
2. Changed consumer expectations: today high fashion content is expected, not only in exclusive brands but also in private labels and no-name clothes offered by supermarkets and low-price retail chains.
3. Consolidation and vertical integration among globalized brand marketers and retail chains.

The globalization of clothing supply markets offers European and American buying companies the opportunity to profit from low factor costs in other parts of the world. Danish clothing companies have profited greatly from these opportunities, but have also been forced to handle the accompanying challenges of distant supply markets. The expanded geographical distance between supply and demand markets increases transportation time and makes it more difficult for buyers (e.g., brand marketers, retail chains, and independent retailers) to monitor their suppliers. At the same time, buyers have tended to increase the number and reduce the size of collections, and now demand rapid delivery of an increasing portion of their assortment in response to end-user demands for high fashion content. This creates an apparent contradiction, as speed is difficult to obtain at low prices over long distances. In addition, an increasing share of the manufacturing capacity, for example, in China for instance, is being used to supply the domestic market,[6] which offers an attractive alterna-

4. For detailed information, refer to the World Trade Organization: http://www.wto.org/english/docs_e/legal_e/16-tex_e.htm.
5. Gereffi and Frederick (2010) offer detailed descriptions of recent developments in global clothing supply networks.
6. In 2007, 56% of apparel production in China was destined for local consumers (Gereffi & Frederick, 2010).

tive for manufacturers. Moreover, consolidation and vertical integration characterize the supply networks. The most valuable activities relate to design, branding, and marketing, not to manufacturing per se. Prices and potential profits increase exponentially from manufacturing to the final sale to end users, and the downstream part of the supply network is the most interesting, profitable, and risky part of the clothing industry.

There is an incentive for the actors in the network to get their share of, or increase their profit from, sales to end users. Retailers are increasingly bypassing brand marketers and developing their own private labels, which they source directly from suppliers as a means to earn a share of the profits that brand marketers would otherwise extract. At the same time, brand marketers are involving themselves in retail through shop ownership and franchising to earn a share of the profits from sales to end users. The distinction between retailers and brand marketers is therefore becoming blurred. This context is the new arena for specialized intermediaries who can help coordinate sourcing activities and integrate functions among actors in the upstream and downstream parts of the clothing supply chain.

Sourcing Strategies Reflect Marketing Strategies

To varying degrees, the clothing industry is a buyer-driven and volatile industry due to the high fashion content of its products. Markets for white T-shirts, basic jeans, and cardigans are relatively stable, whereas those for tops and light dresses are much more responsive and vulnerable to sudden appearances and disappearances of trends. The pink embroidered top that was the top selling item yesterday may be out of fashion tomorrow. Moreover, the demand for fashion varies across end-user segments. Marketers targeting and serving first-mover segments of fashion aficionadas must be able to capture, process, and interpret trends faster than marketers serving mature customers with a classic taste in clothing. The latter type of customer is less interested in the flavour of the week than in a validated design that is distinct and durable. The sourcing strategies of brand marketers, retail chains, and independent retailers therefore differ depending on their business models, which reflect the specific combinations of types of garments, fashion content, and price that their targeted end-user segments demand.

As the clothing industry is relatively labour intensive, sourcing from developing countries with low factor costs offers potential cost savings. There are two ways to profit from these advantages: by either sourcing directly from supply markets or establishing one's own operations in low-cost countries. The choice between the two is a matter of governance modes: keeping control (hierarchy) versus simply reaping the price advantages of competition (market) (Williamson, 1979). However, not all activities are necessarily sourced from abroad. For example, it is not unusual for brand marketers to supplement/replace their in-house staff of designers with local freelance designers. This offers two advantages: first, the fixed cost of staff is replaced with the variable costs of freelance partners; in addition, new innovative ideas may be introduced as the freelance designers are connected to different networks, offering the potential for more varied interpretations of the same basic trends. Design is an activity that is difficult to source abroad without encountering problems related to cultural differences. The same basic trend tends to have a global impact, but the interpretation of the trend differs from place to place, simply because taste, for example, in terms of colours, patterns, and surface finish, differ from Scandinavia to Southern Europe and China. It is still relevant for marketers to consider sourcing both globally and domestically. Table 10.1 illustrates the basic combinations of location and governance modes.

Table 10.1. Location and governance: four strategies.

	Domestic	**Foreign**
Market	Domestic sourcing	Regional/global sourcing
Hierarchy	Domestic in-house activities	Relocation of production

Notably, the choice of location and governance must be made for each activity or function (e.g., design, production, and logistics), and within the same company, this choice may vary among brands reflecting different levels of fashion content and price sensitivity. The resulting activity structure is very complex. The choice between market and hierarchy when organizing production activities separates wholesalers into two distinct groups: brand manufacturers and brand marketers.[7] Both types of wholesalers often own or use more than one brand name. The brands are marketed to corporate chain/voluntary retail chains and independent shop owners. The difference between brand manufacturers and brand marketers concerns the extent to which they own manufacturing facilities, regardless of their location. Our investigation confirmed the tendency of brand manufacturers to give up manufacturing and instead source from suppliers and specialized manufacturers. Wholesalers therefore profit from low factor costs, not by owning manufacturing but by sourcing from global supply markets. By choosing the market solution instead of ownership, wholesalers avoid the risks related to ownership in geographically, culturally, and politically distant supply markets. However, global sourcing entails its own set of risks, complexities, and coordination challenges. These circumstances create the opportunity for sourcing intermediaries to specialize in various functions and activities that support wholesalers and retail chains trading in the global supply market for clothing. The intermediaries' business models mirror the customers' changed sourcing strategies and business models, which in turn reflect the end-user markets served by different wholesalers.

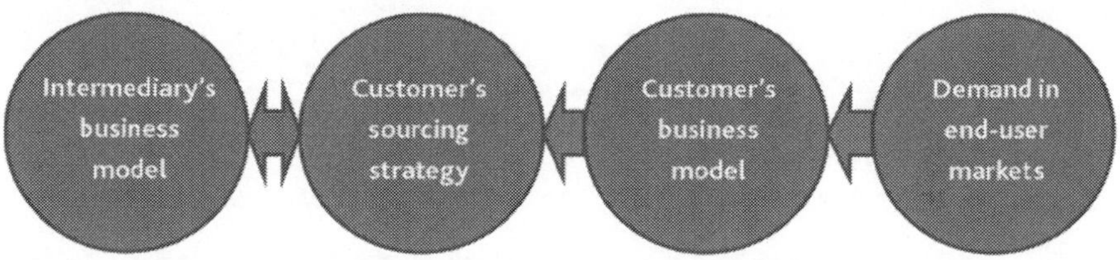

Figure 10.1. Changed intermediary business models as a result of changed customer sourcing strategies and business models.

7. The concepts of brand manufacturer and brand marketer are described in detail by Gereffi and Frederick (2010).

Sourcing Strategies and Globalization

Literature on the global clothing industry tends to focus on whether activities are performed domestically or abroad when categorizing sourcing strategies (e.g., Tran, 2008). However, as pointed out above, the buying company may source some activities domestically and others globally, and each activity in the supply chain may be made or bought, as discussed above. Our data indicate that the cut-make-trim (CMT) and source own design (SOD) sourcing strategies (described in Table 10.2) represent dominant activity patterns in the clothing industry.

Table 10.2. Dominant sourcing strategies in the clothing industry as combinations of make and buy.

	Sourcing Strategies		
Functions	**CMT: cut, make, and trim**	**SOD: sourcing own design**	**BPM: business process management**
Marketing/business concept	Make	Make	Make
Design	Make	Make	Buy
Logistics	Make	Make	Buy
Purchase of materials/fabrics	Make	Buy	Buy
Cutting	Buy	Buy	Buy
Sewing	Buy	Buy	Buy
Packaging	Buy	Buy	Buy
Quality control	Buy	Buy	Buy
Distribution	Make	Make	Make

These strategies were not developed specifically for global sourcing but have been applied in coordinating and integrating specialized domestic actors for several decades. Consequently, we focus on the make (i.e., in house) versus buy (i.e., source) aspect, not on geography, in describing sourcing strategies in Table 10.2. The above sourcing strategies are often described as patterns that gradually replace one another over time as buying companies become increasingly competent in sourcing. This is a process whereby the CMT strategy is gradually replaced by SOD, which is eventually replaced by a third strategy, business process management (BPM), in which only the marketing/business concept and distribution are handled in-house. We are not delving deeper into the evolutionary aspect here, but simply observe that there are three prevalent basic combinations of in-house and sourced activities in the clothing industry, and that these combinations of activities coexist across the industry and within large brand-marketing companies.

Though the differences between CMT, SOD, and BPM may initially appear small, they are actually significant. For brand marketers, the design is a distinct element of the brand and their dominant sourcing strategy is SOD; this also applies to large retail chains with private labels. SOD entails a decision not to source fabrics directly, but to have others buy fabrics as part of a 'package' of activities, which reduces complexity for the buying company. The buyers still approve the fabrics and consequently control designs very closely, but are not involved in coordinating fabric suppliers and clothing manufacturers.

However, the brand marketers' gradual involvement in retailing entails a shift of focus towards the consumer demand market. As consumer markets are characterized by an increasing demand for high fashion content across segments (i.e., high-, medium-, and low-priced clothing), marketers are increasingly choosing a BPM strategy for some of their brands or parts of their collections. BPM implies that all supply-related activities, including design, are sourced externally, and the focus is on the conceptualization and marketing of the brand. The decision to source design externally is a radical change, as design is regarded as a core element of a clothing brand. The choice of a BPM strategy allows the marketer (i.e., brand marketer or retail chain) to focus exclusively on the demand market (i.e., marketing/business concept and distribution). Consequently, another party must handle the functions related to the supply side of the clothing supply network. It is in coordinating these buying companies and their suppliers that novel types of sourcing intermediaries have found their specific roles in the global supply network. Each type of intermediary handles a distinct set of functions, creating efficient and effective links between the market strategies and sourcing strategies chosen by their customers. One increasingly important issue in such coordination is the ability to offer speed and timing.

Design, Timing, and the Distribution System

The challenge of capturing the trend and interpreting it into fashionable clothing is embedded in a complex interplay between brand marketers and independent retailers. The significance of interpreting and validating trends is evident in the distribution arrangements linking retailers and brand marketers. Brand marketers traditionally sold their collections before ordering from their suppliers, whereas retailers bought a clothing assortment in order to have something to offer their customers. The retailer thus invested in speculative inventory, whereas the brand marketer postponed and consequently evaded the speculative risk. Correct timing is a challenge in the fashion industries, as being too early or too late generates losses related to missing the market. Ordering too early involves the risk that the trend may change leading to obsolete styles. Being too late may result in an inability to receive deliveries in time due to deficient logistics capacity, especially in the case of small collections. The collection offered for sale to retailers by brand marketers represents a proposed interpretation of a trend. However, the interpretation is not validated before the retailers have made their choice among the styles and models offered by the brand marketer and have placed their orders. Having done so, they have indicated their preferred interpretation of the trend. They have committed themselves and have reserved liquidity to pay for the order. Still, the final test or validation of the brand marketers' interpretation takes place when the clothes are presented to the end users. Did the wholesaler interpret the trend in an attractive way, and did the retailer spot the styles and models suitable for its specific customer segment or not?

However, this arrangement is under 'attack' partly as a result of consolidation and vertical integration. Retail chains are ordering private label collections directly from manufacturers and suppliers, instead of profiting from the brand marketers' collections. Independent retailers profit from the offerings of specialized express wholesalers, who take the risk connected to speculative collections manufactured abroad and ready for immediate delivery (i.e., in two to three days) when presented to the customers. As these wholesalers enable their customers to postpone their purchasing to the very last moment, they help their customers reduce liquidity strain – a critical problem, especially during times of crisis. Equally important, the express wholesaler enables the retailer to postpone validating the collection offered. The retailer knows what is hot and what is not when ordering, and deliveries are nearly instant. The risk of missing the market is significantly reduced for the retailer, while it is correspondingly increased for this type of wholesaler.

The above descriptions illustrate how the clothing distribution system and supply network have changed and evolved in response to end-user demand and the involved actors' business models. Timing is now crucial in the clothing industry. Moreover, there is no one ideal way to set up a distribution system.[8] Production speed, timely delivery, and design are important criteria, in addition to capacity, correct quality/quantity, and attractive prices, when marketers choose supply network set-ups, which may include a sourcing intermediary.

Findings: Sourcing Intermediary Profiles

Global apparel sourcing used to be dominated by classic agents, who bought products from the suppliers and took title to the deliveries, which they resold to buyers at a profit. In terms of the sourcing strategies described in Table 10.2, they were not involved in any of the listed activities, but simply acted as brokers in the market. At the same time, they bridged distant supply and demand markets and ensured smooth communication and coordination between buyers and suppliers. With increased globalization, these types of intermediaries are, in their own words, a dying breed when it comes to sourcing ordinary clothing from China and other classic clothing supply markets. Buying companies have developed many of the competences that used to define the service offerings of sourcing intermediaries in the clothing industry. For example, our respondents uniformly said that the ability to source in China is common nowadays, as most purchasers in the industry have spent extended periods there. They have learned how to operate in this supply market and have built personal relationships with a number of suppliers, with whom they continue to do business. Note, however, that a few of these classic agents still have roles to play in *specialized* product markets. One of our respondents described such product specialization as follows:

8. See Hulthén and Mattsson (2010) for an interesting account of how distribution systems have evolved over time in the electronics industry.

> If you decide to include sunglasses in a summer collection, and you have no experience at all in sunglasses, it is better to find a competent specialized sourcing intermediary and profit from his services, instead of handling this activity on your own. It takes time to achieve sourcing competence for a specific product. Thus, the total cost of sourcing on your own will probably be higher than the total cost of purchasing through an intermediary.

However, apart from this limited population of specialized agents, our data indicate that two distinct sourcing intermediary profiles dominate, i.e., the production specialist and the full-service provider. These intermediaries can outperform the buying company for certain types of supplies. In the following section, these two profiles, their set-ups, and the division of labour between them, their customers, and suppliers, will be described in detail.

The Sourcing Intermediary as a Production Specialist

Production specialists are sourcing, production, and quality experts, but not designers. They act on behalf of their customers, who source their own designs (SOD), and specialize in a limited number of garments. Their core capabilities are related to in-depth knowledge of manufacturing processes, fabrics, and material processing, for example, various washing processes that are crucial for the final look of jeans. Production specialists are present in the supply market, either permanently or for extended periods of time. Their immersion in the supply market enables them to offer a portfolio of capable and reliable suppliers. At the same time, such intermediaries regard and define themselves as the customer's right hand in the supply market. Their customer relationships tend to be close and committed and they thoroughly know their customers' business models, brands, and designs. One respondent, a customer from a minor retail chain, explained that her relationship with the intermediary was so close and trusting that she felt as if he were part of her own organization. The perceived distance from the supply market is significantly reduced by intermediating production specialists.

Production specialists' more or less permanent presence is the key to their services. They regularly visit suppliers and obtain information, enabling them to find the right suppliers for their customers' specific needs and demands. Such presence also enables them to anticipate potential delivery shortages, for example, when a supplier receives a high-volume order from another customer in the period between delivering sales samples and actual production. In such situations, production specialists with trusting supplier relationships can redirect customer orders to other equally capable suppliers with vacant capacity. This is accepted by the suppliers in the production specialist's portfolio, because they know that next time they might profit from this practice and receive an order if a colleague/competitor has surplus demand. The coordination and integration of orders based on constantly monitoring a portfolio of well-established supplier relationships is a core activity of this intermediary profile. Coordination and integration are very much a matter of creating a good fit between a portfolio of specialized suppliers/manufacturers and customers. The customers' preferred price/quality ratio and the suppliers' capabilities must be compatible. Based on these coordinative and integrative functions, production specialists often possess knowledge of the network that is valuable for their partners in terms of future business opportunities.

Though suppliers are responsible for fabrics and trims, production specialists are closely involved in the selection process. Based on their knowledge of their customers' preferences, they can help suppliers select qualities and designs, for example, of trims and labels that suit individual customers. In addition, these intermediaries act as effective quality inspectors: They can inspect much more efficiently than can many large auditing companies, which can observe deviations from the defined quality but cannot judge whether or not they are of commercial significance. One production specialist offered the following example to illustrate the importance of knowing the customer and the customer's market: 'If the colour of the thread is a tiny bit different it will be of no importance to most customers, whereas few customers would accept even minor changes in the size, colour, or pattern of buttons, because the effect on the design is much greater'. The production specialist eliminates and prevents problems before they occur.

If a buying company chooses a SOD strategy because design is integral to the brand, but is reluctant to invest resources in sourcing part of the collection, the production specialist is an ideal partner. Based on this specialization in sourcing, quality control, and coordination/integration, the production specialist overcomes some of the problems with sourcing from abroad. The resulting division of labour between supplier, customer, and sourcing intermediary in a set-up involving a production specialist is presented in Table 10.3. Sourcing and coordination/integration have been singled out and added to the set of sourcing activities relating to CMT, SOD, and BPM, as presented in Table 10.2.

Table 10.3. Division of labour in a SOD sourcing set-up involving a production specialist.

Supplier	Intermediary	Customer
Purchase of materials/fabrics	Quality control	Market/business concept
Cutting	Sourcing	Design
Sewing	Coordination/integration between suppliers and customers	Logistics
Packing		Distribution

Many large brand marketers profit from the services offered by production specialists, despite having global sourcing departments of their own with knowledge of materials and processes. The production specialists are paid either a fixed fee or by commission for their services. The price paid when using a production specialist may well be higher than the customer would have paid if sourcing directly. However, the total costs are likely to be lower, because integration and coordination are distinct resource-demanding functions that must be considered and incorporated in the calculations when deciding the set-up. In addition, customers can judge for themselves whether the services received are worth the price paid, as production specialists operate with open calculations, which is highly unusual in this industry.

The Intermediary Acting as a Full-Service Provider

This type of intermediary offers a set-up for fast and flexible CMT production, which is otherwise difficult to arrange. The services are contingent on the intermediary's presence in the supply market. Two significant differences distinguish full-service providers from production specialists: 1) Production specialists are paid for the services provided, whereas full-service providers act in their own names and take title to the orders, i.e., they accept the risk on the deliveries they manage and supply to their customers; and 2) production specialists may inspire their customers by presenting fabrics and models that they have seen in suppliers' workshops, but they do not offer designs. This is what full-service providers offer their customers – designs and styles, delivered within six weeks or less from the day of ordering – but the full-service provider does not initiate production before ordering (this is the domain of express wholesalers – see above explanation).

The key to the full-service provider profile is a set-up of activities that reduces lead times significantly by combining presence in the supply markets and in the customers' demand markets. Design activities are based in the customers' demand markets, which overcomes culturally defined differences in taste. Likewise, sales offices are located in customers' demand markets, enabling full-service providers to serve their customers on a weekly basis. Apart from design and sales, all other activities are located abroad in low-cost supply markets such as China. These activities include all functions that customers, who have chosen a BPM strategy, do not handle themselves. Although the intermediary designers are based in the customers' markets, they travel widely and frequently in the supply markets, where they monitor and select fabrics and trims. The chosen fabrics and trims are incorporated into a wide range of basic styles sewn in the intermediaries' own workshops abroad, which function as preproduction laboratories. Based on the manufacture of styles, the intermediary preplans all activities related to the manufacture of each model/style. These include calculating the optimal use of fabrics, specifying trims, and planning and metering the number and timing of manufacturing processes on which price-calculations are made. The patterns and size tables are prepared likewise.

To further reduce time-to-market, the styles to be presented to potential customers are air-freighted to the sales offices, which have a constant flow enabling them to offer up to 50 new styles per week. When the customers come to the sales offices, they pick and choose among the models that fit their mood-boards.[9] They may ask for minor changes to these models, such as changing the sleeve length or replacing the fabric of one model with that used in another. The actual preparation and start-up of the production process is handled by internal sales assistants in China. As the fabric is defined, it can be booked half an hour after the customer has confirmed the order, and then the production planning is set in motion. Each assistant has a portfolio of customers to serve, and the relationships between these assistants and the customers facilitate smooth interaction, which further speeds the process.

One crucial link in reducing lead times is to have sufficient manufacturing capacity that satisfies customer quality demands. Full-service providers pre-book generic production capacity from suppliers, based on the estimated total capacity needed for expected orders. The final definitions of specific orders can then be postponed to a very late point in the production cycle without risking manufacturing shortages. This is a risky part of the service providers' business, but it enables them to offer flexible capacity at favourable prices even for small collections, for which it would otherwise be difficult to obtain production capacity. Finally, the service providers monitor and control quality. In addition, they organize air freight, which can be acquired at a competitive price because it is booked well in advance and specified at the latest possible moment before departure. This unique combination of logistics, design, and production set-up, designed to facilitate speed and flexibility, is the core of the full-service provider's business model. It is an optimal fit for customers who choose a BPM sourcing strategy for some of their brands. However, it is only suitable for garments below a certain size and weight, for which the additional cost of air freight is worth paying in exchange for speed and flexibility.

Table 10.4 presents the division of labour between a BPM sourcing customer, the full-service provider, and supplier in this set-up. Whereas sourcing, integration, and coordination activities are singled out in the case of production specialists, these activities are integral to the full-service providers' own purchasing and sourcing function. They do not

9. A graphic interpretation of trends in terms of colours, patterns, themes, and sketched designs.

handle these activities on behalf of other actors, but in their own names and at their own risk.

Table 10.4. Division of labour in a BPM sourcing set-up involving a full-service provider.

Supplier (manufacturer)	**Intermediary (full-service provider)**	**Customer (BPM sourcing)**
Cutting	Design	Market/business concept
Sewing	Purchase of materials/fabrics	Distribution
Packaging	Quality control	
	Logistics	

Customers who prefer to source their own designs can sometimes also profit from full-service providers, whose services can reduce search times for fabrics, trims, and trend interpretations. Moreover, the set-up enables full-service providers to present very precisely what they can offer as suppliers of clothing manufactured abroad. This is exactly how these intermediaries perceive themselves: As similar to the local domestic suppliers who operated 20-30 years ago. The only difference is that today full-service providers source and manufacture abroad and have relocated most of their activities to these supply markets. In doing so, full-service providers have reduced the risk and complexity involved in profiting from distant supply markets for their customers.

The Changed Clothing Industry and the Sourcing Intermediary

With considerable cultural competence, a presence on global markets, and established relationships with global suppliers and other key actors, many companies have found that the classic agent has become obsolete. Sourcing intermediaries are still widely used, but their profiles have changed as a result of the improved global sourcing competence of clothing companies and the changes in consumer market characteristics. Clothing companies have cultivated an ability to differentiate their sourcing strategies, meaning that for one brand, for example, they may run several different sourcing set-ups. Many supplies may be sourced through a clothing company's own sourcing offices located at home or abroad, but sourcing intermediaries are still needed for certain types of supplies. Even relatively large buying companies cannot profitably invest in global sourcing capacity for each and every type of supply, making it cheaper from a total cost perspective to use an intermediary. In the clothing industry, the question is not so much whether or not an intermediary should be used in distant supply markets. It is more a question of splitting up an increasingly complex and comprehensive product portfolio and matching different consumer market needs with different sourcing set-ups, some of which include the profitable choice of a sourcing intermediary.

What Sourcing Managers can Learn from Clothing Industry Practices

Our study has demonstrated that sourcing managers who exclude intermediaries on principle may be missing out on valuable opportunities. These intermediaries can allow smaller companies to profit from low-cost supply markets without establishing international purchasing offices with high fixed costs. Even when companies are established and experienced in global sourcing, it might pay off to involve a sourcing intermediary for some types of supplies. To determine the real costs of buying directly versus involving a sourcing intermediary, managers must apply a total cost perspective and attempt to identify all relevant costs. If decisions are made merely by adding the intermediary's fees to the direct purchase price, then the intermediary solution can obviously not compete with direct sourcing. However, if the buying company's costs of a sourcing office or sourcing manager, quality management, logistics, and supply market research are all taken into account, then the sourcing intermediary is a highly competitive choice for many types of supplies.

Our findings indicate that, in particular, the production specialist and full-service provider play important roles in clothing industry supply networks. Similar intermediary roles may be equally valuable in other industries as well. But in order to recognize the potential offered by these actors, organizations are required to improve in three critical sourcing areas:

1. Implementing total cost accounting, including systems and procedures for tracking, documenting, and calculating all costs of acquiring a product internationally. We know that keeping track of each and every cost is perhaps unrealistic, but companies must do their best to go at least part way. Without some indication of total cost, the sourcing intermediary will not be 'discovered' to be a valuable option.
2. Loosening faulty ingrained assumptions regarding the feasibility of involving sourcing intermediaries. Some of our intermediary respondents described how using the term 'middleman' when describing their competences would cause customers to dismiss them right away.
3. Tracking the effects of decisions on the sales/marketing strategies and efforts of the company and attempting to align market demands with sourcing set-ups. Involving a full-service provider may be the most expensive option, even from a total cost perspective, but it may allow a company to satisfy the demands of the consumer market for diverse designs and fast delivery.

Finally, sourcing managers from other industries can learn from the highly complex and differentiated sourcing strategies and network structures of clothing companies. Many clothing industry sourcing managers have an impressive overview of their portfolio of suppliers, enabling them to use many different supply network set-ups within the same company, each optimized to meet market demands at the lowest total cost. 'One size fits all' strategies must be abandoned and the strengths of various well-considered strategies be exploited instead.

Conclusion

The literature has been relatively silent regarding sourcing intermediaries. Therefore, we asked 20 highly experienced global sourcing specialists in the clothing industry – one of the most globalized industries – about their experience with sourcing intermediaries. Their unanimous opinion was that specialized sourcing intermediaries generate value for buying companies in the sourcing of certain types of products. We provide evidence supporting the utility of two of these sourcing intermediary profiles. First, the production specialist has specialized in certain products or supply markets and can therefore ensure quality and delivery and provide other services that the buying company cannot itself provide for a reasonable resource outlay. Second, the full-service provider can deliver a portfolio of clothes of various designs at high speed to satisfy consumer demand at a highly competitive cost. These two sourcing intermediary roles illustrate how intermediaries have adapted to the evolved clothing industry characteristics of today, developing specialized sets of services that provide both their customers and themselves with improved profits. They are valuable options for supplying certain types of products, even for large companies with a global presence and sufficient experience to handle bridge building among multiple supply and demand markets on their own.

We believe that sourcing managers from other industries can be inspired by and learn from the clothing industry. An insight of specific significance is how multiple coexisting sourcing set-ups offer the potential to satisfy apparently conflicting demands, such as profiting from low-cost global suppliers without compromising speed and flexibility. Moreover, our study illustrates how specialized sourcing intermediaries can adapt to the evolving context of an industry, supporting their customers' value creation to an extent exceeding the cost of their involvement. For many companies, sourcing intermediaries may not be needed to provide bridge-building services. They are, however, valuable options for supplying certain types of products, so sourcing managers should abandon their reflexive urge to avoid intermediaries and consider them as an option for global sourcing.

References

Alderson, W. & Martin, M.W. (1965). Towards a Formal Theory of Transactions and Transvections. *Journal of Marketing Research*, 2(2), 117-127.

Anderson, P. & Anderson, E. (2002). The New E-commerce Intermediaries. *MIT Sloan Management Review*, 43(4), 53-62.

Balderston, F.E. (1958). Communication Networks in Intermediate Markets. *Management Science*, 4(2), 154-171.

Belevina, E. & Girotra, K. (2010). *Sourcing through Intermediaries*. Working Paper, INSEAD.

Belevina, E. & Girotra, K. (2012). The Relational Advantages of Intermediation. *Management Science*, 58(9), 1614-1631.

Bucklin, L.P. (1965). Postponement, Speculation and the Structure of Distribution Channels. *Journal of Marketing Research*, 2(1), 26-31.

Casson, M. (1997). Institutional Economics and Business History: a Way Forward. *Business History*, 39(4), 151-171.

Cho, J. & Kang, J. (2001). Benefits and Challenges of Global Sourcing: Perceptions of US Apparel Retail Firms. *International Marketing Review*, 18(5), 542-561.

Ellis, P.D. (2003). Social Structure and Intermediation: Market-Making Strategies in International Exchange. *Journal of Management Studies*, 40(7), 1683-1708.

Ellis, P.D. (2006). Factors Affecting the Termination Propensity of Inter-Firm Relationships. *European Journal of Marketing*, 40(11/12), 1169-1177.

Ferber, R. & McVey, P. (1960). Are Channels of Distribution What the Textbooks Say? *Journal of Marketing*, 24(3), 61-65.

Fung, P.K.O. & Chen, I.S.N. (2010). Human Capital for Supply Chain Management Capabilities: a Study of International Trade Intermediaries. *International Journal of Logistics: Research and Applications*, 13(1), 1-12.

Fung, P.K.O., Chen, I.S.N. & Yip, L.S.C (2007). Relationships and Performance of Trade Intermediaries: an Exploratory Study. *European Journal of Marketing*, 41(1), 159-180.

Gereffi, G. & Frederick S. (2010). The Global Apparel Value-chain, Trade, and the Crisis: Challenges and Opportunities for Developing Countries, in Cattaneo, O., Gereffi, G. & Staritz, C. (eds.), *Global Value-chains in a Postcrisis World: a Development Perspective*, The World Bank, Washington D.C.

Horn, P., Schiele, H. & Werner, W. (2013). The 'Ugly Twins': Failed Low-Wage-Country Sourcing Projects and Their Expensive Replacements. *Journal of Purchasing and Supply Management*, 19, 27-38.

Hulthén, K. & Mattsson, L.G. (2010). Distribution Network Dynamics: Evolution in the PC Distribution Network. *IMP Journal*, 3(4), 170-193.

Magretta, J. (1998). Fast, Global, and Entrepreneurial: Supply Chain Management, Hong Kong Style. An Interview with Victor Fung. *Harvard Business Review*, September-October, 102-114.

Mallen, B. (1976). Understanding Marketing Channels. *European Journal of Marketing*, 10(2), 3-24.

Nassimbeni, G. & Sartor, M. (2007). Sourcing in China: a Typology. *International Journal of Production Economics*, 107, 333-349.

Peng, M.W. & York, A.S. (2001). Behind Intermediary Performance in Export Trade: Transactions, agents, and Resources. *Journal of International Business Studies*, 32(2), 327-346.

Popp, A. (2000). 'Swamped in Information but Starved of Data': Information and Intermediaries in Clothing Supply Chains. *Supply Chain Management: an International Journal*, 5(3), 151-161.

Song, N., Platts, K. & Bance, D. (2007). Total Acquisition Cost of Overseas Outsourcing/Sourcing: a Framework and a Case Study. *Journal of Manufacturing Technology Management*, 18(7), 858-875.

Weber, M., Hiete, M., Lauer, L. & Rentz, O. (2010). Low Cost Country Sourcing and Its Effects on the Total Cost of Ownership Structure for a Medical Devices Manufacturer. *Journal of Purchasing and Supply Management*, 16, 4-16.

Williamson, O.E. (1979). Transaction-Cost Economics: the Governance of Contractual Relations. *Journal of Law and Economics*, 22(2), 233-261.

Tran, Y. (2008). Fashion in the Danish Experience Economy: Challenges for Growth. Imagine and Samfundslitteratur, Frederiksberg.

CHAPTER 11

Models of International Entrepreneurship

Morten Rask and Per Servais

International entrepreneurship (IE), which entails new managerial mindsets and ways of framing the challenges of organizing and managing business activities with a global outlook, has received increased attention from a number of researchers over the last decade. Some of their research has examined the early years of international new ventures, stressing the antecedents of and the necessary and sufficient conditions for their emergence (Autio et al., 2000; Chetty & Campbell-Hunt, 2004; Madsen & Servais, 1997; Zahra, 2005). To investigate how international new ventures are established and developed, this chapter reviews extant analytical models of this phenomenon.

'Born-global' enterprises are often established by founders with an explicitly global mindset from the outset (Weerawardena, Mort, Liesch & Knight, 2007), and studying them entails understanding the fundamental transitions of processes, structures, and organizational mindsets at several organizational levels. New managerial mindsets and ways of framing the challenges of organizing, managing, and governing Danish business activities with a global outlook are required.

An international new venture has been defined as a 'business organization that, from inception, seeks to derive significant competitive advantage from the use of resources and the sale of outputs in multiple countries' (Oviatt & McDougal, 1994, p. 9). Due to increasing globalization, we argue that it is particularly important to understand such firms because they represent the new normal in firm internationalization. Using a new longitudinal dataset of the population of start-ups located in Denmark and established between 1995 and 2006, Choquette et al. (2014)

found that 'born-globals' – i.e., firms that within three years of inception export at least 25% of their turnover amounting to around 4% of all start ups, were found to have 79% higher turnover, 60% more employees, and to export to seven more markets than all other types of start-ups (Choquette et al., 2014).

IE research is often regarded as starting with Oviatt and McDougall's (1994) seminal article on international new ventures (Erkko Autio, 2005; Zahra, 2005), which defined the antecedents of as well as the necessary and sufficient conditions for the emergence of 'born-globals' (Madsen & Servais, 1997) or international new ventures (Oviatt & McDougall, 1994). The phenomenon of accelerated internationalization was seen as related primarily to new developments in markets, technologies, and people's capabilities. The entrepreneurship perspective had already been applied by McDougall (1989), but early IE research was dominated by international business viewpoints, which emphasized the time elapsed between new firm establishment and the first international market entry. Since the research fields were young, greater cross-fertilization between international business and entrepreneurship research was called for (e.g., Madsen & Servais, 1997). McDougall and Oviatt (2000, p. 903) then defined IE as 'innovative, proactive and risk-seeking behaviors across borders'. As Zahra and George have also (2002) pointed out, the field lacks definitional rigour, and there is no reason to assume that IE is a phenomenon limited to small firms. 'Indeed, McDougall and Oviatt's (2000) definition of IE is in fact independent of firm size, whereas the 1994 definition of IE (Oviatt & McDougall, 1994) was taken as an empirical 'blueprint' for the many subsequent definitions that focus on how small and young new ventures internationalize' (Keupp & Gassman, 2009, p. 617). Zahra and George (2002) stress the gaps in our understanding of IE that need to be addressed by future research. They suggest that the IE phenomenon should essentially be regarded as independent of firm size and firm age because neither mainstream IB theory nor entrepreneurship theory is confined to specificities of firm size or the micro level of analysis.

Not all researchers have attempted to formulate models based on their findings. This is interesting, because model formulation tells us something about a research area, for example, the definition of the studied phenomenon and the method used to obtain information (Coviello & Jones, 2004). The present paper reviews models used to describe and explain the establishment and development of international new ventures, grouping these models into several 'meta-models'. Rather than taking a partial and/or prejudiced view of IE, these meta-models integrate partial theories and fragments in a more logically connected theoretical area within IE research. In essence, we try to achieve a middle-range approach (Bourgeois, 1979), contrary to the development of general theory. Our intention is to conduct a systematic review that recognizes the various types of research and models. In this review, we focus on the 'model' as an ideal that enables reasoning within an idealized logical framework (Rask, Håkonsson & Strandskov, 2008) to simplify target phenomena whose complexity would otherwise make systematic inquiry impossible (Seelos, 2010). More precisely, a model is a simplified image – an abstraction – of an actual or imagined reality in the form of connected relationships between studied factors.

In this chapter, we focus on explanatory schematic models whose primary purpose is to investigate *how and why international new ventures are established and developed* and which also present answers as schematics comprising boxes, arrows, and letters (Aronsson, Hagg & Wiedersheim-Paul, 1973). Based on these models, theory can be built (Doz, 2011), as models and theories are inseparable (Whetten, 1989). Models benefit researchers because 'visual representation often clarifies the author's thinking and increases the reader's comprehension. In particular, formal models aid theory developers and users to assess the balance between parsimony and completeness' (Whetten, 1989, p. 491). This chapter is not just another review of the field of IE, but a review of models of the phenomenon of infant firms that operate internationally immediately on, or soon after, their inception. It also aims to comprehensively review the models applied to such organizations in the literature from the early 1990s to the present. Based on our review of models, we see a potential for theory development, as many of the reviewed models seem to merge into three meta-models depicting the activities and loci of such firms (Figure 11.1), the motivating factors that give rise to such firms (Figure 11.2), and their growth modalities and strategies (Figure 11.3).

Methodology

Our conceptual review, which 'aims to synthesise areas of conceptual knowledge that can contribute to a better understanding of the issues' (Jesson, Matheson & Lacy, 2011 p. 15), was inspired by Zahra and George (2002) and Rialp, Rialp, and Knight (2005). In reviewing the models, we discuss their foci, types, dimensions, and major conclusions. After screening the reviewed papers, the next step was to describe each model they presented. The *focus* of a model is found in its relationship to the research question concerning how and why international new ventures are established and developed. The *major conclusions* follow up on this focus and suggest directions for future research. We find different *types of models*, such as quantitatively tested models, qualitative case study models, and conceptual models based on theoretical reviews, each with different types of embedded logic. Finally, we also investigate the *dimensions of the models* that relate to the content and the *variables of the models* used to build their logical framework. We used the abovementioned characteristics to create meta-models.

Data

For the review, we used Business Source Premier as it is one of the most popular business research databases, covering the full text of more than 2,200 journals. Moreover, according to the owners of the database, journal ranking studies find its full-text coverage, in all business disciplines, better than that of other databases. We regard peer-reviewed work as certified knowledge that is likely to have the most important impact on a given field (Podsakoff, MacKenzie, Bachrach & Podsakoff, 2005). We accordingly identified the peer-reviewed articles via Business Source Premier by searching the text of article titles and abstracts for ('Born-global' OR 'born-globals' OR 'born-globals' OR 'International New Venture' OR 'International New Ventures' OR 'INV' OR 'International Entrepreneurship' OR 'IE') AND ('model' or 'models' or 'framework' or 'frameworks'). This search identified 84 articles in total. After pre-review screening, we excluded certain articles because they did not present their own distinct models or frameworks. This resulted in the review of only 33 papers, as we chose to focus on the minority of papers that actually presented newly formulated models.

Table 11.1. Summary of papers presenting relevant models.

Publication date	Authors	Research approach	Type of model
MAR 1994	Oviatt & Mcdougall	Literature review	Matrix
DEC 1997	Madsen & Servais	Case study	Multi-stimuli
JUN 2003	Dimitratos & Plakoyiannaki	Literature review	Matrix
SEP 2003	Andersson & Wictor	Case study	Multi-stimuli
DEC 2003	Bell, Mcnaughton, Young, & Crick	Literature review	Stimulus-response
MAR 2004	Knight & Cavusgil	Quantitative tests	Stimulus-response
AUG 2004	Hashai & Almor	Quantitative tests	Matrix
DEC 2004	Knight, Madsen, & Servais	Quantitative tests	Stimulus-response
APR 2005	Rialp, Rialp, & Knight	Literature review	Multi-stimuli
MAY 2005	Jones & Coviello	Literature review	Stimulus-response
SEP 2005	Oviatt & McDougall	Literature review	Stimulus-response
SEP 2005	Evangelista	Case study	Other
JUL 2006	Rialp & Rialp	Quantitative tests	Stimulus-response
JUL 2006	Hallbäck & Larimo	Case study	Matrix
OCT 2006	Mort & Weerawardena	Case study	Stimulus-response
JUL 2007	Fernhaber, Mcdougall, & Oviatt	Literature review	Multi-stimuli
SEP 2007	Weerawardena, Mort, Liesch, & Knight	Literature review	Stimulus-response
SEP 2007	Kuivalainen, Sundqvist, & Servais	Quantitative tests	Stimulus-response
SEP 2007	Gassmann & Keupp	Case study	Stimulus-response
NOV 2007	Aspelund, Madsen, & Moen	Literature review	Stimulus-response

Publication date	Authors	Research approach	Type of model
NOV 2007	Laanti, Gabrielsson, & Gabrielsson	Case study	Stimulus-response
DEC 2007	Freeman & Cavusgil	Case study	Other
MAR 2008	Styles & Genua	Case study	Stimulus-response
MAR 2008	Han Mary	Literature review	Stimulus-response
MAR 2008	Di Gregorio, Musteen, & Thomas	Literature review	Matrix models
JUN 2008	Gabrielsson & Pelkonen	Case study	Multi-stimuli
JUN 2008	Thai & Chong	Case study	Multi-stimuli
DEC 2008	Blesa, Monferrer, Nauwelaerts, & Ripolls	Quantitative tests	Stimulus-response
APR 2009	Boehe	Case study	Stimulus-response
JUN 2009	Keupp & Gassmann	Literature review	Stimulus-response
AUG 2009	Mets	Case study	Multi-stimuli
FEB 2010	Freeman, Hutchings, Lazaris, & Zyngier	Literature review	Stimulus-response
NOV 2010	Amal & Filho	Case study	Stimulus-response

As Table 11.1 illustrates, three research approaches (i.e., 13 literature reviews, 14 case studies, and six quantitative tests) were used to develop and/or test models of IE. Chronologically, the three research approaches were distributed fairly evenly, more or less following each other in sequence, starting with literature reviews, followed by case studies, a quantitatively tested study, and so forth.

Next we synthesize the various models according to their conceptual contents, seeking a better understanding by grouping the models into three groups according to model type, namely, matrix, multi-stimuli, and stimulus-response models. Keeping the models' diverse characteristics in mind, we see a solid basis for creating meta-models of IE. We continue describing the identified model types, often in greater detail than the individual models, using details from the individual models to construct them. After an explorative review of the papers, we define three types of models as follows: *matrix models* delineate various types of firms using IE; *multi-stimuli models* explore various factors influencing IE; while *stimulus-response models* explore the antecedents/drivers, mediators, and performance of IE. The stimulus-response models are far more popular than the other types of models.

Defining Types of International Ventures

Oviatt and McDougall (1994) point out that questions such as why firms are born as international new ventures as well as what their role is on the international market merit further research. The birth of a new venture is explained not only by entrepreneurs' innovative ideas, but also possibly by larger firms' outsourcing decisions and by ideas conceived by existing firms. Different firm origins may determine the different roles of international new ventures and the variations in their relationships with other firms, for example, in terms of interdependence versus dependence on other firms or mutual interdependence within a group of firms. Furthermore, the birth and growth of an international new venture may depend on external facilitating factors (e.g., information and communication technologies) and on factors closely related to the characteristics of the entrepreneur and other business partners (e.g., prior international experience). This suggests that there are four types of new ventures: export/import start-ups, multinational traders (with a multi-domestic approach), geographically focused start-ups (with foreign operations beyond exports), and global start-ups. Of these four types, the first two have not interested researchers of new international ventures as much as have the last two. In the case of firms of the first two types, logistics is the primary activity that is coordinated across countries, so their survival and growth can be understood through well-documented research into exports and early internationalization (Andersson, 2000).

Of the last two types of firms, global start-ups have received the most conceptual and empirical attention in the IE literature, and they will also be the focus of this research. Knight and Cavusgil (1996) called these firms 'born-globals' and many others have adopted this term (Chetty & Campbell-Hunt, 2004; Rialp, et al., 2005). Furthermore, research has discovered new international ventures whose spread fits the definition of geographically focused start-up firms. Researchers from Europe in particular have noted that some born regional or born international firms internationalize rapidly within Europe but do not globalize to other continents to any great extent (Kuivalainena, Sundqvista, & Servais, 2007).

Oviatt and McDougall's (1994) model uses two dimensions that depend on whether a firm coordinates 1) few or many value-chain activities across 2) few or many countries. These two dimensions lead to four types of international new ventures: export/import start-ups (i.e., with few activities coordinated in few countries), multinational trading start-ups (i.e., with few activities coordinated in many countries), geographically focused start-ups (i.e., with many activities coordinated in few countries), and global start-ups (i.e., with many activities coordinated in many countries) (Oviatt & McDougall, 1994). Gregorio, Musteen, and Thomas (2008) consider the firm's opportunities to combine resources and/or markets across borders, and identify four types of new ventures: domestic new ventures, cross-border resource integration, accelerated international sales, and international resource and market combination. Hallbäck and Larimo (2006) use two main classification criteria: 1) does the firm internationally coordinate value-chain activities and (2) in how many countries does the firm have value-chain activities. In studying the internationalization of Finnish firms, Hallbäck and Larimo (2006) found that firms move along the second dimension, starting in few and finally encompassing many countries, depending somewhat on the distance to the foreign markets.

In other words, based on the literature review, the matrix meta-model defines types of international entrepreneurial firms along two dimensions: 1) the degree of geographic diversification and 2) the extent of cross-border coordination of resources and markets.

Geographic diversification			
	High	Multinational trader promoting international sales	Global start-up coordinating international resources and markets
	Low	Domestic new ventures	Import start-up integrating resources across borders
		Low	**High**
		Cross-border coordination of resources and markets	

Figure 11.1. A matrix model of international entrepreneurship.

Multi-Stimuli Modes of International Entrepreneurship

Firms internationalize immediately on their inception or in their first years of existence for various reasons, including the internationalization – or even globalization – of markets, competition, and business networks, as well as organizational issues, such as strategic focus, product specialization, managerial capabilities, and international entry modes. These two major themes – the external environmental factors and the internal organizational and managerial factors influencing IE – have significant implications for how IE strategies are defined with regard to internationalization speed, extent, and scope.

Based on their review of empirical evidence concerning 'born-globals', Madsen and Servais (1997) find that the background of the new venture's founder is crucial to understanding the born-global phenomenon. Their findings are supported by Oviatt and McDougall (1995) and Burgel and Murray (1998). Madsen and Servais (1997) emphasize that factors such as the entrepreneur's education and international experience from former jobs, positions, and living abroad shape the founder's mind and 'decrease the psychic distance to specific product markets significantly' (p. 567). From an entrepreneurial perspective, it should be added that these factors may even create windows of opportunity that spur the founding of the venture. Madsen and Servais (1997) also report on several studies of the role played by the social and professional network of the entrepreneur before and in the years following the birth of the venture.

Rialp, Rialp, and Knight (2005) highlight three key issues, i.e., 1) firms' intangible resource base (i.e., organizational, technological, relational, and human capital), 2) firm-specific international capability (i.e., specialized know-how, core competences, internationally-oriented routines, lack of domestic path dependencies, and absorptive capacity), and 3) the external environment (i.e., type of sector, geographic context, and local and international networks), as influencing the strategic behaviour of early internationalizing firms in terms of pace of internationalization, non-gradual extension of internationalization, enhanced scope of the firm's international strategy, and sustainable competitive advantage abroad. Similarly, Thai and Chong (2008) argue that firm resources and capabilities (i.e., size, international market knowledge, product, technology, entrepreneurship orientation, and network) together with founder/manager characteristics (i.e., age, education, experience in founding businesses, industry and technical experience, international experience, network, entrepreneurial inclination, and global vision) have an effect on the formation of born-globals, while industry structure and attributes (i.e., buyer preferences, market conditions, and industry pressure) and socioeconomic infrastructure (i.e., information and communication technology, production methods, transportation, logistics, trade and investment barriers, financial markets, and investment capital) are factors that influence the formation of born-globals. Fernhaber, McDougall, and Oviatt (2007) emphasize the complex role of a specific environmental factor, namely, the structure of a new venture's chosen industry – i.e., the industry's evolution, concentration, knowledge-intensity, local internationalization, global integration, specialized venture capital, and appropriability regime – in understanding the internationalization of new ventures. Gabrielsson and Pelkonen (2008) focus on the macro environment and the industry's (in this case, digital media) globalization drivers together with the resources and networking that create the international business strategies for addressing markets, operational expansion and contraction, cooperation, and internal operations. Andersson and Wictor (2003) summarize various factors, stressing that globalization, entrepreneurs and their networks, and industry-specific factors foster born-global firms, so that they rapidly create expansive global markets (Mets, 2009).

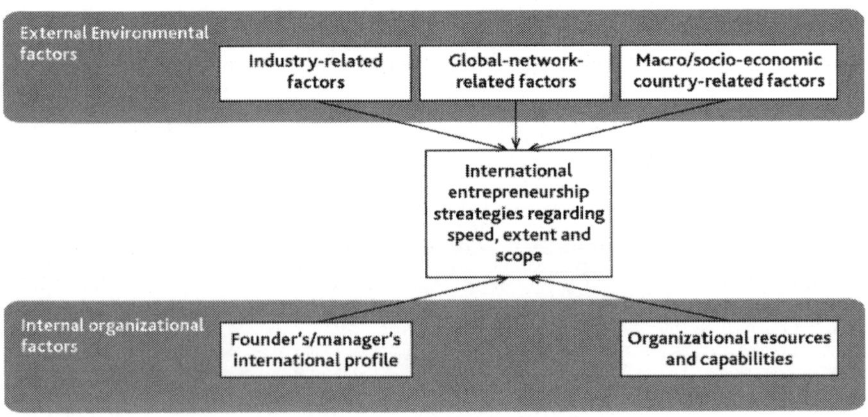

Figure 11.2. A multi-stimuli model of international entrepreneurship.

The above figure shows the reasons given for why firms' internationalization varies immediately after firm inception or in the first years of existence. The external environmental factors and the internal organizational and managerial factors have significant implications for how IE strategies are defined in terms of internationalization speed, extent, and scope.

Stimulus-Response Model of International Entrepreneurship

The focus of earlier research into international new ventures can mainly be divided into four dimensions of rapid internationalization: 1) extent/degree of internationalization of a firm's sales, 2) time elapsed between year of foundation and first foreign sales, 3) scope (i.e., the number and diversity of target countries/markets), and 4) drivers or antecedents (e.g., managerial and firm characteristics) (see, e.g., Bloodgood, Sapienza, & Almeida, 1996; Knight & Cavusgil, 1996; Zahra & George, 2002). As mentioned above, the founder's perceptions are pivotal. Knight and Cavusgil (2004) stress that born-global firms' entrepreneurial orientation is associated with an innovative and proactive approach to internationalization. In addition, the development of new knowledge occurs when there are few or no existing organizational routines to unlearn (Autio, Sapienza & Almeida, 2000; Cohen & Levinthal, 1990). Furthermore, Knight and Cavusgil (2004) emphasize that having an international entrepreneurial orientation implies that born-global firms make the leap into international markets because of unique entrepreneurial competences and outlooks stemming from previous experience. We have tried to encapsulate this process in the model below. The figure shows the antecedents/drivers of IE mediators and performance identified by reviewing the stimulus-response models reported in the literature. External environmental and internal organizational factors defining the founder's/manager's international profile are understood as the antecedents/drivers of IE. Market- and product-focused knowledge development and global networking resulting in marketing competences and market orientation as well as knowledge-intensive, innovative differentiated-quality products moderate those antecedents/drivers. The international performance of IE is evaluated in light of the global strategies for internationalization speed, extent, and scope.

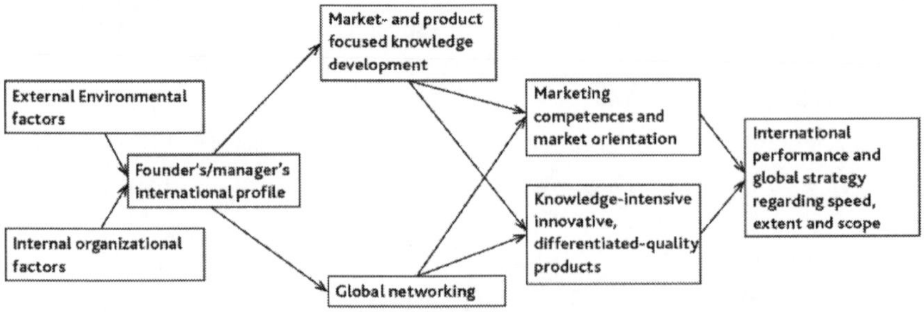

Figure 11.3. A stimulus-response model of international entrepreneurship.

The stimulus-response model is based on conceptual models from the literature review as well as on case studies and papers based on quantitatively tested stimulus-response models. The first studied literature review contributing to the stimulus-response model (Bell, McNaughton, Young & Crick, 2003) found that the external environment (i.e., favourable/unfavourable domestic/foreign market conditions, industry/sector trends, and vicious/virtuous economic cycle), inward technology transfer, and the manager's prior international experience, together with the internal environment (i.e., the firm's human and financial resources, management competences, and knowledge base), shape the managers' characteristics and mental model. The performance criteria are internationalization timing, state of internationalization, knowledge as source of competitive advantage, lead market, and lead home market. For the performance factor accelerated internationalization (i.e., internationalization speed, extent, and scope), Weerawardena, Mort, Liesch, and Knight (2007) regard aspects of the owner's/manager's profile (i.e., international entrepreneurial orientation, geocentric mindset, prior international experience, and learning orientation) as antecedent factors, the mediators being market-focused learning capability (i.e., acquisition, dissemination, unlearning, and integration of market information), internally-focused learning capability (i.e., acquisition, dissemination, unlearning, and integration of technological and non-technological issues), networking capability (i.e., knowledge acquisition and development of complementary resources), marketing capability (i.e., niche market access and global positioning), and knowledge-intensive products (i.e., technological and non-technological). Aspelund, Madsen, and Moen (2007) present and discuss findings related to the antecedent factors affecting firm founding, organizational features, and environmental issues and their influence on market strategy and firm performance, where the international marketing strategy addresses the speed of the internationalization process, niche versus commodity focus, international intensity versus global diversity, and market selection, including the elements of psychic distance, entry mode decisions, etc. Freeman, Hutchings, Lazaris, and Zyngier (2010) note that social networks are drivers of the creation of relational trust and interfirm partnerships in new businesses; this develops tacit knowledge and absorptive capacity, resulting in the faster development of new knowledge in small born-global firms.

In the first case-study-based stimulus-response model paper, Mort and Weerawardena (2006) argue that behavioural characteristics (i.e., proactiveness, innovativeness, and risk-taking) are closely connected to the drivers of fundamental and secondary networking capability (i.e., resource configurations, build, reconfiguring, adding, and deleting). Together with the speed of internationalization (i.e., market exploitation) and knowledge-intensive products (i.e., technological knowledge and market trend knowledge), these behavioural characteristics and networking capability drivers are the mediators of international market performance (i.e., market entry and/or market development). Gassmann and Keupp (2007) find the uniqueness of specialization in international value-chains, homogeneity of products or services, uniqueness of innovation, and scope and extent of intellectual property rights (IPR) protection to be antecedent factors for the mediator rent-generating potential of specialized knowledge. In addition, embeddedness in global communities and networks, geographical location, availability of resources 'on demand', and scope and extent of IPR protection are antecedent factors for the mediator rent-realizing potential of networks. That, together with the mediator rent-generating potential of specialized knowledge, results in the early and rapid internationalization of SMEs, which is the dependent performance variable. Laanti, Gabrielsson, and Gabrielsson (2007) find global and industry-specific environmental-enabling factors to be the drivers of the mediators (i.e., the founder's/manager's international experience, skills, entrepreneurship, innovation, network, and finances), resulting in performance in terms of the implementation of globalization strategies for products, operations, and markets. Boehe (2009) finds that antecedents/drivers (i.e., SME executives' foreign market knowledge, international work experience, language skills, and research partnerships) create the IE, which is positively related to propensity to export.

The first quantitatively tested stimulus-response model was a comparative study of the key marketing dimensions of born-globals in Denmark and the USA: customer focus was the driver; marketing competence, product quality, and product differentiation were the mediators; and international performance was the performance effect (Knight, Madsen, & Servais, 2004). However, other quantitative models were developed after that. Rialp and Rialp (2006) found that intellectual, organizational, relational, and human capital are drivers creating the firm's capabilities and core competences, which are mediators of faster and more successful born-global performance. Kuivalainen, Sundqvist, and Servais (2007) found the antecedents/drivers of born-global strategy to be 'firm resources and founder/manager characteristics' such as international entrepreneurial orientation, while the mediator was the born-global strategy or pathway (i.e., internationalization scale, scope, timing, and speed). The factors affecting export performance were the degree of born-globalness, as well as the competitive advantages and outcomes of born-global strategy. The latest quantitatively tested stimulus-response model identified in this literature review found early international commitment to be the driver of the market orientation mediator, which results in the performance factor international positional advantage (Blesa, Monferrer, Nauwelaerts, & Ripollés, 2008).

Discussion, Conclusion, and Implications

The purpose of this chapter was, through reviewing explanatory schematic models, to investigate how and why international new ventures are established and developed. Based on various types of research and journal subjects, we find the answers in the form of three types of schematic IE models. The matrix meta-model defines types of international entrepreneurial firms along two dimensions: 1) the degree of geographic diversification measured as the scope of foreign market opportunities and 2) the degree of foreign market commitment measured as the extent of the cross-border coordination of resources, actors, and activities. The multi-stimuli meta-model explains why firms' degree of internationalization varies immediately after inception or in the first years of existence. External environmental factors and internal organizational and managerial factors have significant implications for how IE strategies are defined in terms of internationalization speed, extent, and scope. Finally, the stimulus-response meta-model describes the antecedents/drivers, mediators, and performance of IE. External environmental and internal organizational factors defining the founder's/manager's international profile are understood as the antecedents/drivers of IE. Market- and product-focused knowledge development and global networking resulting in marketing competences and market orientation as well as knowledge-intensive innovative differentiated-quality products moderate those antecedents/drivers. The performance of IE is evaluated in light of the global strategies for internationalization speed, extent, and scope.

Researchers, students, and managers in international business and entrepreneurship can use these models as frameworks for understanding IE, illustrating the new managerial mindsets and ways of framing the challenges of organizing and managing business activities with a global outlook.

We hope that the models developed here will constitute platforms for developing managerial mindsets as ways of framing the challenges of organizing, managing, and governing Danish business activities. We also hope that this review can help new researchers in their future work and enable established researchers to set up research projects with a more cross-country comparative outlook, together with more focus on products and business opportunities in relation to international entrepreneurship.

References

Andersson, S. (2000). The Internationalization of the Firm from an Entrepreneurial Perspective. *International Studies of Management & Organization, 30*(1), 63-92.

Andersson, S. & Wictor, I. (2003). Innovative Internationalisation in New firms: Born-globals-the Swedish Case. *Journal of International Entrepreneurship, 1*(3), 249-275.

Aronsson, L., Hagg, I. & Wiedersheim-Paul, F. (1973). *Att Anvanda Modeller i Företagsekonomin.* Lund, Sverige: LiberLäromede.

Aspelund, A., Madsen, T.K. & Moe, Ø. (2007). A Review of the Foundation, International Marketing Strategies, and Performance of International New Ventures. *European Journal of Marketing, 41*(11/12), 1423-1448.

Autio, E. (2005). Creative Tension: the Significance of Ben Oviatt's and Patricia McDougall's Article 'Toward a Theory of International New Ventures'. *Journal of International Business Studies, 36*(1), 9-19.

Autio, E., Sapienza, H.J. & Almeida, J.G. (2000). Effects of Age at Entry, Knowledge Intensity, and Imitability on International Growth. *Academy of Management Journal, 43*(5), 909-924.

Bell, J., McNaughton, R., Young, S. & Crick, D. (2003). Towards an Integrative Model of Small Firm Internationalisation. *Journal of International Entrepreneurship, 1*(4), 339-362.

Bilkey, W.J. & Tesar, G. (1977). The Export Behavior of Smaller-Sized Wisconsin Manufacturing Firms. *Journal of International Business Studies, 8*(1), 93-98.

Blesa, A., Monferrer, D., Nauwelaerts, Y. & Ripollés, M. (2008). The Effect of Early International Commitment on International Positional Advantages in Spanish and Belgian International New Ventures. *Journal of International Entrepreneurship, 6*(4), 168-187.

Bloodgood, J.M., Sapienza, H.J. & Almeida, J.G. (1996). The Internationalization of New High-Potential U.S. Ventures: Antecedents and Outcomes. *Entrepreneurship Theory and Practice, 20*(4), 61-76.

Boehe, D.M. (2009). Brazilian Software SME's Export Propensity: Bridging 'Born-global' and Stage Approaches. *Latin American Business Review, 10*(2 & 3), 187-216.

Bourgeois, L.J. (1979). Toward a Method of Middle-Range Theorizing. *Academy of Management. The Academy of Management Review, 4*(3), 443-443.

Burgel, O. & Murray, G.C. (1998). The International Activities of British Start-Up Companies in High-Technology Industries: Differences between Internationalisers and Non-Internationalisers. In W.D.B.P.D. Reynolds, N.M. Carter, S. Manigart, C.M. Mason, G. Meyer & K. Shaver (Eds.), *Frontiers of Entrepreneurship Research* (pp. 447-463). Babson Park, MA: Babson College.

Cavusgil, S.T. (1980). On Internationalization Process of Firms. *European Research, 8*(November), 273-281.

Chetty, S. & Campbell-Hunt, C. (2004). A Strategic Approach to Internationalization: a Traditional Versus a 'Born-Global' Approach. *Journal of International Marketing, 12*(1), 57-81.

Choquette, E., Rask, M., Sala, D. & Schröder, P. (2014, June 23-26, 2014). *Born-globals – Is There Fire behind the Smoke?* Paper presented at the AIB 2014 Annual Meeting, Vancouver, Canada.

Cohen & Levinthal. (1990). Absorptive Capacity: a New Perspective on Learning and Innovation. *Administrative Science Quarterly, 35*(1), 128-152.

Coviello, N. & Jones, M. (2004). Methodological Issues in International Entrepreneurship Research. *Journal of Business Venturing, 19*(4), 485-508.

Di Gregorio, D., Musteen, M. & Thomas, D.E. (2008). International New Ventures: the Cross-Border Nexus of Individuals and Opportunities. *Journal of World Business, 43*(2), 186-196.

Doz, Y. (2011). Qualitative Research for International Business. *Journal of International Business Studies, 42*(5), 582-590.

Fernhaber, S.A., McDougall, P.P. & Oviatt, B.M. (2007). Exploring the Role of Industry Structure in New Venture Internationalization. *Entrepreneurship: Theory & Practice, 31*(4), 517-542.

Freeman, S., Hutchings, K., Lazaris, M. & Zyngier, S. (2010). A Model of Rapid Knowledge Development: the Smaller Born-Global Firm. *International Business Review, 19*(1), 70-84.

Gabrielsson, M. & Pelkonen, T. (2008). Born Internationals: Market Expansion and Business Operation Mode Strategies in the Digital Media Field. *Journal of International Entrepreneurship, 6*(2), 49-71.

Gassmann, O. & Keupp, M.M. (2007). The Competitive Advantage of Early and Rapidly Internationalising SMEs in the Biotechnology Industry: a Knowledge-Based View. *Journal of World Business, 42*(3), 350-366.

Hallbäck, J. & Larimo, J. (2006). Variety in International New Ventures-Typological Analysis and Beyond. *Journal of Euro-Marketing, 16*(1/2), 37-57.

Jesson, J.K., Matheson, L. & Lacy, F.M. (2011). *Doing Your Literature Review.* London: Sage.

Johanson, J. & Vahlne, J.-E. (1977). The Internationalization Process of the Firm – a Model of Knowledge Development and Increasing Foreign Market Commitments. *Journal of International Business Studies, 8*(1), 23-32.

Johanson, J. & Vahlne, J.-E. (2003). Business Relationship Learning and Commitment in the Internationalization Process. *Journal of International Entrepreneurship, 1*(1), 83-101.

Johanson, J. & Vahlne, J.-E. (2009). The Uppsala Internationalization Process Model Revisited: from Liability of Foreignness to Liability of Outsidership. *Journal of International Business Studies, 40*(9), 1411-1431.

Knight, G., Madsen, T.K. & Servais, P. (2004). An Inquiry into Born-Global Firms in Europe and the USA. *International Marketing Review, 21*(6), 645-665.

Knight, G.A. & Cavusgil, S.T. (1996). The Born-global Firm: a Challenge to Traditional Internationalization Theory. *Advances in International Marketing, 8*, 11-26.

Knight, G.A. & Cavusgil, S.T. (2004). Innovation, Organizational Capabilities, and the Born-Global firm. *Journal of International Business Studies,* Vol. 35, pp. 334-334.

Kuivalainena, O., Sundqvista, S. & Servais, P. (2007). Firms' Degree of Born-Globalness, International Entrepreneurial Orientation and Export Performance. *Journal of World Business, 42*(3), 253-267.

Laanti, R., Gabrielsson, M. & Gabrielsson, P. (2007). The Globalization Strategies of Business-to-Business Born-global Firms in the Wireless Technology Industry. *Industrial Marketing Management, 36*(8), 1104-1117.

Madsen, T.K. & Servais, P. (1997). The Internationalization of Born-globals: an Evolutionary Process? *International Business Review, 6*(6), 561-583.

McDougall, P.P. (1989). International vs. Domestic Entrepreneurship: a Comparison of New Venture Behavior and Industry Structure in the Computer and Communications Industries. *Journal of Business Venturing, 4*, 387-400.

McDougall, P.P. & Oviatt, B.M. (2000). International Entrepreneurship: the Intersection of Two Research Paths. *Academy of Managament Journal.*

Mets, T. (2009). Creating Global Business Model for Knowledge-Intensive SMEs: the Small Transition Country Cases. *Economics & Management, 14.*

Mort, G.S. & Weerawardena, J. (2006). Networking Capability and International Entrepreneurship: How Networks Function in Australian Born-global Firms. *International Marketing Review, 23*(5), 549-572.

Oviatt, B.M. & McDougall, P.P. (1994). Towards a Theory of International New Ventures. *Journal of International Business Studies, 24*(1), 45-64.

Oviatt, B.M. & McDougall, P.P. (1995). Global Start-Ups: Entrepreneurs on a Worldwide Stage. *Academy of Management Executive, 9*(2), 30-43.

Oviatt, B.M. & McDougall, P.P. (2005). Towards a Theory of International New Ventures. *Journal of International Business Studies, 36*(1), 29-41.

Rask, M., Håkonsson, D.D. & Strandskov, J. (2008). Theoretical Perspectives on the Internationalization of Firms. *Journal of Teaching in International Business, 19*(4), 320-345.

Rialp, A., Rialp, J. & Knight, G. (2005). The Phenomenon of Early Internationalizing Firms: What Do We Know after a Decade (1993-2003) of Scientific Inquiry? *International Business Review, 14*(2).

Rialp, J. & Rialp, A. (2006). Faster and More Successful Exporters : an Exploratory Study of Born-global Firms from the Resource – Based View. *Journal of Euro-Marketing, 16*(1/2), 71-86.

Seelos, C. (2010). Theorizing and Strategizing with Models: Generative Models of Business Models. *IESE Business School Working Paper No. 857.*

Shane, S. & Venkataraman, S. (2000). The Promise of Entrepreneurship as a Field of Research. *Academy of Management Review, 25*(1), 217-226.

Thai, M.T.T. & Chong, L.C. (2008). Born-Global: the Case of Four Vietnamese SMEs. *Journal of International Entrepreneurship, 6*(2), 72-100.

Weerawardena, J., Mort, G.S., Liesch, P.W. & Knight, G. (2007). Conceptualizing Accelerated Internationalization in the Born-global Firm: a Dynamic Capabilities Perspective. *Journal of World Business, 42*(3), 294-230.

Whetten, D.A. (1989). What Constitutes a Theoretical Contribution? *Academy of Management Review, 14*(4), 490-495.

Zahra, S.A. (2005). A Theory of International New Ventures: a Decade of Research. *Journal of International Business Studies, 36*(1), 20-28.

Zahra, S.A. & George, G. (2002). International Entrepreneurship: the Current Status of the Field and Future Research Agenda. In D.I.M. Hitt, D. Sexton & M. Camp (eds.), *Strategic Entrepreneurship: Creating an Integrated Mindset* (pp. 255-288). Oxford: Blackwell.

CHAPTER 12

Preparing for the Unexpected: Some Tentative Answers

Hanne Kragh, Poul Houman Andersen and Jakob Lauring

Globalizing Danish Business Organizations

To say that globalization is upon us and is here to stay is self-evident. Conducting global, international, and cross-cultural business has become a normal part of everyday life in many small and in most large contemporary business organizations. For many companies, the key effect of globalization is that of increased worldwide competition and business complexity; even small and medium-sized companies, which themselves may not be particularly active in international markets, experience globalization through their interactions with, for example, customers, competitors, suppliers, and employees.

Due to its pervasiveness, globalization is quickly becoming a catch-all concept. There are many definitions of globalization and many accounts of how it will shape our future, but most people would agree that it is a pervasive concept that both affects various levels of society and creates new interdependences among actors worldwide. Global linkages develop laterally among individuals, organizations, and organizational ecologies. Moreover, global infrastructures for communication and influence mean that these linkages are increasingly effective. Friedman (2006) sees the advance of globalization as a three-phase process starting with the globalization of countries, continuing with the globalization of firms, and ending in the globalization of individuals – which he calls 'Globalization 3.0'. Globalization 3.0 increases the ability of individuals and firms to interact with other actors irrespective of geographical location, cultural divides, time zones, etc. In practice, this also means the increasing influence and interpenetration of several dimensions and aspects of society. Globalization does not necessarily mean that the world is becoming more integrated, however. As Ghemawat (2011) points out, globalization drives both integration and fragmentation in equal measure, and increases a pervasive sense of complexity across society as incumbent and new practices vie for dominance, to promote the vision of engaging in 'the global' while preserving valuable aspects of 'the local'.

Despite its changing governments, Denmark has maintained an ambitious globalization strategy to strengthen future international competitiveness. In particular, the proposed range of concrete resource-enhancing measures addressing educational reform, research, and business start-ups may become major driving forces of increased global integration in the future. In addition, the increasing influx of foreign labour and firms to Denmark could help in achieving this aim. However, as a country with a strong and well-balanced economy with a correspondingly strong national identity, Denmark has developed critical constituents that reinforce among themselves the shared impression that there is no need to accelerate globalization in Denmark. Although the dangers of such a belief seem to have been recognized by the Danish government, the general population may be less convinced of the need for accelerated economic integration. Many citizens seem entrenched in their Euro-scepticism and suspicion of non-Danish values in general, and they may see few economic or other reasons to further integrate Denmark in the world economy.

With this book, we have tried to address the impact that the continuously changing business conditions resulting from globalization are having on contemporary international companies. All chapters, in one way or the other, address challenges related to globalization and various ways of overcoming them. Yet, in a collection of essays like this, the challenges are inevitably addressed piecemeal. Despite taking their inspiration in a set of common changes and challenges described in the opening chapter of the book, the chapters differ greatly in that each scrutinizes a particular, but limited, part of the totality of challenges related to globalization. The chapters address different analytical levels and rely on different types of data from different types of companies in different industries. Glossing over some of these important differences, our aim in this final chapter is to compile the other chapters' main insights, and use these to suggest answers to the three questions raised in Chapter 1.

Chapter 1 raised three key questions concerning the contemporary challenges to Danish firms' involvement and continued growth in an increasingly globalized business context: 1) What critical managerial and organizational challenges face globally expanding Danish firms? 2) How has globalization impacted 'domestic' business practices in Danish society? 3) How do firms that recognize these challenges actively cope with them? After discussing the answers to these questions, we will address the implications of our findings for policy makers.

Managerial and Organizational Challenges Facing the Globally Expanding Danish Firm

Danish firms have come a long way in expanding their international activities, evolving from export-based firms into fully-fledged international organizations operating across international divides. Still, along with this evolution, a certain ethos seems to have developed around the qualities and applicability of the Danish Management Style and the Danish approach to organizing international activities, an ethos rooted in Danish norms, traditions, and approaches. This ethos is challenged by the chapters in the first part of the book. According to these chapters, Danes and Danish managers may have grown accustomed to regarding the Danish Management Style and approach to internationalization as virtues reflecting proud traditions, in some cases even representing a competitive advantage for Danish firms. However, as evidenced by the stories told in Chapters 2 to 4, fashioning organizational design and managerial approaches in accordance with Danish traditions may create challenges.

For example, Klitmøller, Lauring, and Kubovcikova (Chapter 2, 'Open-minded or Self-sufficient? Challenges of Exporting the Danish Management Style to Foreign Business Units') address the challenges of transferring managerial principles and practices rooted in Danish culture to international settings and applying these practices in managing foreign subsidiaries. They illustrate how a Danish Management Style that initially attempts to be open and inclusive may not be perceived positively by foreign subordinates, and how the mismatch between Danish managers' perceptions of themselves and others' perceptions of their management style (as ineffective) may lead to an identity crisis for the managers. As a result, Danish managers abroad may resort to what the authors call 'provincial self-sufficiency' in international settings, where they are seen to develop a much more autocratic and hierarchical management style, which in turn impairs collaboration, communication, and knowledge sharing.

Lauring, Andersen, Kragh, and Storgaard (Chapter 4, 'Parent Company Arrogance: Perceptions and Consequences') address the related problem of parent company arrogance. They illustrate how many of the attitudes and actions of Danish parent company managers are perceived as arrogant by subsidiary managers, even though they may not have been intended as such. The authors organize the various perceptions of parent company arrogance into three distinct categories – i.e., ignoring, bypassing, and educating – reflecting the feelings of subsidiary managers when exposed to managerial actions from the parent company. The authors use these results to advocate increased awareness of the negative emotions that can result from acting in ways perceived as arrogant.

Together, these two chapters indicate that the Danish Management Style, typically regarded as effective at advancing dialogue and eliciting diverse and innovative perspectives, may indeed be very difficult to apply in encounters with other nationalities with different values and expectations. Klitmøller, Lauring, and Kubovcikova (Chapter 2) also describe the negative effects that may occur when managers accustomed to this management style try to adapt it to other contexts and cultures, once they find that it does not work as intended in its original form. As the authors suggest, the inability to effectively delegate authority, as is customary in a Danish context, can lead Danish managers to completely invert these principles and instead apply an autocratic type of leadership.

The chapter by Lindekilde and Klitmøller (Chapter 3, 'Being Close at a Distance: Exploring Technological, Temporal, and Linguistic Challenges to Global Virtual Team Effectiveness') addresses a different challenge facing globally operating Danish organizations, i.e., the use of IT in organizing work teams. Due to their cost effectiveness and flexibility, 'global virtual teams' have become a popular way of connecting individuals located in geographically dispersed sites. Yet, as discussed in the chapter, this way of organizing international activities not only entails communication challenges but also hampers the development of a shared identity within a team. Ultimately, technological limitations, along with differences in time zone and language between members of global virtual teams, severely affect communication, identity, and perceived proximity in such teams, negatively affecting team performance.

Altogether, chapters two to four identify significant challenges, but also potential benefits, if these challenges are addressed properly by the management and boards of internationally operating Danish firms. As we see it, these chapters hold important insights for current management practice. Instead of understanding the Danish way of management as a coherent whole with certain characteristics, managers need to pay closer attention to which particular aspects of Danish management work well and which do not – and under which circumstances. One important lesson concerns managerial and organizational abilities to use Danish management traditions as a best practice. In other words, rather than defining Danish Management Style as a particular 'guiding light', it should be understood as an internalized practice based on assumptions about societal structures, individual behaviour, and social behaviour that are not directly transferable. At the same time, and at a less aggregated level, Danish management practices may mix and work well with traditions from other cultures, and managerial values rooted in a Danish democratic context may effectively guide managers as well, if they are less hard-wired to specific managerial practices and take into consideration the contingencies of the context in which they operate.

In this way, these managers stand a better chance of continuing to uphold and develop those aspects of the Danish way that work well, and of adapting those aspects that work less well. This is no trivial exercise as it involves rethinking the role and perspectives of Danish managers in a globalized world. While Danish managers have so far often perceived themselves to have superior skills for dealing with international issues, this may not be true in all respects. As such, some soul-searching on the part of Danish managers working abroad is required. This challenge is tied to a classic question in subsidiary management, i.e., whether subsidiaries should be staffed with home- or host-country nationals. Putting greater effort into identifying which aspects of the Danish Management Style work better where and when may lead to changes in how foreign subsidiaries are staffed and in how managerial tasks are divided, not only between HQ and subsidiaries but also internally in individual subsidiaries.

Aligning Danish Business Practices with Global Influences

Along with the interconnectedness of markets for capital, labour, and other resources arising from increasing globalization, Danish work life faces transition challenges. The second part of the book describes what happens when Danish business practices meet their more globalized context on Danish ground. This part is less about how to make Danish practices work abroad and more about how to react to and align oneself with new practices, expectations, and inputs arriving from new and perhaps as yet unknown directions, so that globalization can work not only as a distant phenomenon but as a phenomenon penetrating our daily lives (Giddens, 1984). Many of the contextual changes described in chapters 5 to 7 are so persistent that Danish businesses are forced to find ways of adapting and aligning with them, even though they severely challenge culturally and socially rooted ways of working. At the same time, these chapters note that the local Danish context also affects and shapes incoming inputs and practices, making them compatible with existing systems and practices. These chapters address the challenges of aligning domestic business practices with influences from a changing global context at three levels, i.e., the individual level (Normann & Bjerregaard, Chapter 5), the organizational level (Madsen and Rask, Chapter 6), and the business system level (Rocha and Wigand, Chapter 7).

First, in their chapter, Normann and Bjerregaard (Chapter 5, 'Retention of Highly Skilled Expatriates and the Danish work-life Balance') address a potential downside of the Danish work-life balance, in which Danish managers and employees alike usually take much pride. The chapter describes how foreign expatriates coming to Denmark to work for shorter or longer periods are often surprised by the 'Danish way' of working, especially when it comes to balancing the time and effort spent on work versus the family. For foreigners, this work-life balance may create a barrier to socialization and integration into Danish society, because it requires a work culture that promotes focus and efficiency on the job so that employees can spend sufficient time with their families. Even though this work culture may come to be appreciated by foreign expatriates once they are accustomed to it, it currently seems to be more of a barrier to attracting the highly skilled labour that Denmark needs in order to stay competitive in the future.

Second, the chapter by Madsen and Rask (Chapter 6, "Flexpatriation': A View from the Engine Room of Sub-Suppliers in the Maritime Sector') addresses a particular organizational response to the globalization of the maritime industry. Here, the new realities are reflected in the extension of global value-chains, which means that maritime industry suppliers, traditionally serving a domestic customer base, must now find ways to reduce the liability of the geographical and cultural distance from their main customers in distant countries. This results in new roles and responsibilities for the boundary spanners of supplier firms. The industry has traditionally had a proud tradition of 'flexpatriation', but with the changes in the organization of value added and the position of Danish suppliers in this process, the role of these boundary spanners has shifted substantially. It has become much more one of actively orchestrating and constantly looking out for changing contingencies rather than merely nurturing relationships and occasionally forging new ties to prospective customers.

Third, Rocha and Wigand (Chapter 7, 'Translating Private Equity in Denmark: The Impact of the TDC Buy-out on the Danish Private Equity Industry') describe the effect of the increasing importance of private equity firms on the Danish business system. Using the example of the leveraged buyout of TDC by a consortium of foreign private equity firms, the authors describe how the managerial tools and modi operandi of private equity firms are often in tension with what are understood as the characteristics of the Danish business system. The case clearly highlights the clash between the administrative heritage of the Danish business system and the business strategies imported into the Danish context by foreign private equity firms. As illustrated in the chapter, however, the pressure goes both ways. The chapter explores how local actors are affected by the actions of foreign private equity firms, but also how private equity firms are under pressure to gain legitimacy in the business systems they are entering.

On the surface, the chapters in this part of the book are quite dissimilar from each other, addressing various topical issues. However, in addition to being concerned with the meeting between globalization and various domestic business practices, all the chapters in this part revolve around a common paradox that calls for careful managerial consideration. It seems that the special 'Danish way' is a double-edged sword. On one hand, we typically see the good balance between work and social life as a positive characteristic of Danish society partly accounting for why the Danes repeatedly vote themselves the happiest people in the world (Normann and Bjerregaard, Chapter 5). On the other hand, these chapters also indicate that what Danes regard as a positive trait of Danish society in general, and of Danish work culture specifically, can sometimes impede the integration of highly skilled professionals with other cultural and work-related backgrounds into Danish workplaces and, hence, into Danish society in general. In light of the increased need and competition for highly skilled foreign professionals, this constitutes a severe challenge for Danish firms. Danish managers are faced with the difficult balancing act of holding on to, and promoting, those aspects of the local work culture that help attract and retain the best talent while taking a critical look at those aspects that make integration difficult for foreign colleagues. As opposed to the often-expressed view that this responsibility lies mainly with policy makers and public administrators, the evidence presented here indicates that this is also a managerial responsibility.

Common to the chapters in this part of the book is attention to the increased demands placed on boundary spanners in Danish international firms. Boundary spanners simultaneously perform an information-processing function, selecting and interpreting information from external stakeholders, and an external representation function, conveying their organization's ideas and strategies to these stakeholders (Aldrich & Herker, 1977). In this way, boundary spanners represent the perceptions, expectations, needs, and ideas of each side of a relationship to the other side and are subject to pressure from both sides (Walter, 1999). Several of the chapters in this book consider changes to the boundary spanning role occurring as firms are faced with new, complex, and varying inputs. This puts pressure on the capabilities of boundary spanners, who must increasingly be able to sense, respond to, and integrate such inputs into their organizations. As such, managers should increasingly recognize the boundary spanning role as one of integration and negotiation rather than simply information processing (Levina & Vaast, 2005).

In line with the arguments presented in part one of this book, the chapters in the second part also indicate that to benefit from globalization, instead of losing out to it, one must remain open to alternative solutions. This is not only relevant when working abroad or with individuals situated in foreign countries. Having a global perspective and openness to different ways of operating seems to be increasingly relevant, even when doing business in Denmark. The challenge is not just to be open to new ideas and solutions to problems but, even more importantly, to be able to process, adapt, and integrate such inputs into the local context. The former requires diversity and openness, whereas the latter hinges on a certain level of homogeneity and the creation of shared norms. The key to success seems to lie in being able to balance these contradictory requirements, whether at the level of business systems, organizations, or individuals.

Seizing Global Business Opportunities in an Increasingly Dynamic Context

In the final part of the book we address the initiatives of Danish firms to address global challenges and seize global opportunities. Although Denmark has an open economy and Danish firms started working determinedly early on to expand from a relatively small home market, this has not led to any permanent competences in international business. The pace of globalization has been increasing in recent decades, forcing firms to become more dynamic in how they organize activities and frame business models. A common overall theme of the chapters in this part of the book is the shifting role of the (Danish) international firm. In particular, each chapter addresses more or less explicitly the increased reliance of the international firm on external resources and activities. The most obvious manifestation of this is perhaps the shift from 'internalized' to more 'networked' firms relying on various collaborative architectures. The ability to carefully balance the process of transitioning to increased externalization against the ability to maintain an identity and create value are at the core of the studies presented in this part of the book.

In their chapter, Andersen and Kragh (Chapter 8, 'Managing Strategic Transition in an Age of Accelerating Globalization') provide case examples of established Danish MNCs that have made the shift to becoming more network oriented, doing so with varying degrees of success. The authors claim that changing a firm's ability to dynamically adapt activities to changing global realities is not merely a matter of organizational boundary design and externalization. Rather, in adjusting to the changed realities of a globalized world, established firms face great transitional challenges with respect to aligning organizational designs with managerial mindsets in order to act effectively, not only in terms of shifting boundaries relative to other firms but also in terms of organizational design and managerial mindsets. Changes in organizational form refer to the structures, roles, and processes a firm installs to align itself with its (global) environment. The managerial mindset determines how managers view the roles of the actors, resources, and activities accessible from their current positions. The changes made by Danish international firms in these three areas all point to the importance of developing abilities to 'stitch together workable ways of organizing, which may look more like organizations of loosely patched teams and units than finely tuned organizational charts' (Chapter 8).

Similarly, Linneberg and Andersen (Chapter 9, 'Collaboration in the Dynamic Organizing of Global Business Networks: CSR in Commons, Protocols, and Infrastructures') address, in an investigative case study, the concept of collaborative architectures and how these are applied as a principle for coordinating complex webs of actors. The studied case company caters to a highly specialized global market, using CSR standards and processes as an important lever for achieving coordination throughout the value-chain and dynamically aligning external stakeholders with internal competences and project organizers. The case company maintains a varied infrastructure to support dynamic organising and collaboration. In this case, the infrastructure is also a shared set of protocols and values, which is maintained through a relatively small, but globally distributed, set of actors, all of whom ascribe to the corporate social responsibility agenda.

The chapter by Ellegaard and Vedel (Chapter 10, 'Sourcing Intermediary Profiles in the Global Clothing Industry') looks at a particular role in the global value-chain in the global clothing industry: the sourcing intermediary. For many years, the focus of sourcing organizations has been on global sourcing efficiency, which many firms equate to direct sourcing, avoiding presumably price-raising intermediaries. The authors take issue with this perspective on global sourcing. Their chapter sheds light on how sourcing intermediaries generate value for buying companies and help reduce, rather than increase, total cost. They do so by helping solve their customers' problems in various ways, for example, by extending the scope of the offered problem solving to encompass more of the services their customers need. The chapter presents an example of a particular type of firm that assumes or helps other firms assume a constantly shifting role in the global economy, the need for which is argued by several other chapters.

Finally, the chapter by Rask and Servais (Chapter 11, 'Models of International Entrepreneurship') takes its starting point in the increased importance of 'born-globals' in Denmark. Fast international start-ups were the biggest group of start-ups in Denmark between 1995 and 2006. Taking this as their cue to look closely at the establishment and development of such firms, the authors review existing models used to describe and explain the establishment of international new ventures.

Several rather similar managerial challenges emerge from the findings of the divergent chapters in this part of the book. As stated above, a shared characteristic of the opportunities outlined in chapters eight to eleven is that they require that managers and employees alike operate in a much more dynamic and interdependent business world. The implications of the increased reliance on external relationships are profound and require that firms implement entirely new structures and behaviours (Andersen & Kragh, Chapter 8; Gulati & Kletter, 2005). Managers in traditional hierarchies must understand that implementing a more network-oriented organizational structure requires opening up their organizational boundaries to other organizations to a much larger extent than previously. The fundamental role of management in network organizations has changed from the planning, organizing, and controlling of internal resources associated with the traditional hierarchy to creating and assembling resources located outside the firm (Linneberg & Andersen, Chapter 9; Snow, Miles, & Coleman, 1992). Accordingly, many firms are increasingly assuming the role of a 'network choreographer' (Shuman & Twombly, 2010) responsible for designing a collaborative network and for organizing and engaging the network members, including motivating them, facilitating communication and decision making, and managing governance structures (Linneberg & Andersen, Chapter 9). To the extent that firms are increasingly assuming such a role, they must develop entirely new competences and mindsets that fit their changed role.

Implications

In the above, we have attempted to extract the key insights of the individual chapters and use them in making tentative suggestions about what we think managers of contemporary international organizations should attend to when considering the future organization of activities and resources. Common to all our suggestions is that they require that managers look carefully at many of the unquestioned assumptions about how things are done in international organizations, whether related to the internal organization of the firm or to interaction with the firm environment. However, our findings also point to challenges and opportunities for those involved in providing and securing the best possible conditions for internationally operating Danish firms.

How does this book seek to inform current industrial policy and efforts to support the globalization of Danish enterprises? There is no doubt that business support schemes have evolved in recent decades, as industrial policy makers have become increasingly aware of the changing prerequisites for developing better conditions to support the globalization of Danish firms. While both political debate and public policies used to take a protectionist stance towards Danish industry and keeping certain jobs in Denmark, despite changing competitive realities, this is now seldom the case. Today, several regulatory and supportive bodies at the national, regional, and local levels are working to strengthen the competitiveness of Danish enterprises. Initiatives concerned with positioning Denmark in the global division of labour, rather than shielding Danish enterprises from the effects of globalization, constitute an important step towards a more integrative industry policy. Policies helping Danish firms to reach out and integrate new ideas from global hot spots (e.g., so-called innovation centres) are part of this development.

That being said, parts of the underlying beliefs and mindsets guiding industry policy are still rooted in another time and – in Drucker's terms – in another theory of how the world works and to what end. This is perhaps best reflected in a recent and comprehensive review of the Danish business support system, Erhvervsfremme (Damvad, 2011). From this review, it is clear that the main industry policy actor is the Danish Export Council (Danmarks Eksportråd), established in 1998 in an attempt to strengthen policies to support the internationalization of Danish enterprises. In particular, the challenges facing SMEs in initiating exports are identified as a focus area. There is little doubt that this is an important area for industrial policy initiatives. SME growth through international expansion is a job creator and increases the wealth of Danish society at large. That the current export activities of Danish firms are conducted by only 7% of the entire population of Danish firms suggests considerable untapped potential. However, it is also worth noting that Danish industrial policy supporting the internationalization efforts of SMEs has a remarkably long history, this policy area having been emphasized since the 1990s. Although policy in this area has been further developed and probably also made more effective, it still brings to mind Drucker's notion that changes in political measures to provide more effective export support seek primarily to do differently what is already being done. These measures are 'how to' tools.

However, the realities reflected in the research and case studies presented here suggest that the problems faced by internationally operating Danish firms differ from those addressed by supporting institutions such as the Danish Export Council. First, what seems to be a major neglected area is that of promoting the international activities of firms. Adapting a business enterprise to confront international challenges and exploit international opportunities entails more than simply identifying and assessing export possibilities; rather, it is a process of organizational transition. During this transition, organizational processes, structures, mindsets, and competences co-evolve with the enterprise's exposure to multiple international business conditions. As businesses seek new ways of aligning the expected and unexpected and learn new practices and procedures, they also work hard to discard what used to be effective recipes for success. An entire cohort of medium-sized Danish enterprises has undergone the 'tortuous' evolution into fully-fledged global enterprises in recent years. They repeat avoidable mistakes made by other firms in similar situations, and find little support from 'supportive' political institutions in their endeavours. Some of this variety has been captured in the case studies presented here, but the variation in experience is much larger, and much more can be learned from enterprises undergoing the readjustment from being export-based firms to integrating and coordinating activities in multiple international task environments. As we see it, those responsible for the Danish export support system need to rethink the needs of their clientele and consider whether the axiomatic notion underlying the current organization of the export support system – i.e., that the interests of boosting Danish competitiveness are best served by supporting SME export activities – is still the most important mission.

A parallel problem affects other parts of the Danish industrial support and innovation system. The set-up of the current support system could be compared to that of a traditional exporting firm, i.e., one in which internationalization is something that disrupts the organization and that, although necessary for survival, should be taken care of by a specialized export function and preferably be dealt with outside the core of the organization. Seen as a business system, Denmark has been described as coherent, possessing complementary institutions with systemic qualities and capacities, advancing the ability to produce remarkable industrial successes and further innovation (Kristensen, Karnøe & Andersen, 1999; Lundvall, 2002). There is no doubt that these qualities are challenged by globalization's impact on Danish society and, as illustrated in the case studies in this book, a broad range of Danish institutions is struggling to cope with external sources of capital and influence and with the work-life expectations of highly skilled workers entering the Danish labour market. Again, in line with Drucker, we must realize that a primary drive of such institutions is to stabilize and develop predictable outputs while also perpetuating a theory of how the interests of private enterprise and public institutions are best aligned. However, the realities and corresponding assumptions that shaped this system have changed dramatically, and the question is what part of Danish society has the requisite variety to adjust intelligently to these changes. This relates to the role of 'the state': the national, regional, and local political bodies that constitute the regulatory context of business activities (Pedersen, 2011). What we are seeking here is not a resolution to the ongoing debate on what metaphor for the state best suits global competitive realities. Rather, we are interested in understanding how the changing realities of globalization and increased interdependence should be reflected in a broad range of industrial policy measures, and not be viewed as things that are only happening 'outside' Denmark.

References

Aldrich, H. & Herker, D. (1977). Boundary Spanning Roles and Organization Structure. *Academy of Management Review, 2*(2), 217-230.

Damvad Consulting (2011). The Impacts of Innovation Networks in Denmark – an Impact Study on Behaviour and Possible Economical Effects. Report for the Danish Agency for Science, Technology and Innovation. May. Copenhagen.

Friedman, T. (2006). *The World is Flat. Updated and Expanded.* New York, NY: Farrar, Straus and Giroux.

Ghemawat, P. *World 3.0: Global Prosperity and How to Achieve It.* Harvard Business Press, 2011.

Giddens, A. (1984). *The constitution of society.* Cambridge: Polity Press.

Gulati, R. & Kletter, D. (2005). Shrinking Core, Expanding Periphery: the Relational Architecture of High-Performing Organizations. *California Management Review, 47*(3), 77-104.

Hofstede, G. (1980). *Culture's Consequences: International Differences in Work Related Values.* Beverly Hills: Sage.

Karnøe, P., Kristensen, P.H. & Andersen, P.H. *Mobilizing Resources and Generating Competencies.* Copenhagen Business School Press, 1999.

Levina, N. & Vaast, E. (2005). The Emergence of Boundary Spanning Competence in Practice: Implications for Implementation and Use of Information Systems. *MIS Quarterly, 29*(2), 335-363.

Lundvall, B.Å., Johnson, B., Andersen, E.S. & Dalum, B. (2002). National Systems of Production, Innovation and Competence Building. *Research Policy, 31*(2), 213-231.

Pedersen, O.K. (2011). *Konkurrencestaten.* Hans Reitzel.

Pezzini, M. & Byrne, E. (2007). *Globalisation and Regional Economies: Can OECD Regions Compete in Global Industries?* Publications de l'OCDE.

Quah, D. (2011). The Global Economy's Shifting Centre of Gravity. *Global Policy, 2,* 3-9.

Shuman, J. & Twombly, J. (2010). Collaborative Networks Are the Organization: an Innovation in Organization Design and Management. *Vikalpa, 35*(1), 1-13.

Snow, C.C., Miles, R.E. & Coleman, H.J. (1992). Managing 21st Century Network Organizations. *Organizational Dynamics, 20*(3), 5-20.

Walter, A. (1999). Relationship Promoters: Driving Forces for Successful Customer Relationships. *Industrial Marketing Management, 28*(5), 537-552.

Author Biographies, List of Figures and List of Tables

Author Biographies

1. *Poul Houman Andersen* is Professor of Business Marketing at the Department of Economics and Management, Aalborg University. He previously headed the research group Design of Global Enterprise at the Department of Business Administration, Aarhus School of Business. His research explores organizing and managing buyer-supplier relationships, with a particular focus on international exchange. He has published extensively in journals such as *Journal of World Business, International Business Review, Strategic Organization, Research Policy, Industrial Marketing Management,* and *California Management Review.* He is an adjunct professor at NTNU, Trondheim, Norway, and a visiting professor at University of Stellenbosch, South Africa.

2. *Toke Bjerregaard* is a postdoctoral researcher at the Department of Business Administration, School of Business and Social Sciences, Aarhus University. His research treats the intersection of organization studies and international management, in particular, the global careers and work of professionals and how organizations and individuals manage institutional complexity. He has published in a number of journals, such as *European Management Review, Technovation,* and *British Journal of Management.*

3. *Chris Ellegaard* is Professor of Business-to-Business (B2B) Marketing and Sourcing at Aarhus University, where he heads the B2B research

group. He has conducted a number of research projects and published many articles on subjects such as international sourcing, buyer-supplier relationships, and strategic purchasing.

4. *Anders Klitmøller* is an assistant professor at the Department of Language and Communication, University of Southern Denmark. His research examines the headquarters-subsidiary relationship, practice transfer, and global virtual teams in multinational corporations. Klitmøller has received several international research awards, and his work has been published in national and international peer-reviewed journals, including *Journal of World Business* and *Critical Perspectives on International Business*.

5. *Annamária Kubovcikova* is a PhD student at the Business Administration Department of Aarhus University and a member of the Management and Leadership research group. Her research mainly explores cross-cultural issues, especially expatriation, and she is working on a project entitled 'Self-initiated Expatriates in their Institutional Context: The Combined Effects of Multilevel Factors on Adjustment'.

6. *Hanne Kragh* is an associate professor at the Department of Business Administration, School of Business and Social Sciences, Aarhus University. Her research examines the organization and management of international B2B marketing activities, including the management of inter-organizational relationships. Her work has been published in *Industrial Marketing Management* and *Electronic Markets*.

7. *Jakob Lauring* is a professor at the Department of Business Administration, Aarhus University. His research explores international management with a particular focus on multicultural teams and expatriates. He has published more than 100 articles in publications such as *Journal of World Business, International Business Review, British Journal of Management, Human Resource Management Journal,* and *International Journal of Human Resource Management*. Lauring is an associate editor of *Journal of Global Mobility*.

8. *Rikke Lindekilde* is an Industrial PhD student from the School of Business and Social Sciences at Aarhus University. Her PhD project, 'Leading Global Virtual Teams', represents collaboration between Aarhus University, CfL, and Grundfos. Lindekilde previously worked for 11 years as a business psychologist and she holds an MSc in psychology from Aarhus University. She is currently a Fulbright Scholar at the University of San Francisco and a member of Pamela Hinds' research group at the Center for Work, Technology & Organization (WTO), Stanford University.

9. *Mai S. Linneberg* is an associate professor and member of the Design of Global Enterprise research group at the Department of Business Administration, Aarhus University. She researches international management, publishing primarily in two sub-areas, i.e., practice transfer and implementation in the MNC and the utility and challenges of CSR practices, in publications such as *Journal of Public Policy, Nordiske Organisasjonsstudier*, and *Business and Society Review*.

10. *Mona Toft Madsen* is an associate professor at the Department of Business Administration, Aarhus University. Her research explores middle management identities, roles, and discourses with regard to organizational change. As a spinoff project, she has investigated international business travel among Danish managers in the marine sector. Madsen has published in journals such as *Scandinavian Journal of Management, Human Resource Management Journal*, and *Critical Perspectives on Accounting*.

11. *Jan Normann* is a research assistant at the Department of Business Administration, School of Business and Social Sciences, Aarhus University. He is currently researching global leadership adjustment and expatriate entrepreneurs. He is also an editorial assistant at *Journal of Global Mobility: The Home of Expatriate Management Research*.

12. *Morten Rask* is an associate professor at the Department of Business Administration, Aarhus University. His research focuses on international management, global business models, and international entrepreneurship. He has contributed to journals such as *Electronic Markets, European Journal of Purchasing & Supply Management, Marketing*

Intelligence & Planning, European Journal of International Management, Journal of Teaching in International Business, Energy Policy, and *International Journal of Sustainable Strategic Management.*

13. *Robson Sø Rocha* is an associate professor at the Aarhus School of Business and Social Science, Aarhus University. His research into international business treats the MNC, internationalization, and the transformation of managerial models across national borders. He has published in the areas of management, industrial relations, human resources management, corporate governance, and health and safety. He has also taught at the Copenhagen Business School, École de Management de Lyon (France), and the Fundacão Getúlio Vargas, Brazil.

14. *Per Servais* is an associate professor of Marketing at the Department of Marketing & Management, University of Southern Denmark. His research explores international marketing, the formation and growth of international new ventures, and industrial firms' international purchasing and sourcing activities. He has published many book chapters and articles, for example, in *Industrial Marketing Management, International Marketing Review, Journal of International Marketing,* and *International Business Review.*

15. *Marianne Storgaard* is a postdoctoral fellow at the Department of Entrepreneurship and Relationship Management, University of Southern Denmark. Her research focuses on the challenges of managing multinational corporations, in particular, ethnocentrism in the headquarters-subsidiary relationship. Recent teaching and research also explore design management and strategic design. Her work has been published in *Advances in International Management.*

16. *Mette Vedel* is an assistant professor at the University of Southern Denmark. She received her PhD from Copenhagen Business School and carried out postdoctoral research into the use of global sourcing intermediaries in the Danish clothing industry. Before entering academia, she worked for almost two decades in a regional development organization, focusing on Danish SMEs.

17. *Duncan Wigan* is an assistant professor at the Department of Business and Politics, Copenhagen Business School. His research explores various aspects of the international political economy of finance, including derivatives, private equity, and international taxation. He has published in *Competition and Change, New Political Economy,* and *Global Policy* and contributed to several edited volumes.

List of Figures

List of Tables

Subject index